Tamed

Tamed

EFFECTIVE SELF-CONTROL STRATEGIES TO TAME YOUR DARK HORSE AND KEEP YOU FOCUSED, MOTIVATED, AND IN CONTROL.

Guilherme F. C. Albieri

New York, New York
Library of Congress Control Number: 2019906810
Typeset by Amnet Systems

ISBN (paperback): 978-0-578-50257-1

To my wife Vera Lucia, my kids, Victoria and Vinicius, my parents, my grandparents, and all those who selflessly sacrifice their own journeys for the benefit of others.

A special thanks to my friend Francisco Lucio who encouraged me to put my thoughts on paper.

Table of Contents

CHAPTER 1

Introduction

"WHAT IS THE SINGLE THOUGHT you are most proud of?"

This is a question no one has ever asked, or will ever ask, in a job interview. On the other hand, the question—or a version of it—that is invariably asked, is: "What are the achievement(s) you are most proud of?"

We live in a society that values achievement—specifically personal achievement, in the form of implemented ideas and goals that improve our lot in life personally and the lot of society as a whole. Not only is achievement valued by society, but through a feedback loop, it also provides us with the motivational fuel we need to keep going.

In other words, the more we achieve, the better we feel. Our sense of autonomy and control over our environment and our future increases, providing us with additional mental and physical energy and ultimately catapulting us to higher grounds. Achievement generates achievement.

The good life, self-leadership, and happiness have one common thread: they all entail living the life we set out to live, the life we choose for ourselves. A good, happy, and fulfilling life is at least partially secured through the continuous achievement of self-imposed goals and standards. Leadership is no different: it's about achieving either personal or shared goals.

Yet achievement doesn't come easily.

A few years ago, Lydia came to see me seeking counsel. She had high aspirations in life. She wanted to be a doctor. Her desire to do this seemed sincere. Her resume, on the other hand, told a different story. Although she told me she had tried hard to develop her GPA, her grades were below par. Her interests in jazz and soccer consumed most of her time, leaving very little room for the incredible level of dedication that science courses require. She also had a knack for watching TV and spent many hours each week catching up on her favorite shows. Being a jazz dancer and highly acquainted with pop culture gave her a certain importance amongst her friends, making "friend management" a considerable part of her day. With so much going on in her life, she really tried hard to become a competitive applicant, but she was far too entangled in a self-created web of activities that did not support her ultimate goal of becoming a doctor.

Moz was a successful software engineer and received many accolades for his work. He also had many goals outside of his work, such as starting up his own consulting business. However, finding the time and energy required to launch his ideas felt like catching the wind. By the time he got home, he was drained, and as a stress reliever spent copious hours immersed in the parallel universe of online video games. As a tech-savvy guy, he was constantly connected. An endless flow of incoming messages, alerts, and emails made him feel pulled in hundreds of different directions, resulting in a lost sense of purpose. He was busy but not productive. He was tending to an avalanche of incoming messages, but he couldn't pay attention to what really matters.

Moz, Lydia, you, and I all have a few things in common:

1) We want to maximize our potential and achieve an idealized version of ourselves.
2) We want to reach our personal glory and be the heroes of our own life stories.
3) We want to feel the sweet taste and satisfaction of achieving desirable goals, yet we frequently fail at fulfilling some element of that vision.
4) We fail to control our thoughts, actions, feelings, and how we manage time, and we often go against our best interest and intentions, or we fail to adapt to internal or external standards.

The good news is that there is a solution to this pervasive problem. Psychologists agree that the most powerful tool at our disposal, to close this gap, is our ability to self-regulate through self-control.[1]

I wrote this book out of frustration with myself. Just like Moz and Lydia, I felt (and still feel) that there are certain areas of my life that are out of whack—I want something, yet I behave in ways that are in exact opposition to my intended goals. I procrastinate when I need to get work done, I multitask when I need to focus, I indulge when I need to restrain, I doubt when I need to believe, I slack off when I am supposed to take charge, and I use harsh words when I should be gentle, caring, and compassionate. To make matters worse, modern life and our amazing technologies

1 Baumeister, R. F., & Tierney, J. (2011). *Willpower: Rediscovering the greatest human strength.* New York, NY: Penguin Books.

have immersed us in a sea of distractions, which are continually begging for our attention.

We often sabotage our noble aspirations by getting into impulsive emotional states or by losing ourselves in unimportant activities that bring us immediate gratification. Both our hearts and our rational minds desire certain outcomes, yet we frequently act on primitive emotions that are contrary to our aspirations, creating a classic mind-body dualism—we think one thing yet do another.

This internal conflict can be maddening, making us wonder, "who is the real me?" I have often questioned myself: am I the confident, goal-setting, persistent voice that pushed me to succeed in my career or am I the doubtful, unfocused, insecure voice who nearly derailed my goal? Am I the determined voice who controls my basic instincts to indulge or am I the voice who succumbs to temptations? Do I control environmental forces or do they control me? Am I the voice of reason or the voice that reacts emotionally to life events? Is the real me this person with lofty goals who wants to live the life I have designed for myself or am I a weak, unfocused individual who succumbs to the smallest distractions?

The reality is that, to a certain degree, we are both. Our brains (the hardware) operate using a type of software that was beautifully described by Plato as "the chariot triad."

The Dark Horse, the Bright Horse and the Charioteer

Plato gave us the allegory of the charioteer and the two-winged, flying horses to illustrate the human journey towards achievement. This allegory will be used throughout this book to exemplify concepts of self-control. While I've diverted considerably from Plato's original idea to make my point, it forms a useful base for our explorations. According to the chariot allegory, there are three elements that make up the human spirit and determine our ultimate destiny, a triad of achievement: a dark horse, a bright horse, and the charioteer.

Our lives are partially controlled by a mortal, dark horse—one that is wild, instinctual, and dominated by human passions and basic needs. This part of us doesn't respond well to reason (or to a good whipping). The dark horse often pulls the chariot towards unimportant, irrelevant, and hedonistic ends, ultimately limiting our ability to achieve our highest aspirations.

We are also controlled by an immortal, bright horse, representing temperance and virtues. The aspirations and virtues driven by our bright horse, if realized, bring us to our personal glory.

Finally, the charioteer represents human reason and executive decision-making, and strives to bring the three pieces of this allegory into one cohesive whole. The charioteer has the capacity to mediate the relationship between the two horses and guide them toward a common end. The goal of the charioteer is to make the chariot airborne—these are flying horses, after all—and to achieve its highest potential.

The problem most of us face is that when the charioteer attempts to take off in pursuit of our highest aspirations, she feels the pull of the dark horse in the opposite direction. For instance, you want to become a better student and do well in a rigorous curriculum, but the dark horse has more pleasurable plans for you: how about watching your favorite TV show instead? You desire to be more physically active and get in shape, but your dark horse wins and orders a chocolate-covered banana split for dessert. It is your goal to achieve your sales target at work, but your dark horse, in search for immediate gratification, would rather browse the Internet or focus on brainless activities that add little value to your work and to your future. Maybe you want to control what you say, but your dark horse convinces you that you should spill the beans (every single one of them).

The chariot stumbles, loses momentum, and tips over. If the dark horse is not properly tamed and controlled by the charioteer using the required strength, momentum, and rigor, it will derail the chariot endlessly.

Although the temptations luring the dark horse are the major reasons why the chariot is pulled in unintended directions, our bright horse may also not always pull its weight towards our desired destination. Representing virtues such as courage, confidence, pride, integrity, and determination, the spirit of the bright horse is often influenced by experiences, other people, and our own interpretation of facts and events. These experiences can either strengthen the bright horse or drain its determination to pursue our most important goals.

The charioteer must drive both horses towards our most noble aims using strength and vigilance. To do so, we must understand the nature of the two horses and harness their energies towards a desirable, common end. We must also understand the nature of the charioteer. The charioteer, in her efforts to control the dark horse, grows depleted, exhausted, and may sometimes suffer momentary lapses of reason.

When the charioteer and the two horses are aligned, however, we achieve unity—engaging not in conflicting, disjointed goals, but living one harmonious life: the life that we are intended to live. As I will explain in this book, the mechanism to bring unity to this triad is exercising and strengthening your self-control muscle in order to tame your dark horse, strengthen your bright horse, and focus your charioteer.

Modern psychology often refers to the triad of the charioteer and his horses using the terms "hot" and "cold" systems, or System I and System II.[2]

The "hot" system, or System I, is the automatic, fast-acting, emotional part of our cognition and is located in the most primitive part of our brain, the limbic system. It houses our desires, emotions, impulses and habits. The hot system is equivalent to the dark horse.

The "cold" system, on the other hand, is the rational, executive, strategic, self-controlling part of our brain, and is located in the pre-frontal cortex. It houses rational decision-making, discipline, and delayed gratification. It is the equivalent of the charioteer in the chariot allegory.

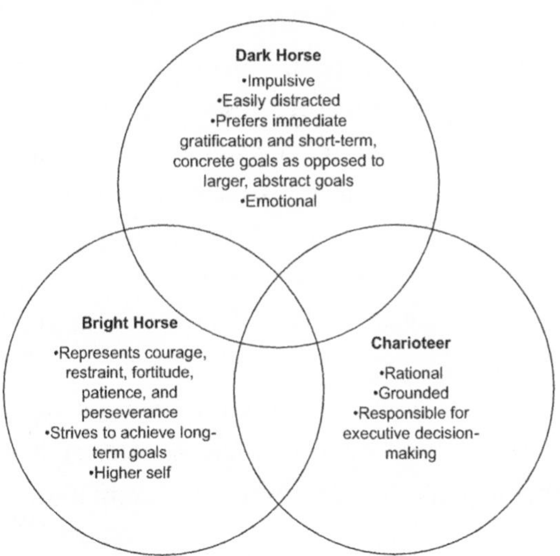

2 Kahneman, D. (2011). *Thinking, fast and slow.* New York, NY: Farrar, Straus & Giroux.

We are the dark horse, the bright horse, and the charioteer. However, although helpful, Plato's allegory has an important missing component... *you.*

In reality, there is a bright horse, a dark horse, a charioteer, and in the background, overseeing this complex system, is you. We often romanticize the figure of the charioteer as being the "certified agent of logic," who always acts in our best interests. But this can be a costly mistake to make.

We must have a system to watch the watcher—to control the controller. This is important because of a small quirk in the brain. Our pre-frontal cortexes give us this amazing ability to think rationally and strategize, but this comes with some side effects.

The paradox is that, because we have the ability to be rational, we often rationalize. We come up with well-crafted reasons and excuses for engaging in behavior that is counter-productive, such as succumbing to our temptations. The charioteer too can be corrupted, and become uncomfortably cozy with the dark horse. Because of that, we need a system to watch the rationalizer from a distance. Furthermore, as explained later in this book, maintaining executive control of our brain is a resource-intensive endeavor, rapidly draining energy from the charioteer.[3] An exhausted charioteer easily succumbs to the demands of a capricious dark horse.

By carefully observing this system from afar, you will be able to fully understand how each element of the triad is behaving. Moreover, this will give you an enhanced, critical perspective on

3 Baumeister, R. F., & Tierney, J. (2011). *Willpower: Rediscovering the greatest human strength.* New York, NY: Penguin Books.

your own system and will allow you to make changes to each player.

Above all, being able to observe your triad gives you control of it. Control is freedom.

This is probably one of the most puzzling paradoxes in life. Freedom is often associated with a lack of control and the ability to move or act freely. But I argue that having control of your triad is one of the most liberating and freeing experiences imaginable. Control is also a basic need of the human psyche. Think about the last time you pressed the elevator button even though the button was lit, a clear indication that it had already been pressed. Pressing it puts you in control of the elevator experience, instead of a random stranger. And being in control makes you feel good.

That is exactly what this book will show you how to do: harness the power of self-control, to live the life you want.

About This Book

The title of this book, *Tamed,* intentionally suggests that what you are embarking on is not going to be an easy journey. Keeping the chariot airborne and pointing toward our highest aspirations requires effort, sweat, energy, and time. On this journey to tame your dark horse, you may at times lose control of it, the chariot may waver and lose momentum, the charioteer may be thrown from the commanding seat, or you may need a change in strategy.

But whatever happens, don't give up. In the end, what is most satisfying about this journey is the thought that you are conducting the chariot in the direction you choose—you are setting your own course. Arriving is not nearly as exciting as the journey itself.

The impetus to write this book also came from a genuine concern about the kind of self-indulgent and distracted society we live in. This is an age of pure delight for our dark horses and of sensory overload for the charioteer. Distractions are everywhere. This hyper-connected world moves at an excruciatingly rapid pace—information, entertainment, data, the ability to communicate with others no matter where we are, or where the other party is located, are literally at our fingertips. The dark horse is nurtured 24/7.

This environmental noise demands more of the charioteer. More than ever, the charioteer has to be constantly alert, reining in the dark horse while steering the chariot towards her desired destiny… No easy feat!

This book was written as a user's manual to help you understand and tame your dark horse, and guide your chariot along life's journey. It is also a training manual to strengthen your self-control muscle and help you fight the many battles you will encounter along the way—particularly your most intimate inner battles, those that take place between you and yourself (between you and your dark horse).

In Part I of this book, I discuss why we need to exercise self-control and tame our dark horses more than ever before, along with what self-control is, and concepts of time—all of which are essential in self-control and goal achievement. You will find valuable information on how our dark horse acts, how to tame it, and how to circumvent failures of the dark horse and the charioteer that are embedded in our systems.

In Part II, I introduce proven strategies to improve self-control using the "EAT" system. The "E" stands for "Environment"; here, I discuss shielding strategies and changes you can make to your surroundings that will help diminish potential distractions for the dark horse and alleviate some of the burden placed on the charioteer. The "A" stands for "Act"; in this section, I will share some valuable strategies for pursuing your desired goals without letting the dark horse lure you towards immediate gratifications that do not support your long-term achievement. The "T" stands for "Think," and here I share strategies that the charioteer (the rational self) can apply in order to stay focused, on track, and in control. At the end of this book, I recommend a 20-day self-control workout using all the strategies you have learned, and provide a template for you to use.

Although I recommend that you read this user's manual from cover to cover, feel free go straight to Part II and select strategies at will. However, remember that self-control is like a muscle: the more you use it, the stronger it gets. Reading this book in full is in itself an excellent exercise in self-control.

So shut out any distractions and immerse yourself in this journey. To take full advantage of it, I encourage you to complete the exercises proposed in each of the chapters and reflect on the questions posed.

Now, let's get to work!

Part I

CHAPTER 2

Why Self-Control?

LET'S SUPPOSE THAT WE LIVE in a world where intelligence, mental health, access to opportunities, and luck were equally available to every human being. We know that they are not, but for the purposes of this mental exercise, we shall hold these variables constant. In this scenario, what would determine one's success?

The main thesis of this book is that when everything else remains constant, self-control—our ability to bring ourselves together to act upon our goals and vision, without succumbing to distractions or other forces that derail us from what we truly desire in the long run—is the most powerful human strength we have at our disposal.

Over the course of our lives, we all have encountered those with amazing talent and intelligence who haven't amounted to much. We have also experienced those who fought through the most challenging odds to fully claim their personal glory. Again, if intelligence and luck are assumed to be constant, they have reached their personal glory through hard work, discipline, focus, determination, and resilience—all of which are characteristics of self-control.

It is also a thesis of this book that time is the true common denominator, particularly mechanical time. We all operate under the same watch. Every hour—for everyone, regardless of financial status, race, creed, intelligence, or personality traits—has 60 minutes; a minute has 60 seconds; a day has 24 hours; a year has 12 months. Thus, our ability to exert self-control in order to get things done in the amount of time that is equally available to us will be a significant determinant of our accomplishments.

The main benefit of developing the self-control muscle is its consequences and benefits. Like many authors, I wrote this book out of frustration... with myself. Since I was a teenager, I was amazed by the disconnect between my thoughts and my actions. I wanted one thing and did the exact opposite. I convinced myself numerous times that I would take a certain action, only to let the opportunity slip through my fingers.

As I started studying the science of self-control, self-regulation, and achievement, I realized that I was not alone. In fact, I realized that creating an idealized and abstract world in our minds that does not correspond with our actions is a basic quirk of our inherently faulty human brains. The science of self-control made me realize that I had a planning charioteer and a bright horse that propelled me towards my goals, but also a dark horse that controlled my actions more often than not.

Two Disappointments

Two moments in my childhood were crucial in shaping my desire to seek a life of self-control. All two were disappointments that still ring clear in my mind, often lighting the necessary fire under me to keep on pushing, trying, and probing.

My family has always been marked by a love for airplanes, largely due to my grandfather's profession. He was a devoted commercial pilot, with the most interesting stories to tell about the early years of commercial aviation. I also had a passion for making things like flashlights, fans, and remote control cars. As a kid, there was nothing that I loved more than high-speed mini-motors, a 9v battery, and LED lamps. With my passion for airplanes and for making things, I one day committed to building a cockpit inside my bedroom. Everything had been worked out in my mind, down to the minutest details. I was going to build a cockpit from plywood, complete with real airplane instruments and a control panel that would shine brighter than the Milky Way. I never cut the first piece of wood.

As a child and a teenager, I had another passion that shaped me in ways that I still can't truly comprehend—my father's weekend farm. We had a small farm where we used to spend most of our weekends. I still remember it as if it were yesterday. Each week, by Tuesday, I was already daydreaming about what I would be doing that coming Saturday: riding my horse Baluarte, eating persimmons from the tree, riding a tractor, fishing, and frog hunting. The lake was the area where I spent most of my time. Some days I would fish from morning until early evening. One day, I had the idea of asking my father to give my brother and I a small piece of land next to the lake, where we could develop our own mini farms. My dream was to fence off a small piece of land where we would have total freedom to raise small animals and plant whatever we desired. My father agreed. The first fence post was never raised.

Although they all happened a long time ago, these were ideas or activities I dreamt about at that time, day in and day out. By reflecting on these experiences, I became fascinated with the pervasive gap that exists between thinking and doing, and the role of the dark horse in pulling me away from my intentions. On the other hand, now that I am a grown man, these experiences serve as reminders and inspiration to never let the things I really want in life slide.

The fact that these unfinished projects still resonate with me until today is called the "Zeigarnick Effect."[5] Have you ever wondered how you can list all the things you need to do but can't remember what you had for breakfast yesterday? A Lithuanian psychologist, Bluma Zeigarnick, was amazed by how a waiter in a café in Vienna was able to remember exactly what people had ordered and at which table, delivering each order with precision. But as soon as the orders were delivered, they were gone from the waiter's memory. She studied this phenomenon and concluded that incomplete tasks in our brains are like open order tickets. The order will linger on in our minds until it is completed. After completion, they disappear without a trace.

The projects mentioned above are open orders in my mind that were never closed, and so they keep coming back as unfinished business. As a result, I promised to myself that I

5 Alter, A. (2017). *Irresistible: The rise of addictive technology and the business of keeping us hooked.* New York, NY: Penguin Press.

would have as few open orders as possible—not by not having goals, but by achieving all the goals I set for myself.

Gaining the Edge in a Competitive World

The ultimate benefit of self-control is creating and living the life you have visualized in your mind. It is merging the imagined reality with the lived reality. It is doing what you say (or think or imagine) you will do. In order to survive in a highly competitive world, students, entrepreneurs, and employees need creativity, imagination, and—above all—the ability to execute.

Cal Newport, author of *Deep Work*, reminds us of a macro reason for developing our self-control muscle and taming our dark horses.[5] He points out the great restructuring that has taken place in our economy: a new world of technological advancement in which our technologies advance while we lag behind.

As this new economy evolves, some skills will become obsolete, leaving a number of workers behind, while other skills will become highly valued, creating amazing new opportunities. Those who will be highly valued are divided into three categories:

- Highly skilled workers who have highly specialized knowledge that is hard to obtain.
- Superstars who perform at the highest level in any given profession, who are so good at what they do that there is high demand for their services, which comes at a premium.

6 Newport, C. (2016). *Deep work: Rules for focused success in a distracted world.* New York, NY: Grand Central Publishing.

- Capital nodes, who have access to capital and can direct new capital to growth sectors of the new economy; namely, startups that generate great value using a very small labor pool.

There is not much that you or I can do about the latter category, unless we have access to capital. Newport argues that entering the two first categories is possible. For that, we need to develop two core skills: 1) swiftly master things that are difficult to master, and 2) produce at an elite level, in terms of both quality and quantity.

Self-control is all about execution. It is about getting things done. It is about bridging the gap between imagining and realizing, knowing and taking action, saying and doing, promising and delivering. And, as we are reminded by Newport, it is also about developing the skills needed to survive in the new economy.

Self-control means autonomy and freedom. Autonomy—a basic human need, as suggested by Matthew Crawford—is setting the laws for oneself.[6] The opposite of being autonomous is being controlled by something foreign to oneself. Autonomy is our ability to set rules and standards for ourselves and live by these rules. It is our ability to set personal goals, establish rules for our horses, and deploy the charioteer to achieve them.

I am not suggesting that contextual factors don't influence behavior. They do, more than we care to admit. I argue that a person can conduct his/her chariot in spite of, or within, the constraints of this external context. An elevated level of autonomy leads the charioteer to experience freedom; in other words, the

---

6 Crawford, M. B. (2015). *The world beyond your head: On becoming an individual in an age of distraction*. New York, NY: Farrar, Straus & Giroux.

sensation of being in control, not being controlled by impulses that do not support one's goals.

Although highly fulfilling, creating such a life is not an easy feat.

Understanding Non-Achievement

To understand achievement, it is important to understand non-achievement. Just like to understand change, it is important to understand non-change—the forces preventing us from changing (or achieving).

The state of quasi-equilibrium

According to Kurt Lewin, the father of Social Psychology (1958), every system (and here, I am qualifying our lives as a system) is in a state of quasi-equilibrium—quasi meaning "almost."[7] There are two types of opposed directional forces holding a system in this state: forces which are pro-change and those which are pro-status quo.

We are all, at this very moment, in a state of quasi-equilibrium, with both pro-change and pro-status quo forces determining where we stand in relation to our achievements. It is as if the dark and the bright horses, as well as the environmental conditions that surround them, have reached a point of common understanding while flying toward the goal at a compromised speed and altitude. The charioteer tries to move the chariot faster, but the two horses, in their present condition, can only

7 Lewin, K. (1946). Action research and minority problems. *Journal of Social Issues, 2(4)*, 34-46.

achieve so much. As long as these forces remain unchanged, or stable, and unaffected by external factors, you will continue to achieve what you are achieving now.

If you wish to achieve new results, the balance between these forces must be upset, either by enhancing the pro-change forces or by eliminating the pro-status quo forces. In other words, either the bright horse must be strengthened or the dark horse tamed.

For instance, if you want to start a new business, the desire to do this is a force in favor of change. Your busy schedule at your current work, other distractions, your fear of failure, the availability of resources, and your family responsibilities are forces in favor of maintaining the status quo. Working together, these two forces keep you where you are—with a desire to open a new business but not moving ahead with your plans.

To actually open your business, the state of equilibrium must be broken. You could do so by working after-hours on your personal project, eliminating distractions, quitting your day job, borrowing money, or a combination of all of these tactics. Without either increasing the forces pro-change or removing the forces pro-status quo, you will remain where you are. This is a basic understanding of the science of action and achievement.

One of the strengths of Lewin's theory is that it is non-prescriptive. Lewin does not specify which forces hamper or aid us in achieving our goals. Instead, we must diligently and judiciously seek to identify and understand the forces at play in our own lives, and then change them. The main theme of this book is that our dark horse and the charioteer, with their strengths and limitations, are two important forces acting in this equation, either pro-change or pro-status quo. The state of quasi-equilibrium in our lives can be represented by the line in the graph below:

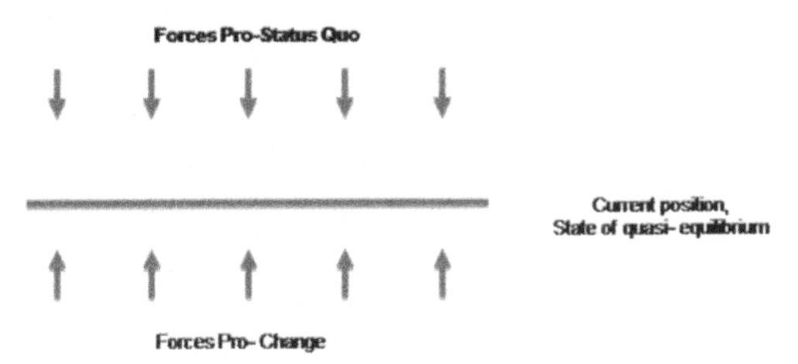

Think for a moment of a goal you want to achieve and draw the graph above, with the forces working in favor of your goal and those against it. In recent achievement theory, the exercise of imagining a goal and determining the barriers between you and your goal has proven to be an important and effective strategy in goal achievement.[8] Focusing solely on the goal without taking an inventory of the barriers will be unrealistic, while focusing solely on the barriers without acknowledging the forces that support your desired future will be counterproductive, if not outright depressing. Also, focusing on your goals without considering the environmental forces at play causes old behaviors to kick in: your goal may be temporarily achieved, but the environment remains the same, activating old habits and bringing the line back to its original position.

Interestingly, lofty goals may require you to make radical changes to the forces acting both in favor of change *and* against it. This may include changes to your surroundings, the people you hang out with, the time you wake up, or your daily routine.

---

8 Gollwitzer, P. M., & Oettingen, G. (2011). Planning promotes goal striving. In K. D. Vohs & R. F. Baumeister (Eds.), *Handbook of self-regulation: Research, theory, and applications* (2nd Ed., pp. 162-185). New York, NY: Guilford Press.

The mistake is trying to move the line without addressing what is keeping it there.

Regression toward mediocrity

Another interesting phenomenon directly linked to the concept of quasi-equilibrium is our tendency to regress back to average performance or mediocrity. Mediocrity, for the purpose of this discussion, is defined as the line that represents where we are at present. It is the same line of quasi-equilibrium we looked at above.

In trying to achieve new goals, we are trying to move away from this imaginary "average" line. We want to improve our future prospects and our lot in life, to (metaphorically speaking) raise the bar. Lewin tells us that the bar is set where it is for one simple reason: forces pro-change and pro-status quo are keeping it there. We may strive hard to move the bar, but the bar keeps on going back to its initial point… mediocrity.

Proponents of the theory of mediocrity converge on one point—the remarkable tendency of systems to reach stability or to regress towards the mean. One of the first scholars to unearth this tendency was Sir Francis Galton.[9] Galton was a Victorian English statistician who created the concept of correlation and was a firm proponent of "regression toward the mean." Galton, in his studies of human difference (particularly height), discovered that the offspring of tall parents were, as a whole, closer to the mean of the population than to the height of their parents. Yes, tall parents tend to have tall offspring, but not necessarily

9 Ellenberg, J. (2015). *How not to be wrong: The power of mathematical thinking.* New York, NY: Penguin Books.

only tall offspring. In fact, they tend to have offspring that are closer to the average height.

In business, this concept was confirmed by Horace Secrist, who, after studying the performance indicators of dozens of companies across multiple industries, concluded that over time great companies become mediocre. The once-outstanding performance indicators of these companies, after a while, become not so outstanding. In other words, "excellence doesn't persist. Time passes and mediocrity asserts itself."[10]

This concept is further sustained by statistical observations that one extreme event will eventually be followed by an event that is fairly close to the usual, or typical, mean. As a result, that one extreme event cannot be taken very seriously, since subsequent events will typically not be as extreme.

For example, think of an unknown soccer player who scores three goals in her first match. She is elected the best player of the match. Sports news outlets notice this extraordinary performance and write, blog, and tweet about it. In the next couple of matches, however, the player does what she does, plays to the best of her ability, but fails to produce out-of-the-ordinary results. She falls from grace rather quickly. How to explain this phenomenon? What happened in the first game was an anomaly in a very small sample size (only one game). In subsequent games, with a larger sample size, she performs as she usually does—she plays well, as usual, but not extraordinarily well. In other words, she regresses toward mediocrity. That is why major sports leagues do not report the results of players who have played only a few games—the margin for variance in a small number of games is too great.

---

10 Ibid, P. 301.

Here is another practical example: Let's suppose you get hyped up about creating a major behavioral change in your life: you have decided that you will become an avid blog writer. In the first two weeks you write quite diligently. Your confidence increases and you gain more followers, beyond your spouse, your mother, and some friends. You are excited.

Five months later, you look back and you realize that those two first weeks were actually your most productive weeks. After that, life got in the way and you went back to doing what you typically do—you regressed towards your mean. That is not to say that your life before blogging was mediocre, but that in light of the new change you expected to create, you went back to what you have always done. Thus, it is mediocre compared to the new goals you had set for yourself. Mediocracy is where the dark horse feels most comfortable.

Entropy

Finally, there is the concept of entropy, a phenomenon that is all too common in our lives and is often disregarded.

Entropy is defined as a system's tendency to gradually decline into disorder and for energy to dissipate. If you have a house that you try to keep organized and tidy, you know what I am referring to. (If you have kids, you know even better!) You wake up on a Sunday morning and decide that you can't live like a teenager anymore, and that from now on, you will keep your house as polished as a diamond. In other words, you decide to tame the dark horse.

You gear up and spend a lot of energy cleaning and organizing. Five hours later, you are exhausted but feeling great—your house looks like it has never looked before. You make a personal vow to keep it like that for the rest of your existence.

Monday arrives. You come home from work tired and leave your shoes in the living room and your socks discarded on the bathroom floor. Entropy is weaseling itself into your vow. That focused energy that was necessary to clean your house is now dissipated and applied to other areas of your life. By Friday, you are living like a teenager once again. You feel trapped on a never-ending hamster wheel.

Entropy is the dark horse showing the charioteer who is boss, bringing the chariot back into the well-established rut it has developed over the years. Entropy reminds us that as we try to organize, structure, and change, there are forces bringing the system back to how things used to be. The natural state of some systems is dissipated energy. You temporarily apply energy towards a certain goal, improving things for a while, but after a while other things in your life require energy (energy is dissipated towards other goals) and all goes back how it used to be. You blink and the system enters a downfall towards mediocrity.

Untangling the Web and Setting New Patterns

The concepts of quasi-equilibrium, regression towards the mean, and entropy have major implications when it comes to personal change and goal achievement.

Firstly, they shatter the view that it is enough to want something in order to achieve it. They remind us that there is a web-like interaction between the forces in your life which dictate what you are doing. To change the results, you must untangle yourself from that web.

Secondly, it shows us that life is not as linear as we might like to think. While simply making an effort today may create results tomorrow, we must analyze a pattern of results over a period of time and not simply count a couple of isolated wins as real change. In other words, creating change requires establishing new patterns. However, old patterns are established patterns for a reason, and the new patterns will not be completely new, but rather an evolution of current, established patterns. To think that new patterns can be easily established is to deny both reality and the self.

This is not to say that change is unattainable. On the contrary, this is a reminder that change is hard and requires a judicious understanding of where you are, what is keeping you there, and where you want to go, as well as substantial amounts of effort, energy, and time.

Feeding the cravings

The dark horse is easily distracted and quick to indulge, while the charioteer tires quickly. And I would argue that modern life has exponentially increased opportunities to feed the cravings of your needy dark horse, thereby overtaxing the charioteer. The factors that feed these cravings and drive the charioteer insane, keeping your chariot stuck in its present location, are discussed below.

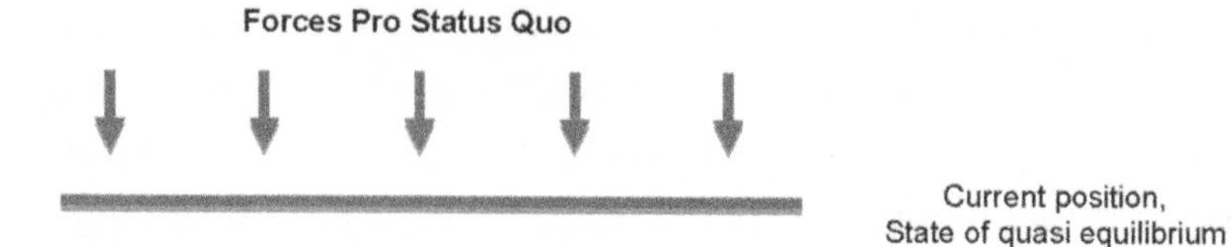

Technology

A recent interaction with one of my students encapsulates the challenges associated with new technologies. This student had done extremely well in a standardized test and I asked her what she attributed her success to. Before hearing what she had to say, I had already imagined her likely response in my mind. I was expecting a report on how she had studied diligently for long hours over an extended period of time, that she had superb time management skills, and that she had sought help from tutors. My mind couldn't help but create these picture-perfect scenarios typical of highly focused and diligent students.

To my surprise, the answer fell as far from my mental imaginings as it could. She matter-of-factly told me, "I lost my iPhone." This was one of those sweet moments when you are hit really hard by a curve ball. I had to smile.

Anywhere we go, we look around and find people diligently tending to their smart phones— talking, texting, browsing the web, posting, liking, taking pictures, or chasing Pokémon. Never in the history of humankind have we had so much information available to us, quite literally at our fingertips. Never have we had so many tools at our disposal within a single device (apps, books, newspapers, cameras, speaking capabilities, and so on).

Technology has changed—and will continue to change—how we interact with the world and each other:

- **Technology has dramatically accelerated how we communicate and do business, changing expectations and communication patterns forever.** Today, we are always connected, always on. Everything is instant.[11] A text message or email sent now is expected to be answered immediately. Speed is the name of the game. If you don't respond immediately, eyebrows start to rise. (I confess I am still adept at letting the message simmer for a while before responding). I stopped counting how many times I have seen people interrupt meetings, conversations, meals, and movies to attend to incoming messages on their smartphones. Does it really need to be answered at that precise second? When I started my career, we did not have emails. How did we survive in those days?

- **New technologies have taken instant gratification to a whole new level.** New technologies, and smartphones in particular, place the most addictive type of gratification, *instant gratification*, at the tips of our fingers. Our dark horse is a self-indulgent beast that constantly seeks gratification and rewards, bringing this issue to a whole new level. Feeling anxious? Reach out to your pocket and ease the emotional pain causing you to be anxious by pressing a couple of buttons. Feeling bored? Play a game, read the news, text your friends. I am convinced that with the proper apps on our smartphones, we will never be bored again. There are, however, important unintended consequences of attending to instant gratification to consider. Most things worth acquiring in life are not instant, requiring years of dedication, preparation, and focus. Instant gratification, on the other hand, steals time,

11 Ramo, J. C. (2016). *The seventh sense: Power, fortune, and survival in the age of networks.* New York, NY: Little, Brown and Company,

energy, and attention away from higher-level goals—the very type of goals that really matter.

- **Technology has exponentially increased the amount of distractions and interruptions in our daily lives.** Push notifications, audio notifications for email, information available at any time in any place, distractions, and interruptions have taken control of our lives. There is an important distinction to be made between distractions and interruptions, however.[12] Distractions temporarily interrupt our focus on a given task, while interruptions cause us to interrupt the pursuit of one goal in favor of pursuing a new, unrelated goal. While distractions and interruptions may seem harmless, their compounded effect can be devastating. Research on distraction suggests that at work, we may lose hours of productivity per day by paying attention to distractions and interruptions. When a distraction occurs, it costs us time and energy to revert to our original task.[13]
- **Technology is burying us in information overload.** Information overload kills focus, time, and attention. Think about the "information rabbit hole." There is always another email to respond to, another article to read, or another website to visit. Once down the information rabbit hole, it is hard to find your way back. You have probably experienced this phenomenon yourself. Not

12 Gazzaley, A., & Rosen, L. D. (2016). *The distracted mind: Ancient brains in a high-tech world*. Boston, MA: MIT Press.

13 Mark, G., Gonzalez, V. M., & Harris, J. (2005). No task left behind? Examining the nature of fragmented work. In *Human factors in computing systems: Proceedings of CHI'05* (pp. 321–330). New York: Association for Computing Machinery Press.

long ago, I was searching online for a paper I remember having read on the topic of information overload. As I searched for it, I found an interesting article on the subject. The article made reference to an author who wrote prolifically about the perils of information overload, so I visited his website. There, the author had links to other interesting and "relevant" blogs and sites. Pretty soon, I was lost. "What was I looking for again? What was my original goal?" I asked myself in dismay. Thirty minutes had passed and I had read a lot of interesting material that may have some value to me someday, but had forgotten the initial intention of my search—to find that paper. The good news is that as I went into that rabbit hole, I was able to escape with a valuable... well, rabbit. I found Jonathan Spira[14], an expert in information overload. Spira has some staggering statistics about the time and money lost as a result:

- Information overload costs national economies a substantial amount of dollars due to lost productivity.
- Millions of hours are lost each year around the globe to information overload.
- Reading, processing, and responding to emails has gotten out of control and can occupy half of a typical worker's day.
- A substantial number of professionals surveyed felt incapacitated by information overload.
- Information overload respects no barriers (off-work hours, weekends, nights); we are now connected

14 https://iorgforum.org/?s=spira

24/7, which is having a negative impact on our quality of life.
- Information overload causes us to lose our ability to manage thoughts and reason well.

A major aggravating factor is that we are information-seekers by nature. That is to say that if new technologies are not naturally overloading the system, we will make sure that it is. Gazzaley and Rosen argue in their book, *The Distracted Mind,* that we are information foragers.[15] From an evolutionary perspective, information gives us an adaptive advantage. Our ancestors survived by seeking information about their surroundings, their enemies, and the things that could kill them or would help them survive. Our minds have evolved from this starting point and have not changed much since. The authors claim that, just as a squirrel will forage for food in a certain patch of land before making a decision to move on to a new patch with more resources, we do the same with information. We seek information from a certain source and as soon as it has provided us with what we need, we move on to a different source. It is not hard at all to see this phenomenon play out in real life. We visit the CNN app until the perceived value of the information goes down and then we immediately move on to Fox News or the *New York Times.* After a couple of finger swipes on Facebook, we move on to Instagram.

15 Gazzaley, A., & Rosen, L. D. (2016). *The distracted mind: Ancient brains in a high-tech world.* Boston, MA: MIT Press.

> Not only do we move from one information patch to another just like squirrels searching for food, we also save information for later. (I can't help but think of that neurotic squirrel in the *Ice Age* movie series, trying to save that acorn.) I have the habit of saving academic and newspaper articles, Facebook postings, and bookmarking interesting websites in the hopes of getting back to them later for a more in-depth analysis. The reality is that I rarely get back to them. Not only is time limited, but in a world of information overload, there is always something newer, more interesting, and more updated streaming on my media feeds. In this environment of abundance, it becomes increasingly harder to focus, or to delve deeply into a topic.

If, as discussed before, the winners in today's economy are truly those who can master things that are difficult to master, it will require tremendously focused attention—attention that is now under fire from a constant cascade of information that may or may not (and most probably not) have any relevance to the problem you are trying to solve.

- **Technology has made content irresistibly sexy and addictive.** Matt Ritchel, author of *A Deadly Wandering*, reminds us that the success of apps and new technologies such as Skype, Facebook, and YouTube are not the result of well-elaborated and executed marketing campaigns. They have unsurpassed appeal due to their incredible utility. That is, "they serve deep social cravings and needs."[16] Our basic need to connect, to bond, to be recognized, to be liked,

16 Ritchel, M. (2014). *A deadly wandering: A tale of tragedy and redemption in the age of attention*. New York, NY: HarperCollins Publishers, p.3.

to share, to rise up the social ladder, to be in control, and to know and make sense of our environment is easily and instantly satiated by these new technologies. The information available to us is now so personal that it makes our technologies irresistible and addictive, Ritchel argues.

Take a TV series as another example of the addictive power of technology. A typical movie requires, on average, 120 minutes of your time. Plots in movies are often predictable and follow a set pattern—there is a crisis or a climax, followed by a resolution. This cycle will repeat itself until the major climatic moment at the end of the movie, which is followed by a final resolution. It is rare that you will finish watching a movie wondering what will happen next. In the end, either the bad guys get busted, the main couple makes up, or the world is saved. There is a clear end to the story. With many TV series nowadays, the scenario is very different. Yes, there will be crises and climaxes throughout the average 45 minutes of any given show, but at the very end, just when you think you can turn Netflix off and go on with your life, a major unsolved crisis presents itself. Your dark horse (and at this point, your bright horse and charioteer too) scream inside your head: "There is no way I can turn this off now... I need to know what happens next!" And Netflix has it all set up for you... all you need to do is click "Watch Next."

This feature is called a "Post-Play." As observed by the author of *Irresistible,* "with Post-Play, a thirteen-episode season of *Breaking Bad* became a single, thirteen-hour film."[17] And because the last episode just ended with

17 Alter, A. (2017). *Irresistible: The rise of addictive technology and the business of keeping us hooked.* New York, NY: Penguin Press, p. 208.

unresolved tension (remember the Zeigarnick effect we mentioned earlier), we click on the option to keep watching, committing another 45 minutes of our lives. We binge-watch because these shows end on unsolved tensions, and like an unhealed wound, we have to attend to it. The developers of these shows and technologies not only understand that, but they capitalize and prey on it.

The irresistible allure of new technologies makes us feel an internal tension, a tug-of-war, between our desires and our sense of being in control. It creates a sense of euphoria and arousal, knowing that the tension can be released, or that immediate gratification, pleasure, and reward is only the push of a button away.

- **Technology opens many new doors.** And your dark horse loves doors. It finds absolute delight in peeking through each open door. This constant peeking bombards our brains with information that may or may not be relevant to our goal, diluting our focus. Our brains, contrary to what many think, have a limited attention span—the cognitive capacity to devote attention to, and process stimuli from, our environment. In other words, we can only productively process so much information from our environment at any one time. Dr. Gazzaley, an expert on attention, asserts that attention allows us to set goals and follow through "without being distracted by every bit of information around us. [...] It allows us to interact with the world through our goals and not be led by, or be a slave to, our environment."[18]

18 Ritchel, M. (2014). *A deadly wandering: A tale of tragedy and redemption in the age of attention.* New York, NY: HarperCollins Publishers, p. 35.

Attention is the art of selecting from a large amount of stimuli and focusing on a small subset of those stimuli—the particular subset that will allow you to further your goals and achieve what you have set to achieve.

The issue we face is that these stimuli have increased exponentially, and will continue to increase; they are omnipresent, readily available anywhere we go—and without discernment, it becomes highly difficult to determine which stimuli we must pay attention to.

The power of new technologies, particularly smartphones, to improve our lives and make us more productive is mesmerizing and unprecedented. Technology allows us to do things that only a short time ago were never thought possible. Yet we find ourselves stuck in a double bind—the same things that save us can also be the main reason for our demise. New technologies can free us, but can also enslave us in ways never imagined.

Multitasking

Let me propose a short quiz. According to research by Clifford Ness, from Stanford's Communication Between Humans and Interactive Media Lab, which are the characteristics of multitaskers?[19] Are they:

a) Better at paying attention.
b) Better at remembering.

19 Gorlick, A. (2009). Media multitaskers pay mental price, Stanford study shows. Retrieved from https://news.stanford.edu/2009/08/24/multitask-research-study-082409/

c) Better at switching from one activity to another than those who complete one task at a time.
d) All of the above.
e) None of the above.

I immediately thought of D as the correct answer. It just so happens that this is a tricky quiz and the correct answer is e) none of the above. Yes, you heard me correctly, *none* of the above. If you aren't shell-shocked to hear this answer, I certainly was.

Interestingly, research by Ness and others suggests that if you went through the options above thinking, "Yes, this is me, I am a great multitasker. I pay better attention to multiple tasks, and I am better at switching tasks," then it is very likely that you are not in fact a good multitasker. A study by the Department of Psychology at the University of Utah found that how well participants performed on a test that actually required multitasking—namely memorizing letters and solving math problems—was inversely correlated to their self-reported multitasking ability.[20] In other words, those who believed they had good multitasking skills actually performed worse on the test than those who had a humbler, and perhaps more realistic, view of their abilities. (People and their inflated view of themselves!) Interestingly, poor performance on the multitasking task was also correlated to speaking on the phone while driving, which led the researchers to conclude that, in this study, the very people who shouldn't be multitasking were actually the ones doing so.[21]

---

20 Sanbonmatsu, D. M., Strayer, D. L., Medeiros-Ward, N., & Watson, J. M. (2013). Who multitasks and why? Multitask ability, perceived multitask ability, impulsivity, and sensation seeking. *PLOS One, 8*(1), 1-8.
21 Ibid.

The study also concluded that people multitask not because they are good at it, but because they generally struggle to focus. Managing a task from start to completion is too much for their scattered brains, so they end up engaging in multiple tasks at once.

When I first began working in the professional world, multitasking was considered a highly valuable skill. I believe it still is, as I often hear candidates in job interviews bragging about their ability to multitask. In those days, multitasking was probably one of the first skills a candidate would list on his or her resume.

Being able to juggle multiple projects is indeed a valued and necessary skill. A cook, like most other professions, should be able to multitask—you can't operate a professional kitchen by focusing solely on the egg frying in front of you. You must be able to fry the egg, cook the fish, and keep the cat out of the kitchen.

However, that's all a cook should do: cook. A cook shouldn't be in the dining hall taking orders or managing the cash register (or texting while he cooks). One needs to be completely immersed at the task—or multiple, related tasks—at hand. Frying the egg and the fish is now vying for attention with incoming text messages, calls, updates, push notifications... and eventually the cat will make its move and the egg will burn.

Multitasking, contrary to what we have been led to believe, overwhelms our brain, impairing important cognitive processing abilities, including focus, memory, and the ability to switch from one task to another. In Dr. Ness' words, multitaskers are "suckers for irrelevancy."[22]

---

22 Flatow, I. (2013, May). Talk of the Nation. The Myth of Multitasking. Retrieved from: https://www.npr.org/2013/05/10/182861382/the-myth-of-multitasking

In studies conducted by his Stanford lab, they tried to identify the "multitasker's edge" by having students undergo a number of computer tests. They couldn't find the edge. In fact, they learned that multitaskers were overloaded with information coming from both the environment and from their memories, impairing their ability to discern what was most important to achieve their goal.

Our prefrontal cortexes have limited cognitive processing capacity. Conducting any task requires mental resources, including energy and attention. Because processing a task is resource-intensive, focusing on one task decreases the resources available for a second task. Adding an additional task to our already occupied brains means that the brain has to divert energy away from the primary task to process this secondary task, delaying or impairing the achievement of one or both tasks.

In short, our brain is really good at concentrating on one thing at a time.

Sophie Leroy, from the University of Minnesota, argues that switching tasks creates an "attention residue," or cognitive processes from a task that are not fully turned off even while we start on another task.[23] This means that even though we have changed tasks, there are residual processes running in our brains from the previous task which continue to use up cognitive capacity. We may switch tasks but not necessarily our attention, and as a consequence the performance of both tasks suffer.

Do you recall the 2017 Oscars' flub? It was an epic ending to the most important night of the year, in an industry that is famous for epic endings. The most anticipated award of the night, the

23 Leroy, S. (2009). Why is it so hard to do my work? The challenge of attention residue when switching between work tasks. Organizational Behavior and Human Decision Processes, 109(2), 168-181.

Best Picture Award, was announced as going to the wrong winner: *La La Land.* After some on-stage commotion, it was revealed that the real winner was *Moonlight.* It must have sucked to be the producer of *La La Land,* interrupted while delivering that acceptance speech. The conspiracy theories rolled in—someone didn't want *Moonlight* to win Best Picture, the decision was racially motivated, and so on and so forth.

At the epicenter of this major flub was the PriceWaterhouseCoopers' accountant who was responsible for handing out the envelopes with the names of the winners. At the Oscars, there are always two envelopes for each category, in case one envelope gets lost, misplaced—or God knows what. The accountant responsible for handing the envelope for Best Picture to the presenters in fact accidentally handed them the duplicate envelope for Best Actress instead. The accountant concerned, minutes before handing over the envelope, had tweeted a picture of actress Emma Stone after she won the award for Best Actress. Backstage pictures also show that moments before the Best Picture award announcement, the accountant was holding two envelopes and a phone. It is still unclear whether the phone or the tweet were the true culprits for this major flub, but there is enough circumstantial evidence to believe so: multitasking diminishes our attention span, period. The accountant switched tasks, but not his attention.

Multitasking also delays the amount of time it takes to finish tasks. The graph below is a simple illustration of how multitasking can hamper our ability to produce results within a certain time frame. This is a graphic representation of the time required to write 500 words in a monotasking condition—when you are writing with no distraction. Under these conditions, we need six chunks of time to write 500 words.

8 a.m.	9 a.m.	10 a.m.	11 a.m.
Writing	Calls	Staff Meeting	Meeting with President

Now let's consider a multitasking scenario below. The black blocks represent tasks unrelated to your writing goal. For instance, the first black box represents you trying to find a perfect song on Spotify or Pandora that matches your writing mood; in the second box you are checking your email inbox just for the heck of it; you then realize that your boss wrote to you and you must provide her with an answer right away… and the list goes on.

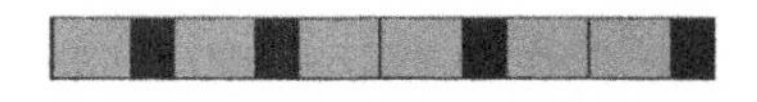

8 a.m.	9 a.m.	10 a.m.	11 a.m.
Writing	Calls	Staff Meeting	Meeting with President

As shown above, you will invariably spend more time and energy on finishing your writing assignment. Also, remember three important points. First, to move back and forth from a black box to our original task requires additional effort and time. Where were you in your writing? What were you thinking when you finished your last sentence? It takes time and energy for your brain to reach peak performance on the original task. Second, as demonstrated above, some actions entice and attract other actions. Peeking at your email inbox will invariably lead to answering emails, further distancing you from what you were doing and the task at hand (writing 500 words). Finally, as you spend more time shifting from writing to managing distractions, you eventually have to move on with your day and attend other scheduled events, leaving your writing unfinished.

Enough of these shaded boxes during our day, and our productivity tanks!

To summarize the issue of multitasking, think of a charioteer who is striving to reach her goal but is being bombarded with stimuli from the environment around her and from her own thoughts. Her eyes are on the goal, but competing distractions and interruptions, both internal and external, draw her attention away from the goal. Multiple cognitive processes running in her head compete for resources, creating a bottleneck. Since we only have limited cognitive processing capacity to deal with stimuli, her processing system heats up. With so many stimuli to choose from, it becomes harder to decide what is important. As a result, she loses focus.

While being able to manage multiple responsibilities is important, it is different from multitasking, which needs to be carefully managed or it can drain our energy and reduce our productivity. New research in the area of multitasking is unveiling its real dangers, which is mainly the cost that our brains must pay for shifting attention between tasks. Self-control helps us choose which tasks to pay attention to and to focus solely on them.

The rise of anxiety

Joshua Ramo reminds us that when we create a ship, we also create the shipwreck.[24] When we created the airplane, we created the plane crash. By that same logic, when we created a superconnected, always-on, and always-engaged society, we also created increased levels of anxiety. Technology and our new devices are not the only causes of this current increase in anxiety—we

24 Ramo, J. C. (2016). *The seventh sense: Power, fortune, and survival in the age of networks.* New York, NY: Little, Brown and Company.

can't discount the impact of terrorism, world crises, an economic crash that devastated numerous households, a polarized political system, helicopter parents, and the list goes on—but it is indeed a major contributing factor.

In part, most of these other issues that may not seem to be technologically-related are aggravated by technology. The overzealous parent reads in a parenting online group, a bucket of think-a-likes, about a newly released study from Harvard showing the quantity of bacteria in various household items and before you know it, prior to dinner, everyone is bathing in Creolin.

According to a *New York Times* article, the number of undergraduates feeling "overwhelming anxiety" increased by 12% between 2011 and 2016. Since 1985, the Higher Education Research Institute at UCLA has been monitoring how overwhelmed undergraduate freshman felt in the previous year. The number of anxious freshmen shot up from 18% in 1985 to 29% in 2010, and to a staggering 41% in 2016.[25]

Our brains possess what one researcher calls a smoke detector.[26] When the brain perceives danger in the environment, the detector goes off, sending a message throughout our nervous system to fight or flight. Anxiety is associated with potential threats in the environment and our perceived ability to manage those threats. Sometimes the threats are real and our ability to do something about them is very little. Other times our

---

25 Denizet-Lewis, B. (2017). Why are more American Teenagers than ever Suffering from Severe Anxiety. https://www.nytimes.com/2017/10/11/magazine/why-are-more-american-teenagers-than-ever-suffering-from-severe-anxiety.html

26 Van der Kolk, B. A. (2014). *The body keeps the score: Brain, mind, and body in the healing of trauma.* New York, NY: Penguin Publishing Group.

high-strung brains overestimate the threat and underestimate our ability to manage them.[27]

Although anxiety often requires professional treatment, self-control and the exercises provided in this book can help us cope.

Pop culture and generational differences

"You are a superstar and you were born this way!" — Lady Gaga[28]

As much as I like Lady Gaga's songs (I really do), I categorically disagree with a comment she made during one of her live concerts. This comment encapsulates the main premise of the "self-esteem" school of thought. As we will see later, although self-esteem is important for achievement and success (after all, if we don't believe in ourselves, including our ability to reach our goals, it is unlikely that we will act upon them), self-esteem is a by-product of our accomplishments. By pumping up people's self-esteem without giving them the tools to succeed, we are not helping them achieve their goals, we are simply creating a false sense of what it takes to achieve a goal. In short, we are instilling the following mindset in them:

---

27 Denizet-Lewis, B. (2017). Why are more American teenagers than ever suffering from severe anxiety? Retrieved from https://www.nytimes.com/2017/10/11/magazine/why-are-more-american-teenagers-than-ever-suffering-from-severe-anxiety.html

28 Baumeister, R. F., & Tierney, J. (2011). *Willpower: Rediscovering the greatest human strength.* New York, NY: Penguin Books.

> *Because you are great (a superstar, and you were born this way), you will achieve whatever you want in life.*

We know that this logic is flawed, and we know that the true logic is:

> *When you work hard, learn from your mistakes, persevere in the face of adversity, and use your talents, you will most likely achieve your goals in life.*

The first logic is deterministic/fatalistic—your fate has already been determined. You are a superstar, you were born this way, and because of that, great things will come to you. (My advice: don't sit around and wait for too long.)

The second logic is conditional. Yes, at the end of the sentence you will achieve (most of) what you choose in life, but a series of conditions must first be met. The word *when* is key here. *When* you do these things, *then* great things will happen. Expecting great things without fulfilling the conditions for them (the *when*), is pure insanity.

The word *most* is also important. We will often not achieve everything we want or desire, and dealing with that reality is a major part of effective life management. From the movie *The Best Exotic Marigold Hotel*: "The measure of success [in life] is how we cope with disappointment."

For years, we have been telling kids and teenagers that they are all "special" and can do no wrong. We have inflated their egos and their self-esteem. We have told them they can't fail. Last place in the soccer tournament? No problem, here's your trophy for participation and for being such a team player. Failed the math test? No problem, you get a B grade for effort.

The problem of inflating people's sense of self-esteem is that, at the end of the day, they have been had so much hot air blown into them that they end up with enlarged, air-filled heads and nothing to show for it. If self-esteem is not backed up by action and accomplishment, it's not a very useful tool. In fact, there is plenty of research showing that self-esteem is not the holy grail of achievement and that it can backfire. Those with high self-esteem are, for example, more likely to engage in risky behavior, think that rules don't apply to them, and believe they can achieve goals with little or no effort.[29] Self-esteem is not the cause of achievement, but the consequence.

Lady Gaga eventually redeemed herself by saying; "I don't like Los Angeles. [...] everybody wants to be famous but nobody wants to play the game."[30]

I would like to draw your attention to those last words, "nobody wants to play the game." Playing the game is such an important point that we will now dedicate a whole chapter to it.

---

29 Baumeister, R. (2005, Winter). Rethinking self-esteem: Why nonprofits should stop pushing self-esteem and start endorsing self-control. *Stanford Social Innovation Review, 3*(4) pp. 34-41.

30 Weiner, J. (2010. March). "Pop Stars Should Not Eat": The 10 Strangest Lady Gaga Quotes from That New York Magazine Piece. *Vanity Fair.* Retrieved from https://www.vanityfair.com/culture/2010/03/pop-stars-should-not-eat-the-10-strangest-lady-gaga-quotes-from-that-new-york-magazine-piece

CHAPTER 3

It's All About the Game: Living in a Socially Constructed World

A RECENT INTERVIEW WITH MIKE Tyson, the controversial boxing champion, stunned me (in a good way). In this interview, Tyson gave Jon Jones—a mixed martial arts prodigy, who saw his title stripped from him after being arrested for a DUI and drug possession—a piece of candid and heartfelt advice: "You know what he has to do? He has to live life on life's terms."[31]

Let's not forget that Tyson's career has been filled with very high highs, and some very low lows, including biting off a piece of an opponent's ear. Even Mike Tyson, whose career seems to have regained some level of normalcy after graduating from the school of hard knocks, has understood a very important truth.

That truth is this: Life is a game. And you have to play the game of life in its own terms. Equally important is that in the

---

31 Fontana, S. (2016). Mike Tyson talks 'Ip Man 3,' boxing, 'UFC 2' video game. *AM NY.* Retrieved from http://www.amny.com/sports/mike-tyson-talks-ip-man-3-boxing-ufc-2-video-game-1.11350592

game of life you must know who the referee is (who is keeping score), what winning entails, and who your competition is.

Playing by the Rules

The world we live in is socially constructed. Unwritten (and written) rules, norms, standards, and laws that moderate social interactions are constructed by and through the interactions between people. In a socially constructed worldview, there is both a material, physical reality and a social reality. Our social reality is constructed through the continuous exchange between members of a group, leading to a general understanding and meaning of the world.

Since most of our achievements happen within the social realm, understanding the standards, norms, and rules of this realm is crucial to success. Abiding by these norms and standards through self-control and regulation is the key to mastering and conquering your environment. Those who successfully read and interpret the environment around them, and are able to meet or surpass its needs, are more likely to succeed.

Those who can't adapt, typically struggle until they start to play by the rules. Teenagers, for instance, are typically anti-establishment. They fight the system tooth and nail, relentlessly trying to assert themselves in a world they perceive as being unjust, out to get them, and plain wrong. The game typically wins.

That is not to say that you cannot change the rules of the game. You can. But first we must play by the rules until we gain enough mastery over the system. Then we can create our own rules.

The Force Field Analysis discussed earlier reminds us that the forces pro-status quo will fight hard to assert themselves and maintain the system in its current form. At a certain point in our lives, we can call the shots and make the rules. But until then...

The "game" metaphor beautifully describes the socially constructed world in which we live.

If you want to be a supermodel, you must have a certain "look" and height. You must also manage your weight, train to move your body in a certain way, attend events where you can see and be seen, and endure long and unconventional work hours. These norms are not necessarily written in stone, but have become accepted and continue to be reshaped by pundits, experts, and consumers in the fashion world. In other words, in order to be a supermodel, besides the physique, you must play and master the supermodel game.

If you want to become a medical doctor, you must demonstrate that you can excel in a rigorous undergraduate science curriculum, volunteer, do well on a standardized entrance test, gain experience in the field, and pass a nerve-wracking interview to only then be offered admission into the medical school of your dreams. After being admitted, you must still endure years of gruesome medical education, complete a residency, and pass a board examination.

You may believe that you will be the first person to ever be accepted to medical school with a 2.1 GPA, but it's just not going to happen. If you want to become a doctor, you must adapt to and master the environmental rules, norms, and standards required by the "game" of admission and the game that is a medical school education.

Architects and engineers often have to deal with limiting standards imposed and enforced by strict building codes. They are also constrained by probably the most universal law: the law of physics. Their creativity is bounded by what physics and the department of building regulations allows them to do. Political power and engineering prowess can be used to challenge these regulations and laws, but their creations are still bounded by these laws and standards. Those who understand and master the laws and design their next mega building around it, will succeed. Those who don't can expect to fight many legal battles, pay fines, and—in the case of the law of physics—experience plain disaster.

Just like with any game, you have other players, competitors, rules that need to be followed, and referees or judges who enforce the rules and give you a score. Your objective is to win. To do so, you must cooperate with team members, understand your competitors, and, if necessary, overcome them.

In the end, in whatever industry or environment you want to succeed, you must embrace it as a game. And you have to play it with gusto. It is your job to understand the rules, the requirements, the prerequisites, the nuances, and the idiosyncrasies of the game and change yourself to fit and master the demands of the game and the environment, not the other way around.

You must also realize that the game is ever-changing. Studies of evolution tell us that an organism's ability to successfully adapt depends on its ability to constantly obtain and process information from the surrounding environment. Once in a while, new players will appear who change the rules of the game. Our ability to obtain this new information, understand that the rules have changed, and adapt accordingly is essential for survival.

Suppose a new breed of zebras emerge that are much faster than their predecessors. Until the lions realize that the new breed requires them to move faster, they will stay hungry.

The Rules Don't Apply to Me

People who are able to adapt to the demands of their environment, whatever that may be, are more likely to succeed. The problem is when the dark horse and the charioteer start to act up. They decide that there are certain rules that don't need to be followed or that some rules don't apply to them. They pick and choose how and where to engage. The dark horse and the charioteer negotiate which rules are worth following, relieving them of activities that they don't "feel" like doing.

In addition—and this is an important point—let's not put all the blame of our failures on the dark horse. As we will discuss later, the charioteer can be just as guilty as the dark horse when it comes to derailing us.

Most weight loss, marketing, sales, and entrepreneurship programs with proven results often fall short of their promised results. You can curse the person promoting these programs as much as you want, to no avail. The problem is not with the system per se, but with how we implement the system. For instance, let's imagine you read a book on how to become a social media whiz. The program is clear:

1) You must post something interesting on social media sites at least three times a day.
2) You must find new people to follow on a daily basis.

Easy, right? If you do these two things consistently and diligently, your social media following will invariably grow. Initially, you get excited and convince yourself that you will follow the plan to a "t"; after all, who can fail a two-step plan? At this point, the new influx of energy stemming from the charioteer and the bright horse subdues the negative energy of the dark horse.

But don't be fooled. Slowly but surely, the dark horse starts quietly asking some intriguing questions and making seductive suggestions that pique your curiosity and make you wonder if you *really* need to post three times a day. Maybe the person who wrote the plan is an obsessive compulsive with nothing better to do. Maybe posting three times a day is only necessary in some industries and not in others. Maybe social media is not that important after all.

Quietly, the dark horse takes control of the situation and has its way. These suggestions are considered plausible by a rational charioteer who then gives in to the dark horse's seductive voice. You fail to implement the two-step program and your social media following is meager. In other words, you failed the social media game by playing your own game.

Take for instance the case of John (a fictitious name but a true story). John was conditionally admitted to his dream school, but because he had not yet taken a required standardized test, his spot in the class would only be confirmed after he passed the test with a certain minimum score. The admissions committee absolutely loved him. He was a vivacious person with a winning personality. I sat down with him and shared a piece of advice I share with all my students: to do well on the test he would need to put in approximately 300 hours of study (Three months of study, 3–4 hours every day.) This is what I told him.

Months later, he scheduled an appointment to see me. Due to the high volume of students I usually counsel, I did not remember his case. He briefly described his situation and shared that he had not passed the test. I gave him the bad news: he would have to retake the test. I went on to say, "*You will need to study for three mon—*" He interrupted me and said, "I know what you are going to say, we already had this conversation before, but I decided not to spend so much time..."

I confess that at this point I stopped listening. My internal voice couldn't help but say, "and that's exactly why we are having this conversation, isn't it?!"

This student had failed to play the game of the test. Certainly the dark horse got its way by insinuating that he was special and because of that, "all those hours weren't really needed." I laid out the rules of the game, clearly, with no ambiguity, but he decided not to play by them. And so he failed in his larger goal: to get admitted to the program. The dark horse insinuated and the charioteer bought into it.

The same is true for self-imposed goals. Goals are self-imposed standards that we commit ourselves to. We carry internal standards for various different aspects of our lives. When these self-imposed standards are established, we then need to change our thoughts, emotions, and actions to comply with and achieve them.

Let's say you learn about a new exercise routine that promises a toned body and healthy living. This routine is in tune with your standard of living a healthy life. You then need to self-regulate to implement that life and live by that standard. The dark horse will kick and scream, but your job is to tame it.

When Liking Becomes Irrelevant

The most important lesson we can learn from the game metaphor is that when the stakes are high—and the stakes are always high, when you want to accomplish something that matters—it is not about *you* anymore, it is about the game. This is probably the toughest medicine I give to my students.

One of the favorite anonymous quotes I carry with me is that, when it comes to most arenas we choose to be successful in, "liking is irrelevant."

You may say to yourself that you don't like organic chemistry and because of that you will focus your efforts on other subjects. You may convince yourself that you don't like managing employees, building personal relationships, or the accounting side of your business and that you therefore prefer to focus on other areas that are more appealing to you.

But by playing to your likes, you are setting yourself up for failure.

This is one of the issues with the self-esteem movement and the career advice industry. In the self-esteem movement, it is all about *you*—you are a rock star, a champion, someone special. The career advice industry has long encouraged us to follow our passion. While it is important to have a high sense of self-efficacy and believe in yourself, pumping yourself up with inflated beliefs about how great you are is often counterproductive.

In the end, the game cares nothing about *you*, including your likes, needs, desires, passions, and wants (stuff the dark horse indulges in). The game doesn't give a rat's a** about your stardom. Winning is about your ability to suppress the needs of your dark horse, empower your bright horse, control your charioteer, and adapt to the rules of the game.

That is where self-control comes into play. Those who adapt to their environment and suppress the demands of the dark horse have higher odds of success.

If you are planning on being an entrepreneur, there are certain fitting characteristics and behaviors that are required by the game of entrepreneurship. If you are planning on becoming a doctor, there are certain milestones and standards that you have to reach, which are determined by the game of medical school admissions. If you plan to successfully launch a product… you get the point. There is a game for everything and our job is to make a wild dark horse play nicely in the game's sand box.

Making Meaning

Humans are meaning-making animals and causal machines. We create meaning in the world around us by creating mental rules about how the world works, based on previous experiences and through inference.

Although these inferences often provide us with very accurate approximations of how things work—that is, how to play the game to win—these self-made rules are often incomplete and not truly representative of how things work in the real world. Expertise in any area of life often requires extensive periods of training and an experienced coach who can guide us through the nuances of mastering the game.

In summary, an optimal fit between the individual and the environment often leads to success. Your ability to apply self-control to become a good fit will determine your ultimate success. An experienced coach or mentor can guide you, helping you play the game to win.

Questions for Reflection

- Do you have a good understanding of the rules of the game? If you don't, where can you learn them? Can you consult a coach or mentor?
- Are you playing by the rules? Is your dark horse in cahoots with the charioteer and trying to negotiate possible ways

around abiding by the rules? Who is in control... you or the dark horse?

- How do you know that you are playing the game to the best of your ability? What is the hard evidence that supports your claim?
- How do you know that the dark horse is not sneaking up on you and making you believe things that are not true?

CHAPTER 4

The Science of Self-Control

Defining Self-Control

Professor Baumeister, a psychologist from Florida State University and one of the foremost authorities on the science of self-control, considers self-control the most promising human strength.[32] He began his career on the self-esteem bandwagon, but soon realized that self-esteem was not the remedy for human achievement that people had expected it to be in the '80s and '90s.

In fact, Baumeister found that self-esteem was often a *consequence* of achievement, not a cause. You do well in school and your self-esteem increases. You do well in sports, you get a boost of self-esteem. Having an inflated sense of self-esteem won't make you a better tennis player or help you do well on a math test. Although very low levels of self-esteem may lead to performance issues, high self-esteem does not equal success.

On the other hand, self-control allows a person to adjust the self to any given situation and apply energy and resources towards achieving their goals.

32 Baumeister, R. F., & Tierney, J. (2011). *Willpower: Rediscovering the greatest human strength.* New York, NY: Penguin Books.

Early studies in self-control began in the '60s and '70s with the seminal Stanford Marshmallow study by Mischel.[33] In this experiment, children could choose a small but immediate reward (one cookie, which, in subsequent studies, was replaced with a marshmallow) or, if they waited for fifteen minutes, they could get a larger reward (two cookies). Follow-up studies showed that students who chose the larger reward later (that is, who were able to delay gratification) were, in general, more successful in life.

Various subsequent studies confirmed the benefits of delayed gratification and self-control. Today, the benefits of self-control are well established in the literature. The literature in the field concurs that those who possess self-control are, in general, more socially-adapted individuals. These individuals find the right balance between the demands of the self and the demands of environment in which they operate.

Individuals who have self-control are:[34]

- More likely to engage in mature behaviors.
- More likely to do better at school and work.
- Less likely to report stress and stress-related illnesses.
- More likely to report having positive relationships.
- More likely to have better mental health.

In short, individuals with self-control have superior physical and mental health, better relationships, and are more accomplished.

33 Mischel, W., Shoda, Y., & Rodriguez, M. L. (1992). Delay of Gratification in Children. In G. Lowenstein & J. Elster (Eds.), *Choice Over Time* (pp. 147–64). Russell Sage Foundation: New York, NY: 147-64.

34 Tangney, J. P., Baumeister, R. F., Boone, A. L. (2004). High self-control predicts good adjustment, less pathology, better grades, and interpersonal success. *Journal of Personality, 72*(2), 271-322.

But what is self-control? Self-control is the ability to override the demands of the ego. In other words, it is the regulation *of* the self *by* the self, or our ability to override default impulses. It is the ability of the charioteer to tame and quiet the dark horse, to control its immediate urges. And it is our ability to control the charioteer. Technically speaking, self-control includes self-regulation, self-discipline, willpower, effortful and executive control, time preference, and the delay of gratification.[35]

The Muscle Metaphor

Empirical research on self-control suggests that self-control is like a muscle—the more you exercise it, the stronger it gets. It also needs fuel to operate well and time to recover.[36] As any professional bodybuilder, Olympic athlete, marathon runner, or Ironman competitor will tell you, to be toned a muscle needs to be exercised, needs energy in order to function properly, and also must get some much-needed rest.

Exercise

The good news about self-control is that it can increase if you properly exercise it. The more you use the self-control muscle, the stronger it gets. As it strengthens, we can then exert it in different domains of our lives. If your favorite TV show is just too appealing to get you focused on your goal, don't despair. You

35 Duckworth, A. L. (2011). The significance of self-control. *Proceedings of the National Academy of Sciences*, 108, 2639–2640.

36 Baumeister, R. F., & Tierney, J. (2011). *Willpower: Rediscovering the greatest human strength.* New York, NY: Penguin Books.

can use the exercises in this book to train for your personal self-control workout.

Just like having a strong muscle in your body has multiple benefits (i.e. a strong biceps lets you lift weights at the gym with ease and also lift furniture when you are helping your friend move), so does the self-control muscle. This is known as the cascading effect: developing self-control in one area of your life also improves your ability to regulate the self in other areas.

For example, research shows that engaging in small self-awareness exercises such as monitoring your posture (sitting up straight) and language (not swearing) are a good warm-ups for your self-control muscle, eventually impacting other areas that also require self-regulation.[37]

John Wooden, the legendary basketball player and coach, who as head coach of UCLA won ten NCAA national championships including an unmatched winning streak of seven in a row, intuitively understood the cascading effect of self-control. Wooden said: "In my 40 years of coaching, you will not find a player that can honestly tell you that he ever heard me use profanity. (…) Self-control in little things leads to control of bigger things." Those with dirty mouths well-suited to become crew members on a pirate ship wouldn't do well on his team. Profanity was prohibited both in practice sessions and in games. "I felt that a player who couldn't control his language when he got upset during a scrimmage would be more likely to lose control in more damaging ways during the heat of a competition," [38] said Wooden.

---

37 Ibid.

38 Daniels, A. (2012). OOPS! 13 Management Practices that Waste Time & Money (and what to do instead) (Kindle Edition). Retrieved from https://www.amazon.com, Kindle Locations 1689–1693.

Energy

In Brazil, whenever a person is in severe distress, the first remedy is to offer a *copo de água com açúcar* or a glass of water with sugar—lots of sugar. I remember as if it were yesterday a shaken neighbor knocking on our door, asking for help as she had just been robbed. Without hesitating, my mother offered her a large *copo de água com açúcar* to calm her nerves. In those days, this was just a customary habit passed down from generation to generation. It so happens that this gesture, embedded in traditional wisdom, might actually really do the trick. There is plenty of evidence in modern psychological literature to suggest that self-control is regulated by glucose.[39]

Baumeister and Tierney recount a number of eye-opening studies linking glucose and self-control.[40] The first such link was established in studies of hypoglycemic individuals. Hypoglycemia, or low blood sugar, happens when blood sugar is below normal levels. People with low blood sugar have trouble concentrating, and are generally found to be more temperamental, explosive, and more anxious.

One of the most fascinating accounts is a study by researchers in Finland who measured the glucose tolerance levels—the ability to convert food into energy—of criminals being released from the correctional system.[41] People with impaired glucose tolerance are able to break food down into smaller glucose molecules, but the glucose is not properly absorbed by the body. The researchers were able to predict with more than 80% accuracy

---

39 Baumeister, R. F., & Tierney, J. (2011). *Willpower*: Rediscovering the greatest human strength. New York, NY: Penguin Books.

40 Ibid.

41 Ibid.

who would be re-offenders, based on glucose tolerance levels alone.

Additional research on high-performance athletes suggests that just a hint to our brain that glucose is on its way is enough to boost self-control.[42]

So far, we have seen that self-control is negatively affected by both low levels of blood glucose and high levels of blood glucose that the body cannot absorb. Think of a charioteer who spends a lot of energy controlling the dark horse, yet has no fuel available to her or has plenty of fuel but no access to it.

To make matters more complicated, high-level brain processes, like self-control, are energy-hungry processes. As we exercise our self-control muscle, it consumes a lot of available energy. Our storage of glucose diminishes, diminishing our ability to exert self-control in future tasks. Although there are other mechanisms that regulate self-control, such as motivation and grit, ego depletion—due to diminished levels of glucose—impacts our ability to perform well in tasks that require regulation.

Thus, eating healthy meals and maintaining appropriate levels of glucose in our bloodstream, particularly when you are exerting self-control, is essential to keep the charioteer alert and in control.

Rest

No matter how rigid the workout regimen of professional athletes may be, they all have one thing in common embedded in them:

42 McClusky, M. (2014). *Faster, higher, stronger: How sports science is creating a new generation of superathletes and what can we learn from them* (Kindle Edition). Retrieved from https://www.amazon.com.

a rest period. This is a period when muscles can recover, repair and strengthen. In fact, rest is essential to high-level athletic performance, while continuous workouts without a rest period can have the opposite effect and weaken the muscles. The same is true of self-control. Overextending your self-control muscle can deplete it, resulting in adverse effects.

To avoid ego depletion and the overextension of the self-control muscle, we need to give ourselves breaks between tasks and after long periods of intense work. We need a break after immediate tasks, such as breaks after twenty minutes to one hour of focused work. We also need weekly or weekend breaks, and breaks after months of work—in other words, a well-deserved vacation.

There are those who mistake self-control for incessant work and who insist that they keep going without a break. The science of self-control suggests that this might in fact be the wrong strategy. As is the case on many occasions in life, we sometimes have to slow down in order to speed up.

Bill Clinton, who made his fair share of not-so-high-functioning decisions, admitted that most of his bad decisions were made when he was too tired. Research shows that although an excuse in Mr. Clinton's case, this claim does have some validity. Being tired lowers the activity in our pre-frontal cortex, our executive center, and defers decision-making to the more automatic limbic system.

In other words, the charioteer goes to sleep leaving the wild horse in total control of the reigns.

John Medina, a molecular biologist, states that "sleep loss means mind loss. Sleep loss cripples thinking [...] attention, executive (brain) function, immediate memory, working memory, mood, qualitative skills, logical skills, logical reasoning ability, and general math knowledge."[43] In other words, a sleep-deprived charioteer is less effective in controlling a willful dark horse.

Arianna Huffington, founder of the *Huffington Post* and member of the executive council of Harvard Medical School's Division of Sleep Medicine, is one of the newest self-proclaimed SEs (Sleep Evangelists). In her book, *Thrive*, she makes a strong case for our need to seek better quality sleep as a means to refresh the self and attain better health.[44] Sleep deprivation has many negative consequences for our health, including mood disorders, and impairment of our ability to focus and to process high-level cognitive functions.

In their book *Scarcity: Why Having Too Little Means so Much*, authors Sendhil Mullainathan and Eldar Shafir remind us that those who have to constantly make decisions about money issues (those who live in a world of scarcity) in fact end up making worse financial decisions.[45] They are depleted, their charioteers tired, therefore impeding their ability to make good decisions, financial or otherwise. In other words, we have a limited bandwidth to deal with problems; when our processing system has to be constantly engaged, it overheats. As a result we make poorer decisions, or we just don't want to deal with making them at all, and so we let our emotions take over the decision-making process.

---

43 Forrester, D. P. (2011). *Consider: Harnessing the power of reflective thinking in your organization.* New York, NY: Palgrave Macmillan, p. 47.

44 Huffington, A. (2014). *Thrive: The third metric to redefining success and creating a life of well-being, wisdom, and wonder.* New York, NY: Harmony Books.

45 Mullainathan, S. & Shafir, E. (2013). *Scarcity: Why having too little means so much.* New York, NY: Times Books.

The mind

So far we have discussed how energy, in the form of glucose, and rest restore adverse effects of ego depletion. It is important to emphasize that ego depletion is a metaphor that illustrates the processes associated with self-control, but just like with any metaphor, it is incomplete.

We tend to think of ego depletion as the exhaustion of a finite resource, which to a certain extent means glucose and the energy we get from it. Our charioteers have full tanks, but overusing that supply causes the fuel to run out, leaving the charioteer with no alternative source of energy for fulfilling her job.

We've all had a certain point in our lives when we experienced a situation in which we felt finished, done, depleted, or exhausted, and yet we somehow tapped into an almost supernatural source of drive and energy that seemed to have been hidden from us before that moment. Where does that extra jolt of energy come from? How is it possible, if we know for a fact we were completely depleted?

A plausible explanation for this phenomenon is found in the study of sports science and achievement.[46] Fatigue is a common experience when we over-extend our bodies physically (and mentally). Fatigue has always been of major interest to sports scientists since finding a way to overcome it could mean the difference between winning and losing, particularly in resistance sports.

We have been often told that fatigue is a physiological process (think of the burning sensation you feel on your calf when you over extend yourself). There are scholars who now propose that fatigue is not merely a physiological process. In fact, fatigue

46 McClusky, M. (2014). *Faster, higher, stronger: How sports science is creating a new generation of superathletes—and what can we learn from them* (Kindle Edition). Retrieved from https://www.amazon.com.

is a brain reading of various signals, including physiological, conscious and unconscious signals that are orchestrated to maintain homeostasis, ensuring that no damage is caused to our hearts and other essential parts of our bodies. This theory is also known as the "Central Governor" theory.[47]

In this case, the central governor is the brain, recruiting muscles according to its perceived level of exertion. The "governor" is a feedback processing machine, fine-tuning feelings of being energized and fatigued, depending on its interpretation of how much you will require of your body to cross the finish line without breaking down the system entirely. Based on the brain's interpretation of the task at hand, its previous experiences with the previous task, various environmental conditions, your physiological capacity, and well-being, the brain makes careful calculations and determines the pace you should take.

In this view, "fatigue is an emotion, a construct in the mind that helps ensure that exercise is performed within the body's ability. That emotion is affected by many factors, such as motivation, anger, fear, memories of past performance, self-belief, and what the body is telling the brain." [48]

It is not only high-performing Olympic athletes who experience the central governor pulling the strings of performance. Think of the last time you were completely exhausted and cranky, with a strong feeling that there was nothing else left in your tank. Suddenly, you were presented with a high-stakes opportunity—the CEO called you into her office and made you the project manager on an important project. You felt a jolt of

---

47 Ibid.

48 McClusky, M. (2014). *Faster, higher, stronger: How sports science is creating a new generation of superathletes— and what we can learn from them* (Kindle Edition). Retrieved from https://www.amazon.com, p 150.

energy and you immediately started planning and taking actions to make that project a success. Where was that dead person from a couple of minutes ago? Gone!

Recently, I spent an all-nighter working on a project. I couldn't start working on my part of the project until a colleague sent me his part. I was idle from 8 p.m. until 11 p.m. waiting for him to send me his part. I had been working on this project non-stop and my son had just been born. By 10:30 p.m., I was convinced I was not going to be able to make it. My eyes were shutting down, my vision was blurred, and my energy levels were depleted. By 11 p.m., when I heard the blipping sound of my email informing me that the material I was waiting for had arrived, I went into production mode for more than six hours non-stop. It is as if my brain was forcing a shutdown when I was idle. But when I needed to perform, since there was no other choice, I was back on the road to high productivity and alertness once again.

Think also of instances when you felt depleted, lacking in your ability to control yourself. You become mouthy with your spouse, short-tempered, a bully, and an unbearable grump. But your boss calls, and instantly you are on your best behavior.

At a certain level, it feels that the brain compartmentalizes experiences, saving the energy available for certain types of interactions in separate buckets. While the spouse/family bucket may be depleted, you will find the energy to exert self-control in other areas where the consequences of losing control of your mouth could be extra costly (for example, it could cost you your job). In the "Central Governor" theory, the brain is making these calculations non-stop as we process the world and the situations around us.

Where is Self-Control Located in Our Heads?

Self-control is often attributed to the prefrontal cortex (PFC) of the brain. This outer, newer part of our brains has gained much prominence lately in cognitive psychology literature for being the place in the brain that houses high-order thinking, executive decision-making power, and self-control. It is often labeled as the "rational" brain.

Although the PFC represents only 4-5% of the volume of the brain, it houses five major cognitive functions, including understanding, deciding, recalling, memorizing, and inhibiting impulses. In short, it is where our ability to think rationally, to plan for the future, and to control impulses resides.[49] By now you probably already know that the PFC is the charioteer in our allegory.

Although the PFC deserves its moment of glory, let's not forget that the brain does possess other systems responsible for self-regulation. These systems are, however, associated with automatic, emotional responses, such as the fight-flight-freeze mechanism, and to a large degree function without much conscious control on our part. (May I suggest here that our love affair with the PFC is partially due to the fact that it is under our direct, conscious control.)

If the PFC is the hero of this story, then the limbic system—the most basic, primitive part of the brain—is often (wrongly) labeled as the villain. The desires emanating from the limbic

---

49 Rock, D. (2009). *Your brain at work: Strategies for overcoming distractions, regaining focus, and working smarter all day long.* Retrieved from http://www.amazon.com.

system are typical of the dark horse. However, the limbic system, including the brain stem, the amygdale, and the hypothalamus, do not need any more bad press; they need the opposite.

Seeking pleasure, avoiding pain

It is part of human psychology to maintain homeostasis—the process of internal regulation to stay in the state of equilibrium needed for survival.[50] The process of homeostasis is achieved unconsciously by the limbic system. For instance, the brain stem and hypothalamus are constantly scanning our internal and external environment in search of information that upsets our internal balance. When disconfirming information is detected, a motivating emotional response prompts us to seek corrective actions, bringing the body back to its original state of equilibrium. Internal balance may be disrupted by internal threats, such as hunger and thirst, as well as external threats, such as the identification of pain or imminent danger in the environment. Thus, the saying that the brain avoids pain and seeks pleasure is equivalent to saying, "the limbic system seeks homeostasis," which does indeed include pain-avoidance.

Environmental threats place the brain in a state of emotional arousal, bringing the emotional temperature up to dangerous levels. The limbic system selects between the alternatives of fight-flight-freeze to respond; unless, of course, the PFC kicks in to take over the situation and you find a way out by employing some good ol' thinking.

---

50 Churchland, P. S. (2011). *Braintrust: what neuroscience tells us about morality*. Princeton, NJ: Princeton University Press.

The limbic system runs the automatic program that evolution has gifted us with to deal with imminent threats to our internal equilibrium. However, we must keep in mind that this sophisticated system has not evolved at the same pace as the world around us. As such, we may have instinctive reactions to potential threats that are disproportionate or completely unnecessary. (I discuss this phenomenon in more detail later in this book.) We also have instinctive impulses and desires that are outright maladaptive and socially abhorrent. And these—for any society to function well and for us to function well in society—must be controlled and tamed. In fact, Freud equaled civilization to the domestication of our instinctual impulses.

Applying the brakes

We also have a mechanism for inhibiting instinctual, "hot" system types of responses. A region in the PFC called the Ventrolateral Prefrontal Cortex (VLPCF) lights up in the brain during functional magnetic imagery if we inhibit motor, cognitive, or emotional responses.

David Rock, author of *Your Brain at Work,* describes the VLPFC as being the brakes in your car.[51] For instance, the brain sends impulses to your body in a process that can be broken down into three parts: brain signal, desire and movement. The brain signal creates the desire, which then may or may not become a movement or action, depending on how effective the VLPFC is at stopping it. Think about the times when

---

51 Rock, D. (2009). *Your brain at work: Strategies for overcoming distractions, regaining focus, and working smarter all day long.* Retrieved from http://www.amazon.com.

you were cut off in traffic. The recklessness of the drivers creates a brain signal and activates a desire: shout at them from the top of your lungs. You may also apply the VLPCF breaks, control your instinctual desire to shout, and wish them a safe drive. Rock reminds us that the VLPFC has some design bugs that have major consequences for us—it is located in the most energy-hungry part of the brain and it only works sometimes. The more we use the brakes, the more our capacity to use it in subsequent tasks decreases.

Another challenge with stepping on the brakes in time to stop impulsive behavior is the speed at which things happen in our brains. The brain decides to act upon something 0.3 seconds before we are conscious of it. Before you consider being cordial to the reckless driver, your brain had already decided to shout. Before you have an emotional reaction that you may later regret, the brain is already a couple of steps ahead of you. The speed between the brain's signal, the desire, and your body's movement is often too great for us to effectively control.

Remember that in our allegory the dark horse is in front of the chariot, being controlled by the reins. The pull on the reins to control the horse is always an after-the-fact endeavor.

There are, however, several ways to manipulate the brain's signal-desire-movement sequencing, which will be further discussed in Part II. For instance, we can avoid cues that trigger the brain signal to begin with, but as suggested by Rock, being aware of the brain signal-desire-action sequencing is a good start.

Renowned psychiatrist and Holocaust survivor, Dr. Viktor Frankl, beautifully stated that "between stimulus and response there is a space. In that space is our power to choose our response. In our response lies our growth and our freedom." Who am I to argue with him? But the truth of the matter is that, yes, there is a space, but the space is short. Very short. So short that in some instances it feels as if there is no space at all. And in some instances, there is no space. We are so conditioned to certain responses that the space disappears.

Unfortunately, there is no recall for this bug. We have to create the patches ourselves. Due to the rapid nature of our responses, probably the best possible patch to suppress instinctual responses is to develop healthy habits. In Part II, I share a proven strategy to build new habits. But before that, let's discuss the anatomy of habits.

Creatures of habit

As is the case with most structures of the brain, scientists only discovered their functions and utility following brain injuries that affect a specific part of the brain. For instance, the role of the PFC as the powerhouse of high-level cognitive thinking was discovered by observing several cases of individuals who lost their decision-making abilities, following a brain injury that affected the outer part of their brains.

When it comes to the part of the brain that houses our habits, its discovery was no different. Scientists realized that animals with injuries to an oval part of the brain, which looks a lot like a bean sprout in its very early stages of growth, developed problems in performing habitual tasks. Meet the basal ganglia. The basal ganglia is the part of the brain that identifies, codifies, stores and repeats habits.

If you have not appreciated the beauty of brain anatomy by now, the basal ganglia will make you fall in love with it. As discussed before, certain brain activities can be energy-hungry. The basal ganglia is an incredible evolutionary device that allows the brain to recognize patterns in your environment and transform them into a habit, saving considerable amounts of energy.

In a fascinating experiment, scientists inserted wires into the skulls of rats to monitor brain activity as they learned their way through a T-shaped maze with chocolate at one end. As the rats learned their way through the maze, considerable brain activity was recorded, particularly in the basal ganglia. As scientists repeated the experiment, they realized that the rats' behaviors started to change. As expected, they engaged in less exploratory behavior and were all business; they wanted the food and knew how to get it. Interestingly, scientists also recorded a substantial *decrease* in brain activity. The rats had become creatures of habit, with little need to process environmental information to make decisions. The brain probes showed that the basal ganglia had stored a sequence of activities and were in high gear when rats were at the maze, while little activity was identified in other parts of the brain.[52]

The basal ganglia is crucial for our discussion on self-control and discipline. As seen before, there are three basic challenges we have to grapple with on a daily basis: 1) the more primitive part of our brain, the limbic system, which often overreacts to stimuli and cues; 2) the prefrontal cortex and the ventrolateral prefrontal cortexes, which are energy-hungry systems that get exhausted after being over-extended, diminishing our ability to inhibit impulses; and 3) even when the PCF and VLPFC are fresh and full of energy, we may still rationalize decisions that go against our best interests in order to protect our self-image.

---

52 Duhigg, C. (2014). *The power of habit: Why we do what we do in life and business.* New York, NY: Random House.

This is a lot to control and to keep in mind. Thus, the best solution is to download cognitive functioning into the basal ganglia through the acquisition of good and healthy habits. In doing so, we train the dark horse not to react to impulses while at the same time releasing the need for the charioteer to be in constant control, which we know by now is not a good strategy.

Conscious mental activity consumes energy at much faster rate when compared to automatic brain functions. For example, think of when you're driving on a flat highway and you reach cruising speed. Inertia kicks in and the green light indicating that you are now in fuel-saving mode flashes on. On the other hand, if you decide to pass the truck in front of you, you must hit the gas pedal, considerably increasing your fuel consumption. Engaging in higher-level cognition is the equivalent to hitting the gas pedal—it requires a lot of energy, and consequently, a lot of fuel (glucose). And just like the fuel in your car, you only have so much of it until it has to be replenished.

The Chemistry of the Brain and Self-Control

The food that fuels the horses, both bright and dark, is dopamine. Dopamine is a neurotransmitter that operates in the brain's reward center. It is responsible for motivation, perseverance, and pleasure. The right quantity of dopamine at the right place at the right time is essential for the functioning of any healthy human being. The problem is when the dark horse overindulges in it.

Dopamine tells us when we have done something good. It is released when we engage in experiences crucial for our survival or intense experiences with high rewards, like eating, accomplishing things, and having sex. The release of dopamine tells the brain that the experience is important, creating a reward circuit. Dopamine is not only released when we engage in pleasurable activities—the sheer anticipation of a reward actually releases dopamine and makes us want more of it. It makes us not only identify and anticipate rewards, but also take action toward them. That is when the dark horse goes a little wild.

Imagine that you update your Facebook profile and 50 people like your update and 5 people comment on it. The social recognition you just received is exhilarating, releasing dopamine. You now feel a sense of arousal and you start to mentally craft your next post, hoping to receive 51 likes. There is tension caused by the anticipation, which gets you excited and releases more dopamine. These releases of dopamine create an anticipatory link—each tiny reward makes you crave larger rewards. And when the rush of excitement fades, the dark horse protests, wanting more of it.

This cycle of arousal, tension, release, pleasure overpowers the logical center of the brain, the charioteer.[53] It is as if your chariot is being pulled without the interference of the charioteer. The charioteer may sense that the action you are about to take contradicts your long-term goals and what you believe in, but the pull of the dark horse has already steered the chariot towards the reward. When dopamine puts our brains on a reward-seeking mission, we

53 Ritchel, M. (2014). *A deadly wandering: A tale of tragedy and redemption in the age of attention.* New York, NY: HarperCollins Publishers.

become the most risk-taking, impulsive, and out-of-control versions of ourselves.[54]

Interestingly, although dopamine is associated with the pleasure center of the brain, this pleasure does not necessarily create happiness. In fact, it can backfire. Engaging the anticipatory link creates anxiety.

To complicate this state of affairs, modern mobile technologies have allowed us to receive incessant rewards. Bored? Press that key on your phone and you shall get endless connectivity, social recognition, news, and entertainment. It's a constant promise of a flood of dopamine through our system. In his book *A Deadly Wandering*, Ritchel asserts that the mere presence of our devices offer the promise of hits—making them, to say the least, addictive.

54 McGonigal, K. (2012). *The willpower instinct: How self-control works, why it matters, and what you can do to get more of it.* New York, NY: Penguin Group, p.116.

CHAPTER 5

Why The Charioteer (Self-Control) Fails Us?

MOST OF US DON'T STRUGGLE with self-control, until we do.

Routine work doesn't require self-control because routine tasks have been downloaded into, and are operated by, the basal ganglia. However, we often encounter what I call "moments of truth," or what other authors call an "inflection point." In calculus, an inflection point is a point in a curve at which the curve changes shape. A curve with a convex shape, at an inflection point, becomes concave.

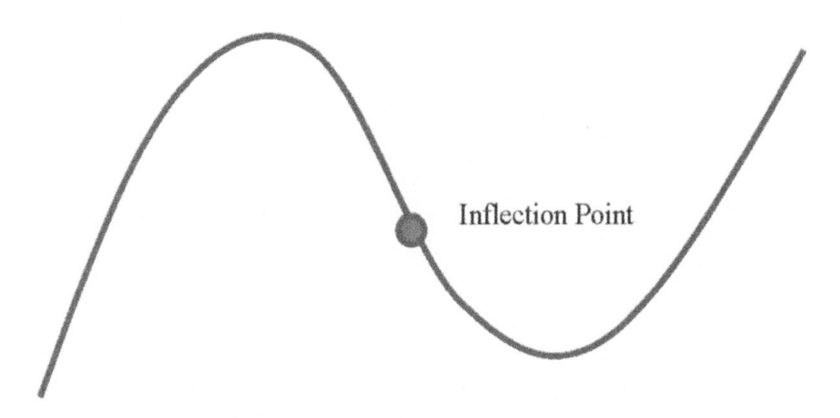

Think of the last time you had to exert self-control. You decided to sit down and write. You wrote for the first three minutes and suddenly you were checking emails and browsing the Internet. When you made the switch from focused to unfocused, that was a moment of truth (or an inflection point), when self-control actually changes the outcome of an event.

Moments of truth typically involve dilemmas, a decision between two choices. On the one hand, you have an option that yields guaranteed, concrete results; on the other, you have an option that yields uncertain results but that in the long term could be very beneficial. You have to choose between this and that, when choosing both is impossible, not ideal, or will have significantly different consequences in the long- and short-term.

We are faced with these moments of truth ignited by dilemmas on a daily basis—to work out or be sedentary, to eat consciously and healthily or pig out, to study or binge-watch your favorite TV show.

Later in this book, I will share helpful strategies for enhancing self-control. But before we take the medicine, we must understand why we do the things we do in the first place.

Taking the medicine without having this understanding would be equivalent to taking diet pills while still consuming 5,000 calories a day—it's not going to help you, unless you understand why you are gaining weight to begin with. The focus of this next section is to try and understand why the charioteer fails us when dilemmas or moments of truth arise.

Failing Twice Over

Scholars at the University of Chicago[55] have developed a two-stage model to explain our failure to control the self. Stage 1 is recognizing the conflict between temptations and goals, and Stage 2 involves implementing actions to avoid succumbing to these temptations.

We typically fail at one or both stages of the model. That is, we fail to recognize that there is a conflict between our temptations and our goals (that there is in fact a dilemma or tension that needs to be solved), or we fail to take appropriate action to deal with our temptations—or both at once.

For instance, if you are planning to implement a project, you can fail to exert self-control by:

Stage 1. Failing to recognize that there is a conflict between temptations and your ultimate goal:	**Stage 2. Failing to implement strategies to avoid succumbing to temptations:**
• Failing to recognize that answering every email as soon as it reaches your inbox consumes valuable time	• Failing to reconsider strategies for how to answer emails effectively

(continued)

55 Myrseth, K. O. R., & Fishbach, A. (2009). Self-control: A functional of knowing when and how to exercise restraining. *Current Directions in Psychological Science, 18*(4), 247–252.

• Failing to recognize that keeping the same schedule of unproductive meetings takes up valuable time that could be devoted to more important goals	• Failing to cancel less important meetings until you accomplish/finalize your project • Failing to start your day early when there are no or fewer distractions in the office
• Failing to recognize that spending large amounts of time socializing with co-workers eats up your time	• Failing to create alone time
• Failing to recognize that certain people and places are cues for undesired behavior	• Failing to eliminate negative people from your life

If you fail to recognize that these temptations or habitual impulses are impairing your ability to achieve your goal, you cannot act upon them to correct them. As Dr. Phil, the celebrity psychologist, is known for saying: "You cannot change what you do not acknowledge." And after acknowledging it, you must have the guts to do something about it.

In the exercise below, first think about a goal you want to achieve. Then write down in the first column the temptations, impulses and other activities that keep you from achieving your goal. Now that you have taken the first step in successfully controlling the self by identifying conflicts, take the second step and identify potential solutions to manage these temptations and impulses.

Goal: ______________________________

Stage 1. Temptations, impulses, activities conflicting with your goal	**Stage 2. What can you do about it**

The challenge with Stage 1 errors—the failure to recognize that there is a conflict between the impulses of the dark horse and our goals—is that our temptations may feel irrelevant or unimportant when, in fact, their compounded effect can be devastating. (More on the issue of compounded effect will be discussed later in this chapter.) And so, to clearly recognize conflicts, you must develop a clinical and self-critical mind, lower all your defense mechanisms, and be highly self-aware and reflective.

This is of course as easy as asking the wind to stop from blowing. Often, working with a coach or a mentor helps you see what you cannot see.

There are several additional reasons for why we fail to recognize conflict and why we fail to act upon it even when we do recognize it. I will argue that the charioteer fails us because:

1. We are irrational, illogical, and unrealistic beings.
2. We are cassette bodies in a digital world.

3. We prefer immediate, smaller rewards now to larger rewards later.
4. We assume that our feelings will be consistent over time.
5. Abstract goals, distant goals in our heads, don't excite the brain for long.
6. We fail to understand the compounded effect of our actions.
7. We get easily depleted.
8. We are fooled by abundance
9. We underestimate unknown situational factors.
10. We ignore or distort disconfirming feedback and data
11. We engage in flawed self-assessment.

Let's look at each of these in turn, starting with the most crucial one.

1. We are irrational, illogical, and unrealistic beings

Kelly McGonigal, a psychologist from Stanford, suggests that our problems with lack of self-control rest in our inability to think logically, rationally, and realistically about the future.[56]

Although we may think of ourselves as rational beings, we are far from it. If we were completely rational beings—as Herbert Simon, one of the most influential social scientists of the 20th century has stated—we would always select the alternatives that would lead to the total fulfillment of our goals and aspirations.[57]

---

56 McGonigal, K. (2012). *The willpower Instinct: How self-control works, why it matters, and what you can do to get more of it.* New York, NY: Penguin Group.

57 March, J., & Simon, H. (1993). *Organizations.* Cambridge, MA: Blackwell Publishers.

In other words, we wouldn't have dilemmas and consequently self-control issues. We would never feel the pull of the dark horse in the opposite direction to our goals. You and I know that this is hardly the case.

To be purely and consistently rational beings, our charioteer would have to:

a) Have complete information about all the options available to us and know the consequences of all the choices we make;
b) Have extraordinary computational capacity that would allow us to take all the variables into consideration when making decisions, and
c) Make consistent decisions throughout our lives, regardless of our emotional state.

According to Simon, we suffer from a condition called bounded rationality. We are rational, logical, and realistic within the limits of the information we have, our capacity to process that information, our capacity to control our emotions, and time constraints.

That is, we are rational, logical, and realistic beings until we aren't. The charioteer is in control until she is not. And given the fact that we more often than not fail to pass the rationality test, we struggle to select the alternatives that best represent our future intentions. When moments of truth arise, we choose the low-hanging fruit.

Okay, so we understand that we are irrational beings. But what are the other factors that make us lose control of the chariot in moments of truth?

2. Cassette bodies in a digital world: Base motivations driving us amok

Self-control involves curbing impulses and instinctual motivations. But, as suggested by psychologists Baumeister and Vohs,[58] shouldn't we want to act upon our most base motivations? We feel the urge to eat in order to supply our bodies with energy and essential nutrients; we feel the urge to go out with others and socialize in order to fulfill our basic need for bonding. Thus, most of our urges are often adaptive responses from our natural bodies in the struggle to survive. What is wrong with following these motivations?

The issue we face is that our bodies were designed thousands of years ago for a very different lifestyle from the one we live today. We are old designs in a changed, evolved world.

Think of someone who, to this day, still listens to music on a cassette player. Evolutionarily speaking, we are like cassette players in a digital world.

We were designed to eat when food was available and conserve energy through fat, because in the Stone Age we didn't know when our next meal would be. We were designed to conserve our energy for times of need. We were designed to spread our genes because infant mortality was rampant and having as many offspring as possible was the only way to ensure the continuation and survival of the species. We were designed to protect our self-interest and the interests of our in-group (as opposed to the interest of out-groups), because we had to protect and maintain our own lot and keep ourselves alive. We were designed to pay attention to noise and movement in our surroundings as an indication of imminent danger.

---

58 Baumeister, R. F., & Vohs, K. D. (2007). Self-Regulation, Ego Depletion, and Motivation. *Social and Personality Psychology Compass*, 1(1), 115–128.

This earlier, outdated design causes us to overeat and gain weight, become couch potatoes, engage in relationships we later regret, take advantage of the system in ways that benefit ourselves, become prejudiced towards those who are not from our inner circle, and pay attention to every push notification that we receive on our phones (Jonathan Haidt, a social psychologist at New York University, reminds us that we are descendants of people who paid a lot of attention to the slightest movement in the bushes).[59]

Attending to immediate instinctual stimuli and motivations and seeking immediate gratification may feel justifiable at a gut level. Our earlier design thrived on activities that would promptly put the more primitive part of our brain, our dark horse, at ease. Short-term rewards gained by immediate gratification are concrete, real, palpable, can be touched, and excite the senses; long-term rewards, on the other hand, are abstract, distant, and improbable. We were designed to seek short-term rewards because in an uncertain and unpredictable world it made sense to think about our immediate survival.

The world around us has changed, with some of the environmental impositions that shaped our bodies and our cognitive circuitry no longer present, but we have not had enough time to evolve. Many of our hardwired responses to stimuli in the environment that once had a survival value have now lost their relevance.[60]

---

59 Rock, D. (2009). *Your brain at work: Strategies for overcoming distractions, regaining focus, and working smarter all day long* [Kindle 6.3 version]. Retrieved from http://www.amazon.com

60 Banaji, M. R.,& Greenwald, A. G. (2016). *Blindspot: Hidden biases of good people.* New York, NY: Bantam Books.

Base impulses and motivations, although part of our human make up and programming, need to be outwitted and overridden by a new mental program, one that is better suited for today's new reality of abundance and multiple interruptions and distractions. We need a new software patch—a piece of software designed to fix bugs, vulnerabilities, or to improve performance or usability of a computer program. This patch is self-control.

3. Temporal discounting and abstract goals

By design, humans tend to favor short-term over long-term rewards. Abstract, distant rewards do not excite the emotional part of our brains. To save money *today*, in order to take advantage of the rewards that this saving behavior may (or may not) bring 30 years from now, is a lot to ask from our self-indulgent and stimulus-craving brains (and horses).

This is a concept referred to as temporal discounting. There are a number of studies in economics and psychology that have demonstrated how temporal discounting plays out in our lives. In these studies, subjects will consistently choose smaller rewards now over larger rewards in the distant future. The dark horse is lured towards the green pastures in front of it, ignoring the even greener pastures at the end of the journey.

This phenomenon has as much to do with our need for immediate gratification as it has with how we interpret future goals.

Consider a student who needs to focus on studying for biochemistry but is lured by the strong gravitational pull of *Breaking Bad*, or any other addictive TV series. Biochemistry is one of the student's gateways to her ultimate dream: becoming a medical doctor. On the other hand, this goal is distant (it takes four years of undergraduate school, then a long application process), it's energy consuming (it requires studying extremely hard, volunteering, and work-shadowing), and, above all, it is abstract and uncertain (competition is fierce, she must excel not only in biochemistry but in a host of challenging science courses, and there is no real certainty she will accomplish it).

Taking into consideration the way the brain is designed, it does make more rational sense to indulge in binge watching *Breaking Bad.* After all, if our brain's modus operandi is pleasure now (instead of later), saving energy, and focusing on activities that offer concrete and certain rewards, then the TV series sounds like a great alternative.

We know the importance of saving today or studying for a test that can define your future, but when confronted with the temptation of instant rewards, the short-term rewards will typically win out. Just like we suffer from bounded rationality (rationality is bounded by our limitations), Kelly McGonigal suggests that we also have bounded willpower—that is, we have self-control until we don't.[61] We can theorize what is the right thing to do, but often fail when the temptations are real and placed right in front of us.

4. Assuming that what I feel now is not what I will feel then

We base predictions of future behavior on abstract, conceptual terms. A case in point are New Year's resolutions. Every year, we tend to align our chariots towards our desired goals and make it airborne again. At the beginning of the year, we are excited, refreshed, and filled with hope. The dark horse is also content,

61 McGonigal, K. (2012). *The willpower Instinct: How self-control works, why it matters, and what you can do to get more of it.* New York, NY: Penguin Group.

as we have allowed it to feast and indulge in various end-of-the-year celebrations. We have been so busy wrapping the year up, attending parties, shopping, and preparing for the holiday season that we typically eat and drink more than we should, spend more money than we should (or have), and forget about goals we have been struggling with all year long, such as exercising and monitoring our weight. But not to worry, because we have New Year's Eve, when all is brought back into perspective, we can press the reset button, and change is again possible.

On that night, resolutions will be made, new goals set, and dreams will become reality... at least, in our minds. You decide that you will now join the gym, you will save more money so that you can go on vacation—not once, but twice a year—you will complete that project that you have been sitting on for a while, and you will be more tender when communicating with your kids and your spouse. And then....

Well, then Monday kicks in and you are back into your old routine (you regress towards mediocrity).

Where did all those new aspirations go? You are too tired to think about it. Reality sets in. We fail miserably. We realize that our chariots are still being dragged towards the ground by the same self-indulgent dark horse and we make very little progress towards our goals. *Why?* you ask in despair.

We often mistakenly assume that our choices are consistent over time. We think that our preferences and behaviors now will be the same as our preferences and behaviors one hour, one day, or one month from now. In technical terms, we think our intertemporal preferences are time-consistent.[62]

---

62 O'Donoghue, T., & Rabin, M. (2000). The economics of immediate gratification. *Journal of Behavioral Decision Making, 13*(2), 233–250.

This is a dangerous and erroneous assumption. If the example above does not relate to you, think of a time when you decided that at the next office happy hour you would only eat healthy food and would refrain from drinking alcohol. But during the next happy hour you stuff your face with chicken wings and drink like a fish.

What is at play here? Not only are we seeking immediate gratification, but we are also making decisions in very different cognitive/emotional states. The same is true for New Year's Eve. On that evening, or before the happy hour, the planner inside of you is making future plans either based on "hot" cognition (excitement and arousal, typically enhanced by one glass of Champagne too many) or "cold" cognition, typical of the charioteer (calling the shots while the dark horse is at bay).

However, when we go back to reality and make in-the-moment decisions in the midst of the chaos that is life, when our hot system is in high gear, when the dark horse is exposed to temptations, our preferences suddenly change—habits kick in, easier targets are preferred, and old patterns are re-established.

Our decisions vary according to our emotional states. Our emotional states when we plan, and commit to a plan, will invariably be different from our emotional states when the time comes for us to implement the plan. Having this understanding allows us to be more careful when planning and more vigilant when the time to implement our plan comes around.

That is why I urge you never to assume that you will behave in a certain way in the distant future based on how you think now. Most likely, you won't. Developing awareness and good habits will prevent you from falling into this trap.

5. More on Abstract Goals

A conversation with my mother illustrates how abstract goals impact our ability to self-regulate. It was the summer of 2013 in Brazil, and my wife, newborn daughter and I were visiting home for the holidays. My parents and I went to a beach resort to unwind, eat some good coastal food, and enjoy the beauty of the Brazilian coastline. My mom and I went into the warm Atlantic Ocean for a mom-and-son chat. As we paddled among the waves, she mentioned how much she loved the beach and the fact that, despite the beach be so close to their home (my parents live about 80 miles away), they rarely took advantage of it. She also expressed how much she would love to bring her grandkids to the beach more often.

I agreed with her that going to beach more often would be fantastic. I also, probably to her dismay, proceeded to give a theoretical explanation as to why this phenomenon happens, using Kurt Lewin's Force Field Analysis described in Chapter 2.

I invited my mom to engage in a mental exercise to define what the forces were pro-change and against change. Her desired change in behavior was clear: travel to the beach more often. We identified the following forces pro-change (or pro the new desired behavior);

1. How close the beach was from my parents' home.
2. The benefits of getting out of the city and enjoying a relaxing weekend at the beach.
3. Breaking routine by doing something different.
4. The beach itself, which she loves.
5. The good food at the local restaurants.
6. Spending quality time with family.

We then discussed the forces pro-status quo or against change. This is when reality came to life:

1. Trips cost a considerable amount of money.
2. The dog needs to be placed at a pet hotel, adding to the cost of the trip.
3. The roads in Brazil can be somewhat dangerous.
4. My father is getting older and does not drive as well as he used to.
5. She does not feel comfortable bringing her grandkids with her with fear that something may happen (consider points 3 and 4).
6. She needs to decide what to do with the food in the refrigerator.
7. The house would be left alone.

Soon, what seemed to be a romantic getaway had turned into a logistic nightmare. No wonder she only went to the beach on very special occasions.

When we are planning for the far distant future, we tend to plan in abstract terms, focusing on the forces pro-change, our desire for better results, for a new "you" and a new beginning. Yet we fail to consider the concreteness of our lived lives, the forces pro-status quo—the forces of inertia that keep us doing what we habitually do. You are living how your life is designed to be, with the forces pro-change and pro-status quo in a state of (quasi) equilibrium.

When we are in the planning mode, our dark horse is at rest. It is when you try to bring the chariot airborne, and real action is actually needed, that the dark horse will scream, recoil, and buck.

6. The Compounded Effect of Epsilon-Costs

Is eating a cookie a sin that needs to be avoided by all costs? Is attending to social media platforms really impairing my ability to reach long-term goals? Will an episode of *Walking Dead* determine my future?

The answer to the questions above is a categorical no. Eating a cookie is not a sin and will not define your long-term health and weight; updating your Facebook status won't have an influence on your future; *Walking Dead* can't ruin your life.

If analyzed in isolation, these activities in themselves are harmless. They don't interfere with your future… until they do. It is when these isolated activities are compounded over time and create patterns of behaviors that we should start worrying about them.

The compounded effect of eating cookies and other high caloric and sugary foods is what, in the long-term, impacts our health (and weight); the compounded effect of attention to social media is what detracts us from other more important activities; the compounded effect of hours spent watching TV shows is what robs us of valuable time to work on other projects.

This is called the "epsilon-cost effect."[63] In calculus, epsilon-cost is the term used to describe negligible quantities that when taken together end up making a substantial difference.

If you have watched the movie *Office Space,* you are familiar with the concept of epsilon-cost. In that movie, a group of colleagues, realizing that they are going to be fired from their jobs, decide to embezzle a fraction of a cent from each financial operation by planting a computer virus in the company's

63 Dube, L. (2010). *Obesity prevention: The role of brain and society on individual behavior.* San Diego, CA: Academic Press.

accounting system. A fraction of a cent is not much. But if you multiply that by multiple transactions over multiple years you will amass a small fortune.

Let's now consider epsilon-costs in our daily lives. One beer does not give you a beer belly. But a couple of beers a week over twenty years, along with the high caloric snacks that go with the beer, and boom, there you have it—a round, protuberant, floppy belly.

Likewise, one unproductive meeting will not impact your achievements or those of your department and your company. But put a couple of unproductive weekly meetings attended by a large number of well-paid professionals, compounded over a number of years, and you have wasted thousands of hours and millions of dollars.

This is what I call the "patchwork quilt" effect. Small decisions, that may seem unimportant in isolation, but when made over a long period of time, will eventually create the quilt of our life. In this quilt you can find patterns or sequences of decisions made that now determine who you are and where you are in life.

The piece you are placing on the canvas of life at this exact instant may not seem to have an impact on the long run, but it will indeed be part of the overall end product. There is no way around it.

Our lives are the accumulation of epsilon-costs. These costs tend to quietly take control of our lives, depriving us of achieving our more honorable goals. The list below shows the intersection between the impulses and temptations that end up becoming epsilon-costs. Identify the items on the list below that are interfering the most with *your* ability to achieve.

Time	• Following a busy schedule regardless of and disassociated from your most important goals • Answering emails frenetically • Dividing time across multiple projects • Long meetings • Unproductive meetings • Keeping same schedule as the one before, regardless of the new goal you are trying to achieve
Social	• Going out with friends to the detriment of your goal • Going out with family to the detriment of your goal • Water-cooler conversations
Diet	• Reaching for high-caloric and satisfying foods • Small snacks • Daily consumption of alcohol
Media	• Watching too much TV • Playing video games • Addiction to social media • Web browsing • Reading too much news • Reading gossip sites

Remember: *Above all, it is the compounded effect of managing mundane, routine events, that prevent us from achieving higher aspirations—unless, of course, we do something about it.*

So far I have shared the negative effects of compounded effects, but of course the power of compounded effects can work to our benefit. Small but important choices, such as choosing the right food and choosing to walk five blocks instead of driving, can have a substantial effect in the long run.

Epsilon-costs also help us better understand the vacation phenomenon. Right before we go on vacation, we become top achievers at work. We accomplish a week's work in the space of a day or two. It is a Herculean feat! What I have observed is that when I am preparing to go on vacation, every second of my day is devoted to accomplishing my goal: eliminating every single item on my To Do list. The accumulated result of strategically and purposefully using every minute of my time pays enormous dividends, as I can finish an overwhelming amount of work in a short period of time. Think of what you could achieve if you applied this same focus the rest of the year.

7. Ego Depletion: Exercise, Energy, Rest, and the Charioteer

By exercising our self-control muscle, we ensure the fitness of the charioteer to tackle any challenge ahead of him; by eating well we are providing him with much-needed glucose and the physical energy he will need to function at an optimum level; and by allowing him to rest we are providing him with a much-needed dose of vitamin S (sleep), the best kind of vitamin known to humankind. Nothing rejuvenates the body better than quality rest.

But what happens when the charioteer is depleted? Can he recognize temptation when it is in front of him? Can he act upon it?

Empirical research shows that a depleted charioteer *can* actually identify situations where self-control is needed. But because he is depleted, he does not act upon it, letting the dark horse do whatever it so desires.[64]

---

64 Hedgcock, W. M., Vohs, K. D., & Rao, A. R. (2012). Reducing self-control depletion effects through enhanced sensitivity to implementation: Evidence

Researchers at the University of Iowa and University of Minnesota set out to understand what was going on inside the minds of depleted charioteers using fMRI (functional Magnetic Resonance Imaging) technology. Their goal was to find out what was going on during the two-stage approach of self-control discussed earlier (Stage 1: Identifying conflict; Stage 2: Acting upon it).

Participants in this study were divided into two groups: a depleted group and a control group. To deplete the charioteers, researchers had participants undergo a common attention-control task used in depletion research. Participants had to look at a fixed point in the middle of a computer screen. Periodically, words would appear in the screen. They were instructed to ignore the words and if at any time their attention was diverted from the fixed point, they were reminded to revert immediately to it. In contrast, the control groups had the choice of following the words or ignoring them.

The results were conclusive. Brain activity in the part of the brain that is responsible for implementing executive control----the dorsolateral prefrontal cortex (DLPFC) diminished when the participants were depleted. Activity in the area of the brain associated with conflict identification, on the other hand, remained unchanged.

The researchers concluded that when the charioteer is depleted, he fails to implement self-control strategies, but his ability to identify conflict between short- and long-term goals remains intact. This is also known as the "it's bad for me but I will do it anyway" syndrome.

After a long day of work when you have exerted a lot of self-control to get things done and to engage in social behavior, you

---

from fMRI and behavioral studies. *Journal of Consumer Psychology, 22*(4), 486–495.

may more easily succumb to the lure of a cookie sitting in the office kitchen. Even worse, you may reward yourself with two cookies. This is the case not because you fail to recognize that the cookie, a temptation, conflicts with your dieting goal. The problem is that although you can recognize the conflict, you fail to act upon it.

This handicap of the charioteer is also evident when my wife convinces me to go shopping with her. There is nothing that depletes me more. At the end of the day, when my wife asks me for the hundredth time which jeans look better, to save me from my misery, I will just say, "take both." I can recognize that taking both goes against my savings goal, but at that point I'd do anything just to get me out of my misery.

When the charioteer is tired, sleep-deprived, lacks energy, and is out of shape (with a weak self-control muscle), controlling the dark horse becomes too much to bear. And although he knows that the horse is out of control, he just doesn't have the stamina to deal with it.

8. Scarcity and Abundance

The model used throughout this book is the scarcity model. The basic premise of the scarcity model is that we have limited resources available to us: energy, time, materials, and finance. In other words, there are limits to what is possible. What can be achieved needs to be accomplished within the boundaries of the resources that are available to us.

Sendhil Mullainathan and Eldar Shafir, in their book, *Scarcity*, argue that scarcity actually changes the way we think.[65] The consequences of scarcity can be positive as well as negative.

---

65 Mullainathan, S., & Shafir, E. (2013). *Scarcity: Why having too little means so much.* New York, NY: Times Books.

On the positive side, it forces the mind to focus on what is truly important, ruling out less important choices and creating a single-minded focus on what deserves our undivided attention. For instance, meetings will typically run loosely until time starts to run short. At this point, a course correction will take place and people will then focus their attention on the agenda items that require tangible actions. College students with tighter deadlines are more productive than those with distant ones. And coupons with no expiration date are less likely to be used. Mullainathan and Shafir argue that deadlines are important because they force us into a situation of scarcity, focusing the mind.

Dr. Carstensen, who studies successful aging, reminds us that as our longevity narrows, we begin seeing our priorities more clearly.[66] I once listened to an inspiring interview with her in which she recounted an epiphany she had when interviewing residents of a nursing home. A couple of elderly ladies told her that they no longer had time for gossip and drama. Inwardly, Carstensen thought that they must have a lot of time in their hands—after all, they lived in a nursing home, without much to do.

It was then she realized what they meant by "time." Yes, they had a lot of time on their schedules but not a lot of time in a larger context: time left to live. And that dramatically changed their priorities.

On the negative side, scarcity creates a form of tunnel vision. Tunnel vision diminishes our visual field, concentrating our focus on the task at hand while neglecting other things we value. When you're in your tunnel, you see only what is ahead of you. For instance, when you are pressured to deliver at work or at

66 Carstensen, L. L. (2006). The influence of a sense of time on human development. *Science, 313*(5782), 1913–1915.

school, you end up neglecting your health by eating poorly or forgetting to go to the gym.

When it comes to achievement though, our biggest enemy is the opposite of scarcity: abundance. Early on in our career we may have the impression that we have abundant time and resources at our disposal. Abundance gives us an often-false sense of security and lack of urgency.

As a result, we may spend more money than we have, focus on unimportant things, spend time on trivial or unrelated issues, or simply ignore the task at hand to attend to other more pleasurable activities.

Professional teams are known to perform better towards the end of a game, when time is of the essence. Projects are delayed until the completion deadline approaches and everyone stops doing anything else, puts in all-nighters, and focuses solely on finishing the project. Students will study for several consecutive hours the night before an exam. Some people think it is acceptable to slack off and work menial jobs for a while, or go on a date with someone they're not really interested in, or endure a toxic workplace, because there will always be tomorrow.

In all these examples, at a certain moment there was a moment of abundance, when anything was possible. Dr. Carstensen's nursing-home residents remind us that this is not always the case.

In the scarcity model, there are two important concepts that we must take into account. Firstly, our resources are finite and need to be used for our survival. Secondly, because these resources need to be consumed, our repository of abundance is constantly diminishing. We will often only notice that it is diminishing when it is already too late, which in turn forces us to focus.

This is also the case with self-control. At any given point we may have an abundant repository of self-control. We don't use it until we have to. And because self-control is a finite resource, when we must use it we deplete it fast, much faster than if we had applied self-control judiciously over a longer period of time.

If you invest your resources wisely, these investments will pay dividends. These dividends then increase your levels of available abundance, which can in turn be used for further investments in your future. When we pace the usage of self-control, we make small but certain progress which, in turn, creates more room for further progress. For instance, you apply dosages of self-control throughout your daily routine at work by focusing and eliminating distractions. As a result, you get more done in less time, freeing up time for other projects.

The challenge for most of us is how to balance abundance and scarcity. Based on the model presented above, there are a few things we can do:

1) *Accept the scarcity model:* realize that we have limited:
    a) energy;
    b) time;
    c) money;
    d) resources.
2) *Be aware (and accept) that abundance is momentary:* abundance levels will invariably change, so abundance will exist until it won't.
3) *Invest your resources wisely:* just like with any limited resource, we must be responsible stewards of these resources and protect them dearly. Internal and external forces will compete for these resources and we must manage them well, so that they can be deployed in the most effective ways possible. That means saying "no" to activities that are not

> important, saying "yes" to those that will pay dividends, and sheltering our goals from resource leeches.

McKeown, author of *Essentialism,* has probably the best test for determining if you should be spending your valuable time and energy on a project.[67] Do the test yourself, by asking yourself one simple question.

When you think of your proposed project, do you feel:

a) Hell yeahhhhh!
b) Yeah!

If the answer is not a), then drop it.

At work you may not be able to only focus on "hell yeahhh!" projects. What you can do is apply the principles of scarcity by limiting how much of your time and energy is spent on tasks that are non-important, non-strategic, a waste of time, or irrelevant. By doing so, not only will you be maximizing your time and energy, you will be opening up space for "hell yeahhh!" projects.

9. Underestimating Unknown Situational Factors

Let's imagine you are planning to work on a project or study for several hours in the afternoon. However, a last-minute urgent request from your boss, or a friend, interrupts your plans, and you fail to achieve your goal.

Particularly in the Western world, we were raised to believe that we are in full control of our destinies. We believe we are in

67 McKeown, G. (2014). *Essentialism: The Disciplined Pursuit of Less.* New York, NY: Crown Business.

charge of our future... when, in fact, we are not. There are hosts of situational factors that influence our ability to reach our goal.

These situational factors will only be known when a particular situation arises and they are difficult to control. Worse yet, we rarely have a plan to deal with them. Later we will discuss the advantages of starting your day early and creating alone time as some of the ways to manage these factors.

10. Ignoring Feedback and Unconsciously Manipulating Disconfirming Data

Every action that we take results in a consequence. A consequence is a crucial piece of information that is fed back to us.

Take, for example, a person who invests considerable time and resources in mastering her craft. An acquaintance takes a pottery class, falls in love with it, and decides that she wants to commercialize her creations and make a living off of it. In the beginning, that craft may be rough around the edges and not very refined. Clients are just not buying her creations. In other words, the response from potential clients (the consequence) is low. She tests new models, techniques, listens to her customers, and makes changes to the product according to their comments. Her product improves considerably and begins to sell.

Or think of the student who despite all his efforts to do well in anatomy and physiology just can't seem to get a breakthrough.

In everything we do, we will receive direct or indirect feedback telling us how we are doing in relationship to an external standard or goal we want to achieve. Direct feedback may come in the form of criticism from others or corrections from a coach, teacher, parent or mentor, as well as from our own success and failure. Indirect feedback is a little more subtle and is embedded in our inability to achieve a certain goal despite our best efforts. Some of us will listen to the feedback and change course accordingly, while others will continue to bang their heads against the wall.

Feedback is an effective mechanism that tells us if we are on the right course or if our strategy needs adjustment. However, negative feedback can be perceived as a threat to the self. And we are very good at rationalizing any threats to our self-image by distorting it.

When we think about a time when we failed to achieve a goal, we can easily come up with hundreds of excuses why it wasn't our fault. It was the economy, my espouse, my father (or mother), the bank, or—better yet—society was not yet ready for me and my amazing idea. We fail to look internally and understand what the feedback is telling us.

I recently had the opportunity to speak with troubled teenagers who were failing in college or losing their jobs due to behavioral issues. I was floored by their ability to distort reality in a way that would aggrandize their self-image. They had very clear ideas in their minds about what they wanted and how to get there, despite all the negative feedback showing them that their actions were not leading to positive outcomes. Worse yet, they were receiving pointed feedback from their parents, partners, and bosses about what to do, but this advice was falling on deaf ears.

When confronted with the question of how they could maintain their stubborn position if they had no results to show for it, they became defiant. The parents, bosses, and partners were always wrong and completely removed from reality. These teenagers knew better.

Failing in college is data. Getting fired is data. Advice from others, particularly more experienced people, is data based on experience. Feedback is data. Personal experience, good or bad, is an amazing source of data. Yet, our charioteer often ignores this data—or worse, it distorts it.

The best way to predict future behavior is to look at past behavior. When planning to complete a project, reason suggests we look at how effective we have been at completing similar projects in the past, as well as how others have done. This would allow us to make a data-driven assessment of our ability to accomplish the task at hand.

However, we tend to take a rosier view. We fantasize about future projects with complete disregard for past experiences, often failing to predict how much time, energy, and money it will take to successfully complete them.

It is said that there are "lies, damned lies, and statistics (data)." In data we trust, or should trust, but the human mind, in search of self-protection and maintaining an unblemished self-image, finds sophisticated ways to distort data. In later chapters, we will discuss the importance of creating a growth mindset, in which data in the form of feedback is utilized to encourage learning and growth. In the meantime, ask yourself these questions:

- How well do you take feedback? Who gives you valuable, honest feedback?
- As you try to implement your goal, what is the feedback that you're receiving that may be signaling that you need to correct your course?
- How is feedback being fed to you? Do you accept it with an open heart/mind? Do you consider the possibility that those giving you feedback could be correct?

11. Flawed Self-Assessment

We tend to be conveniently ignorant about our own shortcomings, including our ability to control the self. A flawed assessment of our own abilities, skills, and character is one of the main reasons behind self-control failure.

Researchers from Cornell University, Stanford University, and the University of Iowa have burst our inflated bubbles by confirming that the relationship between our self-view and our performance is meager.[68] We tend to take an egocentric view of our abilities, thinking that in positive traits we score higher than others while in negative traits we score lower than others.

In other words, we tend to think that we are better than average in various activities, including driving, being charismatic, and self-regulating, when compared to others. We tend to think that we are more self-aware and demanding than our peers, when in fact we are not.

The truth is that this is a statistical impossibility. The majority cannot be above average. Some of us, at something, must be average or below the average. It so happens that others' predictions of our outcomes are often more accurate than our own predictions.

Flawed self-assessment can affect our self-control in a number of ways.

a) Unrealistic assessment of skills and abilities

We may unrealistically assess the gap between our goals and our abilities, failing to implement the necessary actions to fill the gap.

---

68 Dunning, D., Heath, C., & Suls, J. (2004). Flawed self-assessment: Implications for health, education, and the workplace. *Psychological Science in the Public Interest*, 5(3), 69–106.

Achieving our goals and aspirations requires skills, abilities, and self-control. There are often gaps between our goals and how prepared we are to tackle the challenges necessary to achieve it. It's the equivalent of me quitting college to start my own technology business because Mark Zuckerberg, Steve Jobs, and Bill Gates never graduated from college. These individuals are often glorified as people who did not need a college degree to achieve their dreams (and substantially transform the world in the process). However, it is important to remember that before (or even during college) they acquired superior, and I mean superior, technical skills that allowed them to succeed without a college degree. (One could also argue that they may have a well-above average intelligence.)

J. K. Rowling, the creator and writer of the highly successful *Harry Potter* series, is often portrayed as a bilingual secretary and mom who created an amazing character on a delayed train from Manchester to London and wrote it all out while sitting in a café. What a romantic view!

What is little talked about is the fact that Rowling wrote short stories as a child, had a troubled relationship with her father and lost her mother to cancer (experiences that shaped her and colored her stories). She was wildly well read, and graduated with a degree in Classics. *Classics?!* If you have read classics such as Homer's *Odyssey*, it is easy to spot how Greek literature and mythology may have served as potential sources of inspiration for Harry Potter's characters and plot. Her stories and characters are also highly inspired by her own suffering and personal experiences. This is not to devalue her work. To the contrary, it is to show how prepared she was when she came to write *Harry Potter*.

Zuckeberg, Jobs, Gates, and Rowling are all outliers. But they do have one thing in common: they had, at least to some degree, the tools, the skills, and the knowledge they needed to cross from where they were to where they stand today. Sometimes we fail to do an assessment of the gap between where we are and what we want to achieve.

What can we do to identify this gap between where we are and where we want to be? First and foremost, we have to scrutinize our current situation for clues. Is it time, energy, lack of self-control, or knowledge that is the problem? What is standing between ourselves and our goals?

Then, we must do something about it. In the case of self-control, we can exercise the self-control muscle. There are a number of exercises in this book to help you start doing a simple self-control work out.

Knowledge can be acquired through training, coaching, and education. You can also outsource the part of the work that you need help with or don't have the resources to achieve. For instance, I committed myself to creating an app for the iPhone before I died. I downloaded Apple's App Builder for a cost of $90 and started teaching myself how to build apps. After hours wasted on this, I realized I did not have the technical skills, the time, or the energy to develop it.

But realizing the gap between my limitations and my goals made me think creatively. After talking to a couple of people, I learned about an amazing site where you can outsource your work to bidders. I sent out a request for bids and in a few weeks after the realization that I was not cut to design an app myself, I had hired someone to help.

Some questions to think about:

- What are the skills and knowledge that you currently have that can be assets in helping you reach your goals?

- What are the skills, knowledge, and competencies that you need to develop?
- How can you capitalize on your strengths and overcome your weaknesses?

b) I am different (and special)

There is one rule of thumb when managing personal finances that every human being knows: you must set aside money for retirement. Helaine Olen and Harold Pollack, authors of *The Index Card,* suggest that the earlier you do it (preferably in your early twenties), the better; and if you do not do so, you will certainly regret it in the future.[69]

Most of us even have an aunt, grandparent, or someone in our family or group of friends who is struggling financially after they retire.

We see people close to us struggle (financially or in other parts of life), yet only a few of us are actually saving for retirement. Why is that?

Yes, there is the issue of immediate gratification and abstract goals (remember, saving today for an uncertain future goes against the principles of the dark horse), but there is also the fact that we are *special* and *different.* "I am smart and intelligent, I have a good job," we think, and we like to imagine that auntie so-and-so is different from ourselves.

The statistics are clear: half of all people reaching retirement age don't have savings and 47% of us could not come up

69 Olen, H., & Pollack, H. (2016). *The index card: Why personal finance doesn't have to be complicated.* New York, NY: Portfolio/Penguin Books.

with $400 right now. But again, that's not me and that will not happen to me, right?[70] I am special and different.

The experiences of individuals like our aunt and the statistics indicate that there is trouble in the horizon. In the case of retirees with no retirement savings, 50% is an enormous amount of people. Yet we disregard both the statistics and the personal stories. They are part of a different category that does not include us.

The problem is that we are not so different. We are all part of a normal curve. If it happened to them, it can happen to us. When we perceive ourselves to be outside the curve, as if the rules don't apply to us, we fail to self-regulate and will feel the consequences.

c) The restraint bias effect

Along with overestimating our abilities generally, we also tend to overestimate our ability to be in control of our impulses and temptations. We think the charioteer is in charge when in fact the dark horse is. This is one of the reasons why we engage in addictive behaviors and other behaviors that go against our best interests in the long run.

Think of the drug addict who fooled himself into believing that he could handle a couple of hits of hard drugs because he was adamant that he could control his addiction. Or the recovering alcoholic who insists on hanging out with his old buddies at their favorite bar because he is convinced that he is strong enough to restrain himself.

---

70 Rysdall, K. (2016). *If you had to come up with $400 right now, could you do it?* Retrieved from https://www.marketplace.org/2016/04/20/world/why-american-middle-class-broke

Drug and alcohol addiction may seem like extreme cases. But there are plenty more mundane cases in which we are convinced that we are in control, when in fact our impulses control us. For instance, you convince yourself that you will stop at your friend's party just for an hour and then go straight back to working on a project. In reality, that one hour becomes five and you don't get to the project until tomorrow morning.

This phenomenon is called a restraint bias, when exaggerated beliefs about our ability to control ourselves expose us to temptation, consequently inducing impulsive behavior.

We think that we are effective in implementing strategies to control the self, when in fact we are not. We tend to develop inflated views of ourselves, including our ability to self-regulate (for example, saying no to dessert, controlling alcohol intake, or eliminating distractions). We are not as good as we think we are when it comes to controlling the self and we must come to terms with that.

Next time you convince yourself that you are strong enough to be in control of your impulses, think twice. While believing in your sense of efficacy and your level of self-control is key to success, you also have to be realistic about it by studying your behavioral patterns of the past. If you were not able to control the self *then*, what is the guarantee that you will be able to do it *now*?

Admitting powerlessness is, in some cases, an effective first step.[71] Alcoholic Anonymous, a successful addiction recovery program, includes in its 12-step program the tenets of honesty, humility, faith, and hope. Honesty and humility refer to accepting the fact

71 Dunning, D., Heath, C., & Suls, J. (2004). Flawed self-assessment: Implications for health, education, and the workplace. *Psychological Science in the Public Interest,* 5(3), 69–106.

that an alcoholic is and will remain an alcoholic, and that one must acknowledge one's powerlessness over alcohol. Alcohol is in control, not the person; no matter how much an alcoholic may think that he is in charge of his horses, he is not. Faith and hope have to do with turning control of life (our chariot) over to a higher power to help save us.

We can admit powerlessness over other parts of our life; for example, our ability to avoid the lures of the Internet. Millionaire author Amanda Hocking admits her own powerlessness in this regard and sometimes hides her modem to avoid succumbing to the temptation to connect.

Questions for Reflection

Below are some questions to think about:

- How often do you overestimate your capacity to control your impulses? Think of a time when you were determined to get something done but you did something of less value but more pleasurable instead?
- When was the last time you were powerless and succumbed to bad habits and temptations?
- How did it happen?
- What was your emotional state? Where were you?
- Who were you with?
- Did these elements have anything to do with your failure to exert self-control?
- Is this a pattern? If so, what can you do about it?

CHAPTER 6

Time

ACHIEVEMENT AND SELF-CONTROL CANNOT BE properly discussed without first gaining a better understanding of time and its properties.

This is crucial for three reasons. Firstly, time is an essential component in the fabric of our lives; it is where all action takes place and the canvas in which our lives occur. Our achievements are largely determined by how we invest our time.

Secondly, time is the only resource that is equally available to all of us—both my minute and yours contain sixty seconds, period.

Thirdly, time management is in itself a form of self-control. That is, time management is about making sure you do the things you should be doing within the amount of time at your disposal.

Time is seen as a scarce commodity these days, and it only seems to be growing scarcer. This is troubling because if time forms the canvas in which your life is lived and this canvas is quickly disappearing, how can you possibly achieve your goals? As noted by Joshua Ramo, life is accelerating, the delay separating input from response is diminishing, and *instantness* has become the norm.[72] Harnessing time and increasing speed (that is, doing as much as possible in the time available to us) are the only viable solutions.

To better illustrate the concept of time, in this chapter I will discuss four types of time—mechanical, biological, psychological, and built time. Vivaldi's *The Four Seasons,* my favorite piece of classical music, will help us to better understand each of these types of time. In this famous group of concertos, winter, summer, spring, and fall—with their own respective moods and emotions—are beautifully celebrated and personified in the cadence and intensity of each note and each instrument. Through its passion and texture, it is a piece that takes the listener on an emotional journey.

So how is this piece of music related to time?

Mechanical Time

When I play *The Four Seasons* on my computer, my iTunes display keeps track of the time it has been running. For example, it shows me that 0:26 minutes of the first song have elapsed and that there are 4:35 minutes remaining until the end of the song. As I listen, the clock keeps on ticking, regardless of how I feel in that moment.

Mechanical time is the time measured by clocks. It only goes forward: second by second, minute by minute, hour by hour. Once that second is gone, it is gone; there is no going back or reliving it.

---

72 Ramo, J. C. (2016). *The seventh sense: Power, fortune, and survival in the age of networks.* New York, NY: Little, Brown and Company,

Mechanical time has major implications for self-control and time management. Understanding the limits of mechanical time is crucial for goal achievement. Here is why:

1) Mechanical time is a limited commodity. There are only 24 hours in a day. In your lifetime, assuming that you live to the age of 80, you will have 700,800 hours available to you in total—no more, and no less.
2) Mechanical time is the great equalizer. All your accomplishments will have to fall within those 700,800 hours. If we all benefited from the same levels of intelligence, opportunity, education, and mental health, it could be argued that the difference between highly-accomplished individuals and less-accomplished individuals would come down to the choice of how to allocate time. Highly-accomplished individuals use their time wisely, to further their long-term goals.
3) Goals are achieved through action, but action requires time—mechanical time. Action consumes energy, which in turn diminishes our ability to act in subsequent periods of time. So if you are not utilizing the mechanical time available to you towards a particular goal, it means that this time is being used towards some other end. As such, your goal will not be achieved.
4) Mechanical time follows the law of physics: two bodies cannot occupy the same space in the physical world. Time used for one activity cannot be allocated to another. As you have focused your attention during this second on reading these words, that time has been consumed by reading these words and nothing else. Attempts to split attention across different tasks at the same time have proven to produce less-than-ideal results.

Biological time

Biological time is the time of nature, our bodies, and the universe. Our lives are very much controlled by biological time: birth, teenage years, adulthood, and death. Each season has its own developmental milestones, its own peaks or valleys of hormonal activity, and its own eventual transition into a new phase.

Vivaldi's *The Four Seasons* is a celebration of biological time—winter, spring, summer, and fall. During each season, which has its own distinct biological cycle, specific activities take place: during the fall, trees shed their leaves; in winter, all growth comes to a halt, and so on.

Before the introduction of artificial lighting, life was primarily determined by nature's cycle. There was a time to sow, a time for crops to grow and mature, and a time to reap. There was a time to be awake and productive, and also a time to rest. Summer breaks in education allowed families to come together for harvest time. With the advent of the electric lightbulb and the industrial revolution, the separation between daily biological cycles became blurred. There was enough light to keep you working for hours into the night and machines could now operate 24/7.

After the revolution of the electric light came the connectedness revolution. Not only are our machines now operating 24/7, they are connected to infinite streams of information and to others around the globe. Midnight in New York is noon somewhere else in the world.

Despite these external revolutions that have made biological time nearly irrelevant, particularly in industrialized societies, our bodies are still very much dependent on biological cycles. We still need rest, sleep, breaks, and time to refresh and regroup, just as always.

Respecting the flow of biological time is crucial for self-control. As previously discussed in this book, resting and getting proper nutrition—respecting the cycles and needs of our bodies—play a major role in better self-regulation.

Psychological time

When listening to *The Four Seasons*, the music transports you both mentally and emotionally. It takes me places and makes me feel alive. This may be memories of my childhood, or of significant events in my life. Worries vanish momentarily at the sound of the violins; the crescendo of the strings fills my spirit with a sense of confidence, power, inspiration, and energy.

Psychological time is the time that takes place in our minds. A certain emotion may bring us to a different time and place in our minds, stealing our attention away from whatever is in front of us. As we set goals and steer our chariot towards these goals, we envision better, more secure places in a not-so-distant future. We may also be linked to past emotions and thoughts that hold us in place, either through fear, insecurity, or doubt.

Psychological time plays a role in almost everything we do. It shapes our values, beliefs and actions. Teenagers are notorious for having a sense of abundance of time, while the elderly, approaching the end of their lives, realize that there is not much time left and no time to be wasted. These different perspectives will drastically shape the individual's values and preferences. Technology, as discussed earlier, also shapes psychological time. Our devices have made us more anxious, less tolerant, and more distracted.

Built Time

Listening to *The Four Seasons* on my iPhone represents built time—the time when things were built. When I was a child, I had to listen to Vivaldi on a record player. Today, I can listen to music anywhere I want, including songs that are stored in the "cloud."[73]

Our current built time is a time of smart phones, mobile technology, and wireless connectivity. This built time influences all other types of time and has completely transformed the concept of mechanical time. Technology has allowed us to complete multiple tasks simultaneously, in a way that was previously impossible. For example, I recently hired a contractor in Indonesia to help me with a personal design project. I would email him instructions in the evening before going to bed, and by the time I woke up the next day he had sent me my requested changes. During the day I would pick up from where he had left off and at night I would email him when I was done. It was one of the most productive projects I have worked on.

These kinds of transformations have allowed us to be hyper-productive, but also completely wasteful with our mechanical time. It has taken psychological time to neurotic levels (think of FOMO: Fear of Missing Out).

---

73 Thirty years ago, if you explained the concept of a cloud to someone, you would be crucified for heresy. I remember when a neighbor told me that his dad, who worked at an electronics company, was working on a special type of disc that transmitted imagines to a TV set. My reaction was to call him a liar—after all, who would ever want to play a disc and see things on TV? How would it be even possible? Remember that in those days a "disc," for the layperson, meant a vinyl record. Five years later, the LaserDisc hit the market and my jaw dropped. The saddest part of this anecdote is that depending on what generation you are from, you may not even know what a LaserDisc is!

Understanding the different types of time gives us a better understanding of the playing field we are operating within when striving to accomplish our goals. Mechanical time reminds us that how we budget and utilize our time is crucial for accomplishing goals. Biological time reminds us to respect the cycles of our body and the time taken by nature to mature, which is reflective of the time taken for any project to grow, develop, and mature. My entire work in self-control was inspired by built time, when I realized that technology would come to dominate our lives and that it would be our responsibility, as the creators of that technology, to control our creation and not become victims of it. Finally, psychological time plays a major role in how we perceive the past, the present, and the future, with a significant causal impact on our performance. This is, in fact, the focus of our next topic.

Time and Achievement

Our orientation towards time influences, to a large degree, our ability to achieve our goals. Renowned psychologist Philip Zimbardo has written extensively about the impact of time orientation, or psychological time, on achievement.[74] According to him, there are five types of psychological time orientations:

1) **The "past-negative" type:** This person focuses on negative past experiences that still have an impact on them

74 Zimbardo, P.G., & Boyd, J.N. (1999). Putting time in perspective: A valid, reliable individual-differences metric. *Journal of Personality and Social Psychology,* 77(6), 1271–88.

and hold him/her back, such as by feelings of resentment or remorse.

2) **The "past-positive" type:** This person reminisces about the good old days. Their relationships are typically strong and positive. A "better safe than sorry" approach to life may hold the person back—after all, the good ol' days are gone.
3) **The "present-hedonistic" type:** This person succumbs easily to the pleasures of life, and seeks immediate gratification instead of seeking larger rewards in the future. This person is a risk taker, tends to be popular, and engages in less healthy lifestyles.
4) **The "present-fatalistic" type:** As the name suggests, this person believes that the present "is what it is." They may not be happy with it, but they don't believe they have much control over it. Whatever happens is supposed to happen.
5) **The "future-focused" type:** This person is focused on goals and aspirations, lives by "to-do" lists, and is a go-getter. They easily forfeit instant gratification in pursuit of higher goals, which may negatively affect relationships and personal time.

We may have all five orientations operating in our minds at once at any given time, but there are one or two that will usually be our preferred orientation.

The research on time orientation and achievement is conclusive. Those with a future orientation tend to perform at a higher level when compared to all other groups.

In one study, a group of researchers at the University of California, Berkeley, tested the time-orientation of a group of 722 talented middle school students. The findings of this study are telling because, despite the fact that this group was comprised of talented students, time orientation still played a significant role in predicting academic achievement. A "future-focused" orientation correlated positively with academic achievement while a "present-fatalistic" orientation was negatively correlated with academic achievement. In other words, those who had positive attitudes towards the future did better academically and those who had a negative attitude about the present did not perform to their full potential.[75]

My own research with highly intelligent and accomplished professional students in a rigorous health-related program has confirmed the relationship between time-orientation and achievement. Enjoying the here and now (being "present-hedonistic") was negatively correlated to academic achievement in undergraduate science classes as well as in performance in professional schools. Also, the here-and-now group scored considerably lower in self-control than individuals with other time orientations. A "future-focused" orientation was a stronger predictor of self-control as well as academic achievement in professional schools.

Future Orientation and Borrowing From Your Future

A future-focused orientation has long been established as a precondition for goal achievement and success.[76] Future-oriented individuals use the present as a platform for future achievements,

75 Mello, R. Z., & Worrell, F. C. (2006). The relationship of time perspective to age, gender, and academic achievement among academically talented adolescents. *Journal for the Education of the Gifted, 29*(3), 271–289.

76 Zimbardo, P.G., and Boyd, J.N. (1999). Putting time in perspective: A valid, reliable individual-differences metric. *Journal of Personality and Social Psychology, 77*(6), 1271–88.

have superior planning and scheduling skills, and anticipate challenges along the way.

Above all, future-oriented individuals understand that procrastinating today means borrowing from tomorrow, and that borrowing is a costly venture. Borrowing time is to a large degree equal to borrowing money.

Think of a bank loan. When you borrow money from a bank, you are borrowing at a cost. Banks don't give money away for free, after all. That means that by the time you put your hands on the borrowed money, you must have a detailed plan and work really hard not only to recuperate the borrowed amount, but also to pay off the compounded accumulated interest. If you only recover the amount borrowed plus interest, you may still be in the same situation that prompted you to borrow in the first place. Therefore, you must also make a profit from the loan.

That is why banks are, or at least should be, very meticulous when approving a loan. An educational loan typically means that, if you graduate, you will make enough money to pay back the loan plus interest on time and will also make a considerable amount of additional money in your career. Business loans are approved when bankers are convinced that you have a winning business plan, that you have the management chops to implement it, and (most importantly) that you will make enough money to generate a profit and pay off the loan.

The same is true with time. When you procrastinate, you are borrowing time from the future. You are taking out a "time" loan. By doing so, you must ensure that at some point you will earn back the time you borrowed against your future plans plus some "time" interest.

Invariably, not taking care of business now will mean taking care of it later. Not taking care of business now may mean that business will never be properly taken care of. So often, what allows us to procrastinate is that there is no such a thing as a "time bank" that sends collectors after you if you don't pay back what you have borrowed, plus interest.

Our time collector is ourselves alone—our charioteers, our conscience. Unlike bankers who want their money back, we easily forgive our time debts.

We borrow from the future when we aimlessly browse the Internet, waste hours updating and checking social media statuses, create excuses for not getting things done today, and focus on the easy things to the detriment of larger, more important items on our To Do lists.

That chunk of time devoted to the less important and trivial will eventually have to be converted into high productivity time to generate enough returns to pay back the principal and the interest on your time loan. However, the game has now become high-stakes, because if you don't put in substantial effort, you will miss your payments. And if you have not done it in the past, where is the evidence that you will do it now? As Mark Twain once allegedly said, "progressive improvement beats delayed perfection."[77]

Future-oriented individuals understand "time loans" and create a sense of urgency to get things done *now*, not later.

Pancakes and Future Management

To help with this, two students of mine—quintessential future-oriented individuals—devised the "pancake method" of time management.

---

77 Retrieved from http://www.azquotes.com/quote/783090

After enrolling in professional school, they quickly realized that borrowing from their future, which in professional schools takes the form of cramming, was a recipe for disaster. The sheer volume of material they had to cover every single week was so high that it made their stomachs churn.

This physical sensation of thinking about covering all that material before a test was equivalent to the nausea we feel when we think about eating a semesters' worth of pancakes in one sitting. Hence, the pancake method of time and work management was born.

These students considered every class attended in any given day to be the equivalent of one "pancake." Their goal was to eat their daily share of pancakes. This created a common language between students: they would ask one another if they had eaten their share of "pancakes" for that day. If, for instance, the Neuroscience pancake had been neglected on that day, the students knew that on the following day they would have to eat that day's share of pancakes and the neurosciences pancake from the day before. Leftover pancakes are never as tasty and digestible as fresh pancakes.

They also created a very detailed schedule that they still live by. Marked on the schedule are critical dates such as midterms, finals, holidays, and how much in advance they must practice or study for assessments.

In short, these students envisioned the mid- and near-future and reverse-engineered what they needed to do and by when. By eating their daily pancakes and having a full view of a semester's calendar they were able to plan their work accordingly.

In a recent conversation with Dr. Baumeister, he shared with me that his recipe for being a prolific writer was to sit and write something every day. His advice to his graduate students is to make small but steady progress toward their publications on a daily basis; that is, he encourages them to eat their daily dose of pancakes.

In this view, your bright horse is not a glamorous stallion that saves the day and achieves its goal through pure willpower, but more like a bright mule who pulls its weight, day after day after day.

Eat your weekly pancakes

Carve out some time to think about all the things you must, or would like to, accomplish this week. Write down all these things on paper. Separate tasks into daily procedures or urgencies that are part of the job, and pet projects that will advance your career and personal life. Then reverse-engineer your week to identify what needs to be accomplished, by when, and in what order, for you to accomplish all your goals by the end of the week.

In other words, what are the daily pancakes you must eat to take care of business during that week? Can you make any adjustments in mechanical time to ensure you will be able to eat all your pancakes?

Remember, pancakes require time and energy to be eaten. Also, ask yourself if you are adding pancakes to the plate that are not related to your big goals. What pancakes can be eliminated?

The Cycles of Life

Some of us tend to describe life events in terms of past, present, and future, as if these time periods were separate from each other.[78] In this view, the past has already past and there is nothing one can do about it. The future, as long as it depends on our

---

78 Tam, L., & Dholakia, U. M. (2014). Saving in cycles: how to get people to save more money. *Psychological Science, 25*(2), 531-537.

personal actions, will always be better than the past and the present. The actions of today will be reaped tomorrow.

This focus on the forward flow of time is known as linear time orientation. It is quite reassuring to perceive the flow of life in a progressive and loosely connected time continuum.

The reality is that life is less linear than we would like it to be. Life is much more like the four seasons than a straight line: events repeat themselves over and over again in a series of continuous cycles. In this perspective, the future is not much different from the present, as the same behavioral patterns present today will be present tomorrow—unless, of course, something major is done about it.

This is called a "cyclical time" orientation. Because the cycles will be repeated in the future, the individual with a cyclical time orientation builds healthy routines today so that it can be replicated in similar future cycles.

Those with a linear time orientation think:

- "In the future I will resist temptation."
- "In the future I will exercise more."
- "In the future I will use words more carefully."
- "In the future I will treat others as others like to be treated."
- "In the future I will eat healthier."
- "In the future I will start saving for my retirement in the near future."

Those with a cyclical time orientation think:

- "If I have not resisted temptation today, what is the evidence I will resist it tomorrow?"

- "If I have exercised today and in the recent past, I will likely exercise in the future."
- "If I can't control the words that come out of my mouth today, it is unlikely that I will get better at it in the future (unless I start changing my habits today)."
- "If I always struggle to eat healthily, I will face similar issues in the future."
- "If I haven't saved one penny for my future before today, it is unlikely that I will start saving in the near future. "

In the cyclical model, the metaphorical summers, falls, springs and winters of life keep on coming back to either bless or haunt us.

Life is comprised of both small and large cycles, and the behaviors expressed in each cycle defines the quality of each cycle. Smaller cycles define larger cycles, and larger cycles define even larger cycles, the cycle of life being the ultimate cycle to be complete.

In the cyclical view, the quality of one's life is measured by the quality of smaller and larger cycles. For instance, going to the gym is a cycle. Within the larger gym cycle there are smaller cycles embedded in it: the bench press, the squats, and the sit ups. The quality of each smaller cycle defines how good (or poor) your workout session is. The combination of the larger gym cycle with other gym cycles will form the overall exercise cycle, which in turn will define your overall fitness.

A bodybuilder has much more frequent and intense gym cycles than I do, and that is why I don't look like they do (it's all about the quality of each cycle). In the linear mindset, I see myself working out today and envision a well-defined six-pack in the near future. In the cyclical mindset, I realize that my workout sessions have not yet produced the six-pack abs I was expecting, and it probably won't in the future either... unless... unless I make major adjustments to each gym cycle.

Most of us are trapped in a hamster wheel, a sequence of continuous cycles that cause us to only achieve the results we are currently achieving.

The good news, however, is that vicious cycles can be changed. Cycles can be broken or enhanced if we have 1) understanding; 2) motivation; and 3) skills.

First we must understand the nature of cycles and accept the fact that they keep on reoccurring in our lives; then, we must identify which cycles to change. After we understand that something needs to be done, we must be motivated to act towards the desired change, pressing forward long enough to allow for the creation of new habits, which will in turn change the quality of each cycle. Finally, we must have the appropriate skills required to change a cycle.

For instance, if I want to be healthier I must first recognize and understand the cycles that are trapping me in an unhealthy lifestyle. I must then want to change my lifestyle. And finally, I need to have (or develop) cooking skills and start exercising.

Research on cyclical and linear modes of thinking shows that how we perceive time impacts our ability to accomplish our goals.[79] One study on personal saving habits show that those with a cyclical mindset are more likely to save than those with a linear mindset. Individuals with a cyclical mindset not only provided higher saving estimates but also actually saved on average 78% more than those with a linear mindset. The authors

---

79 Tam, L., & Dholakia, U. M. (2014). Saving in cycles: How to get people to save more money. *Psychological Science, 25*(2), 531–537.

of the study propose that cyclical individuals have lower future optimism concerning their ability to save money and are better at implementing savings plans, including having more concrete, as opposed to abstract, implementation planning.[80]

The Rhythm of Time

So far we have discussed different types of time orientation and how they impact our ability to succeed. It's also very important to understand that not all time is created equally.

As we have seen with biological time, there is a time to sow and a time to reap, a time to take action and a time to rest. If we were to plot out our levels of energy at different times of the day, or during different activities, we would notice that our energy levels fluctuate and have a certain pre-established pattern or rhythm to them.

Let's revisit Vivaldi's *The Four Seasons* for a moment. Each song evokes certain emotions from the listener by a change in the tempo for each season. The "La Primavera" (Spring) concerto has an allegro tempo—bright, vivid, fast—and the first movement in this concerto ends with a beautiful battle of violins at high intensity (for me one of the most exciting pieces of classical music ever written). Other songs evoke different feelings and their tempos change accordingly.

In musical terms, tempo is the speed or pace of a piece of music—how fast or slow it should be played. All things have their own tempo, their own cadence. A few days before vacation you are in a high-strung tempo, getting multiple things done at once; on Mondays, on the other hand, your tempo may be a little

80 Ibid.

slower. My tempo after three cups of coffee is very different than after a heavy meal.

Productivity experts are advising us more than ever to understand, anticipate, and manage our tempo as a means of managing and increasing our personal productivity. For instance, working at an intense pace for approximately one hour followed by a 15-20 minute break is deemed to be the ideal work-to-break ratio, making us more productive over the long haul.[81] A period of high intensity tempo followed by a moderate tempo is in harmony with our biological time, by respecting our brain's propensity to oscillate between high- and low-energy spurts.

The figure below is a graphic representation of the typical tempo of a normal day. We wake up in the morning (low energy), dress, drive to work, have a first cup of coffee, answer some emails, work on an important project, have lunch, and so on. As we move through our day, we are constantly interrupted by our phones, incoming text messages, and colleagues (represented on the graph below by the vertical lines).

Notice that the oscillation between valleys and peaks of energy does not dramatically change. In a normal week, this tempo is likely to repeat itself each working day, as we often wake up at the same time, get dressed at the same time, and answer emails, have meetings, and work on projects in a pattern-like manner.

---

81 Bradberry, T. (2016). *Why the 8-hour workday doesn't work*. Forbes. Retrieved from http://www.forbes.com/sites/travisbradberry/2016/06/07/why-the-8-hour-workday-doesnt-work/#74401d3a7981

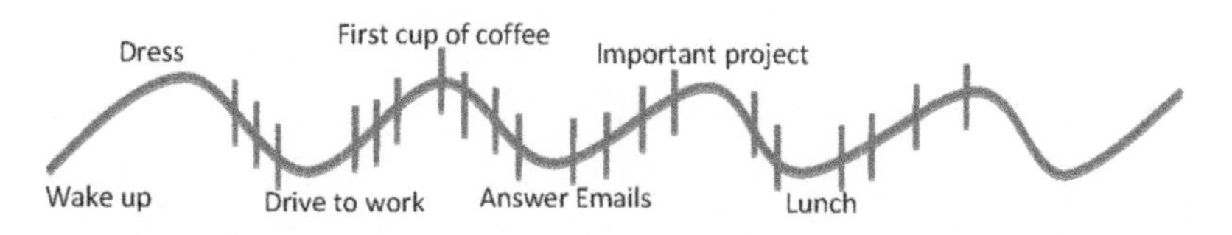

Often our lives feel more like the graph below, with very little space between tasks and still a lot of interruptions.

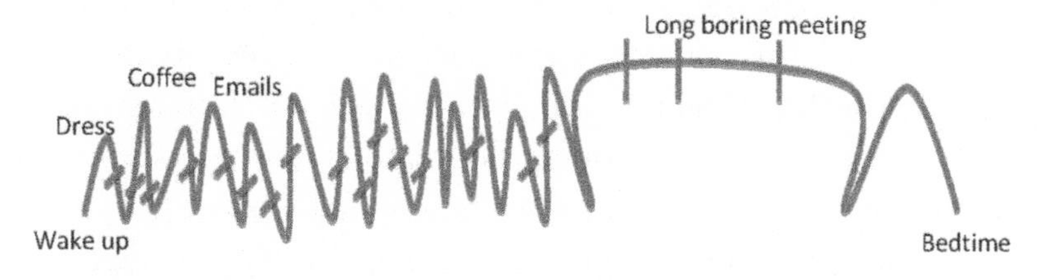

Maintaining the frantic pace of the graph above for too long may have major negative consequences, including burn out and fatigue (think biological time).

Now try and insert the implementation of a new project or goal, your big goal, within the tempo described on either of the graphs above. You quickly discover that it is almost impossible to manage your daily routines and at the same time implement your new goal. Trying to create change with the same tempo as the graphs above is utterly impractical and marks the onset of career suicide.

Only by dramatically changing the tempo, the cadence of your day, can you get everything done. Your new tempo will look more like the graphs below: peaks of high, focused energy that last longer.

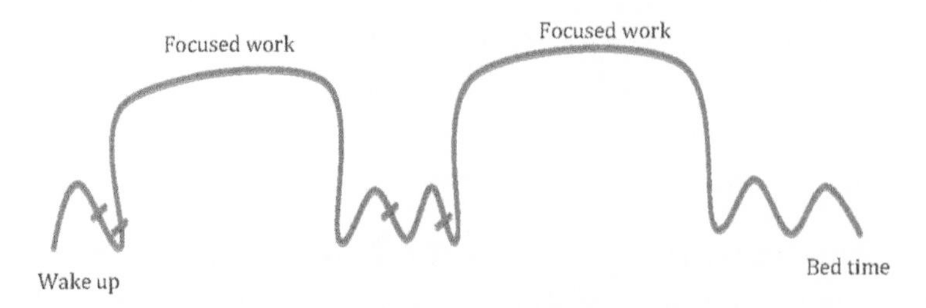

In fact, having two periods of highly focused work may be impractical. I, for instance, due to the nature of my job, can only focus at this level from 7 a.m. until 9 or 10 a.m. at most (or in airplanes or on Amtrak trains). Many of the highly accomplished individuals discussed in this book have specific hours of the day when they are highly focused. Anything that falls after those hours is play time.

Time management specialist Elizabeth Saunders encourages us to reflect on our monthly, weekly, and daily tempos and manage our schedule accordingly.[82]

1) **Monthly tempo:** Focus on one major project during a month and make as much progress as possible toward that one project. Adding too many big projects during the same month will mean that your energy and focus will be diluted, only making small progress towards each project. Also, don't forget that your focus will invariably be diffused by daily activities and tasks.
2) **Weekly tempo**: Every week has its own tempo, which is largely determined by your calendar. Plan your week in advance based on your own intuitive knowledge about

82 Saunders. E. G. (2016). How to get into a rhythm at work if you can't stick to a schedule. *Harvard Business Review Digital Articles,* p. 2-5. Retrieved from https://hbr.org/2016/04/how-to-get-into-a-rhythm-at-work-if-you-cant-stick-to-a-schedule

your weekly tempo. What days are busiest for you? Are there days when your energy is lower or higher? Are there days in the week when you are out of commission due to mandatory meetings/tasks? For instance, I schedule all my weekly staff meetings for Tuesday and leave Wednesday free for major projects. Why Wednesday? Because I know I'll still have Thursday and Friday to manage the consequences of the actions I took on Wednesday.

3) **Daily tempo:** It is ultimately your daily tempo that will determine how much you achieve in any given week or month. Most successful students I know manage their daily tempos with major TLC (tender loving care). Students preparing for high-stakes standardized tests will tell me that they set aside at least two or three hours daily to study for a given test, and will save one day of the week for long-haul study sessions of up to eight hours. I try and manage my daily tempo with great care. I have long realized that there are few times in my day in which I have full control of my own daily tempo, a time when I control what I do and any outcomes that I derive from it. Most of the rest of the time, I am managing other people's interruptions, attending to fires, and dealing with important, but low-yield, activities.

When thinking about your monthly, weekly, and daily tempo, consider this one question proposed by the inventor of the revolutionary Scrum system for software development, Jeff Sutherland:

how many things can you do in a month, week, or day? And by "do" he means "done"—completed, delivered.[83]

By critically analyzing this question, you will invariably have to relook at your To Do list to prioritize and focus on those tasks that are critical to fit within your tempo (the speed you get things done) or increase intensity of your tempo to ensure that your list can be accomplished within the available time.

Final words on time orientation

A future-focused orientation is developed in a stable and reliable environment, which allows people to make realistic predictions about the future. Having grown up in a very unstable Brazil, I remember the economy fluctuating considerably and regularly. As the ups and downs of the economy affected our home, I had no choice but to question the value of planning for the long term. After all, if we were all at the mercy of this invisible force that did not always play in our favor, why bother?

The same is true in unstable households where promises are broken and trust shattered. A child growing up under these circumstances may have a difficult time planning for the future, because in their view the future is nothing but broken promises. In fact, recent studies show that reliable environments and trust significantly increase people's ability to delay gratification.[84]

The good news is that although time-orientation may be a preference, it is not a fixed trait. If you are a present-hedonistic,

83 Sutherland, J. (2014). *Scrum: The art of doing twice the work in half the time.* New York, NY: Crown Business.

84 Severns, M. (2012). Reconsidering the marshmallow test. *Slate.* Retrieved from https://slate.com/human-interest/2012/10/the-marshmallow-study-revisited-kids-will-delay-gratifcation-if-they-trust-their-environment.html

like I used to be in my college years, you can become future-oriented. You are not cursed to live for eternity with one time orientation. Although time orientations may be strong personal preferences, the research discussed later in this book on the nature of mindsets tell us we can indeed change how we see and interact with the world. It may require effort to make any real progress, but it is possible.

Time is King (and Queen)

Time is probably the most valuable commodity that is being slowly, without our conscious realization, being stolen from us. Now more than ever, time rules. The effective and judicious use of your time is paramount.

The Japanese, renowned for their efficiency (and like most war-torn countries), consider waste a crime. Wasting time is a crime as it robs you of your future.[85]

Time is one of the most sacred resources we have at our disposal and should be treated as such.

Let's not only consider the time on our clocks, but the time on calendars and that of a life-span. Days, months, even years go by in the blink of an eye. In our college years, we have our entire careers in front of us. In those days, energy (and hormones) abound, as does time: we are usually single with pockets of free time readily available to us at night and during the weekends.

As we enter the workforce, the horizon is distant and the possibilities are endless. Levels of energy are still high and time is in our hands.

---

85 Sutherland, J. (2014). *Scrum: The art of doing twice the work in half the time.* New York, NY: Crown Business.

But before we know it, time creeps on us like a dark wolf that unexpectedly strikes our horses without giving you, the charioteer, the opportunity to respond.

Reflection Activity

You can find out your time preference by taking Zimbardo's Time Perspective Inventory, available at http://www.thetimeparadox.com/zimbardo-time-perspective-inventory/.

Afterwards, ask yourself:

- Does your score reflect your personal experiences?
- Do you believe you need to change your time orientation to better accomplish your goals?
- How would you go about changing your time orientation?
- Are you in charge of your time, or is it being eroded by distractions?

Part II

CHAPTER 7

The EAT Path to Self-Control

IT'S CLEAR THAT WE HAVE a lot of work to do. As we learned in Part I, the people who will succeed in the future are those who can master difficult problems and produce at high levels. For that, we require a two-dimensional canvas (time and focus) on which to build our lives, spend our time, and focus our attention.

Due to all the reasons we have looked at so far, both canvases are literally disappearing, being consumed mainly by interruptions that lure our dark horse away from our goals.

I created the EAT system to strengthen the charioteer's self-control muscle, to tame the dark horse, and to free the bright horse to pursue productive ends.

In the EAT system of self-control:

- "E" represents the Environment
- "A" represents our Actions
- "T" represents the way we Think.

For each of the letters in this acronym, I will share with you proven self-control techniques.

This model was created based on the Force Field Analysis concept presented earlier. The main premise is that there are environmental factors (Environment), internal factors (Thinking), and behavioral factors (Actions) that influence our self-control and our ability to achieve our goals.

These influences can be either positive or negative: just as there are EAT factors that support the achievement of our goals, there are other EAT factors that go against our best interests. Based on this model, we have to identify the EAT factors for and against change, and either diminish the forces pro-status quo or increase the factors pro-change.

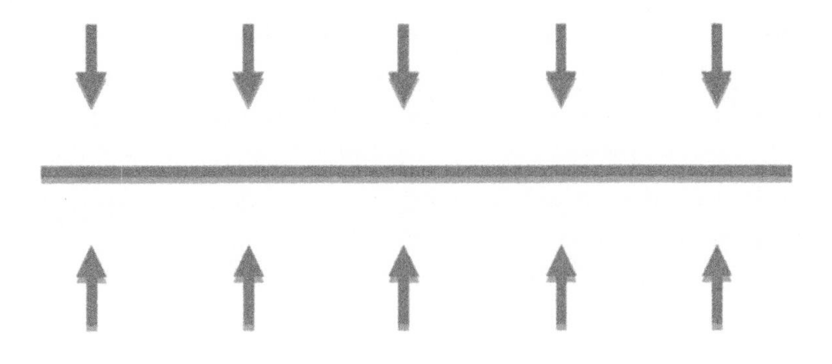

This model was also inspired by biological models of successful adaptation. Julian Huxley, a British evolutionary biologist, was eager to find a common variable that changes as lower-level organisms evolve into higher-level organisms. His conclusion was that there were in fact two common threads or variables: an organism's ability to control its environment, and inner homeostasis (independence from the environment).[86]

The EAT process suggests that we can self-regulate to achieve our goals by controlling the environment around us (the E), or changing internal states to better adapt to the environment (the T, changing how we think and interpret events). Action, on the other hand, changes us and our environment at the same time: as we act, our environment responds and we are able to adjust our internal state to become more adaptable.

But before I delve further into the EAT system, we must first discuss preconditions for self-control. Without these preconditions, there is no dose of self-control that can help us.

Strategy #1: Dream, Believe (With Caution), and Become: A Somewhat Demotivating Speech

When I first moved to the United States to attend graduate school, I became a member of the student organization SIFE (Students in Free Enterprise). Only weeks after I arrived, still fresh "off-the-boat", a representative delivered a speech at a SIFE national event entitled "Dream, Believe, Become."

Do *not* worry. I am not going to begin a motivational, wishy-washy, "believe in yourself" type of narrative here. Although the speech was highly inspirational, I was (being a bit of a skeptic) reluctant to fully embrace the concept of "dreaming and believing." I now have to admit that the research evidence is loud and

86 Calcott, B., & Sterelny, K. (2011). *The major transitions in evolution revisited.* Boston, MA: MIT Press.

clear—yes, dreaming and believing are not only important, they are crucial! But there are also some important caveats to this rule.

Dreaming

Dreaming, for the objective mind, may sound like a motivational speaker's smoke and mirrors. It is a word that has been repeatedly overused and abused. Let's remove whatever preconceptions and emotional value the word "dream" might carry for us, and focus instead on an objective definition of the word: dreaming is our ability to envision a different, better future for others and ourselves.

A dream is an ideal state, an abstraction. It's what our horses and the charioteer are flying towards. If our species hadn't had the capacity to dream of a better future, we wouldn't be any different from other primates and mammals.

Dreaming can be highly motivational and function as a powerful source of energy for goal attainment. In fact, psychologists consider this type of fire or motivation to be a basic ingredient of self-control. In other words, without motivation, it is very hard to meet a goal or standard.[87]

The word "ingredient" is used by psychologists deliberately, meaning that it is a necessary precondition for self-control. It is the equivalent of baking bread without flour—impossible. To make bread, you need flour. To self-regulate, you need motivation. Moreover, motivation is actually an effective energy booster

---

87 Baumeister, R. F., & Vohs, K. D. (2007). Self-regulation, ego depletion, and motivation. *Social and Personality Psychology Compass, 1*(1), 115-128.

for when you have run out of self-control, or when the ego is depleted.

However—and here is the twist—*how* we fantasize (or dream) about the future is equally important in determining our ability to fulfill those aspirations.

Simply fantasizing or dreaming of an idealized future as an act of pure indulgence is a poor predictor of achievement. Studies show that people who only fantasize about the future display low effort, engage in behavior that is not conducive to the achievement of their fantasized goal, and have the sensation that the goal has already been attained without the need for further action.[88]

Think of a time when you fantasized about how easy it would be to get a good grade in a difficult course, or how easy it would be to complete a project. Then life hits you with something called reality: obstacles, pushbacks, and life itself.

In our idealized view of the future we rarely take into consideration the amount of sustained effort, time, and energy required to achieve the fantasy and keep it alive. That is when dreams fail—when we realize that so much is needed to achieve the dream that it is easier to start dreaming about something else. Moreover, we also fail to consider the level of skill needed to make the dream a reality, or we over estimate our own skills.

One of my favorite documentaries is *Jiro Dreams of Sushi.*[89] Jiro is an elderly sushi master who reportedly makes some of the best sushi in the world. When culinary connoisseur Anthony Bourdain was asked during an interview what his ideal last

---

88 Oettingen, G. (2012). Future thought and behavior change. *European Review of Social Psychology, 23*(1), 1–63.

89 *Jiro dreams of sushi* (2012). United States: Magnolia Home Entertainment.

meal would be, Bourdain answered without hesitation: a meal at Jiro's restaurant. The documentary is called *Dreams of Sushi* for a good reason—Jiro dreams about the perfect sushi, and has made it his daily commitment (and motivation) to achieve an unsurpassed level of perfection in the sushi he serves. He dreams about the perfect sushi, then plans it, executes it, and consistently delivers it.

His daily routine is exhausting. Early in the morning—and I mean the wee hours of the morning—he is up and visiting his suppliers at the local markets, seeking only the freshest ingredients. His routine is repetitive. He repeats his techniques consistently, daily, incessantly. We are told that the only difference between Jiro today and Jiro 40 years ago is that he has quit smoking. Other than that, the repetitiveness of his actions is still intact, including where he sits in the train each day.

He has been honing his skills on a daily basis for a lifetime. It is through relentless discipline that he was able to achieve the status of one of the most prominent sushi masters in the world.

Now think of a friend in college who shared his dream with you of opening a restaurant or a bar. I think we all have encountered someone who has dreamed of opening a restaurant. Most of these dreamers never get anywhere, primarily because the dream dies off. Those who actually implement it face a disturbing truth: the rate of failure for new restaurants is massive. For the most part, restaurants and bars fail because of poor management. Maintaining food and service quality is a daunting quest, one that requires uncompromising effort and skill. Few have what it takes to sustain this effort over long periods of time.

One of the solutions for this phenomenon is to engage in "bounded" dreaming—to dream while at the same time taking into consideration the challenges, obstacles, and potential difficulties along the way.

This mental exercise is called "mental contrasting" and you will learn more about it in Chapter 10. Research in this area reminds us that contrasting dreams with reality allows us to get sufficiently energized to attain the goals we know are within our reach, while de-energizing those whose dreams are beyond their reach.

This is not to throw a bucket of cold water over dreams and fantasies about a better future—just the opposite. Our unique perspectives, including our ability to dream about the future and to set standards for ourselves that push our limits, define who we are. Our achievements *depend* on our capacity to dream and embrace a more desirable future.

You may ask, "but what does dreaming have to do with my need for self-control to finish that dreadful report, study for biochemistry, or hit the gym?" The answer is that you must make these smaller goals part of a larger future fantasy: finishing a report becomes part of the larger goals of career advancement; dreadful biochemistry becomes part of the dream of getting into medical school; and hitting the gym is a subset of the larger goal of living a life of health and fitness so that you can spend more time with your kids and see them grow up.

Even if you have to exaggerate or lie to yourself to temporarily increase your enthusiasm to act—that is, to create a lofty goal just to justify achieving a smaller goal—that's fine with me. You may be preparing a presentation and you may tell yourself that this presentation will change the course of how things are done in your company. The truth may not even be close, and you know it, but if dreaming big has given you the motivation to start working on your presentation, then you have accomplished your goal... and I'll bet that by starting with such a framework, your presentation will be damned good.

The reality is that any goal worth achieving demands sustained levels of effort and energy over a long period of time. To sustain these high levels of energy and effort, we need fuel to keep us going. This fuel is the allure of reaching that envisioned future reality. This is a gift from evolution to us. An enlarged prefrontal cortex has given us the ability to imagine the future and exert self-control to achieve it.

Just don't forget, at some point, to add a good dose of reality into the equation.

Believe

Dreaming alone will not make you achieve your envisioned, preferred future. You have to believe in both your dream *and* in your capacity to reach it. Believing in this context is different from the "you are perfect no matter who you are and you were born this way" kind of belief discussed in previous chapters.

Research has confirmed that those who believe that they can achieve a goal are more likely to achieve it.[90] In fact, dieters who believe in their ability to stick to a diet are three times more likely to stick to it. But we have to go deeper than that to understand the power of believing.

It is hard, if not impossible, to picture Jiro waking up, week after week, for years, in the wee hours of the morning to select the freshest fish from the local market if he did not believe that achieving a nearly perfect sushi was possible. If that was the case,

---

90 Halvorson, H. G. (2010). *Succeed: How we can reach our goals.* New York, NY: Penguin Publishing Group.

he would have probably given up by now. Instead, he built a host of intricate daily rituals that bring him closer and closer to the perfect sushi.

Albert Bandura, one of the most prominent psychologists of our times, developed the concept of self-efficacy, a person's belief that he or she can deliver certain levels of performance.[91] People with high levels of self-efficacy embrace difficult tasks, such as puzzles, as challenges to be solved instead of problems to be avoided. They tend to set stretch goals that will challenge them and will keep them committed to their goals over the long term. Failures and setbacks are perceived as lack of effort or of skills that can be developed.

Belief alone is not sufficient. Belief must be grounded in facts, data, past performance, and previous demonstrations of the strength of your character. Beliefs should also be open to feedback from those around us—belief without a strong foundation is a recipe for disappointment.

When I coach students on gaining admission into competitive healthcare programs, I often encounter candidates who overestimate their ability to achieve good scores in standardized scores. They tell me not to worry because they know they will do just fine. These are the candidates that often worry me. They are overconfident, and their overconfidence blinds them.

Believing in ourselves is often ignited by vicarious leaning—watching others succeed. We see people who we compare ourselves to and convince ourselves that "if they can do it, so can I." Seeing others achieve goals is a potent trigger for goal achievement. However, what is often discounted is the level of

---

91 Bandura, A. (1997). *Self-efficacy: The exercise of control.* New York, NY: W. H. Freeman and Company.

skill, maturity, the number of hours, the sacrifices, contextual elements, and sheer luck that others have combined to achieve their goals.

According to Nigel Nicholson, a professor of organizational behavior, believing too much in ourselves is a genetic gift from our Stone Age ancestors.[92] Humans had to be confident to survive the uncertainties and perils of the Stone Age. Confidence gave them the strength to secure resources essential for survival, attract more mates (as they seemed more likely to prosper), and allow them to gain more allies.

However, as is the case with any good medicine, one must take the right dosage. Overconfidence can also work as a blinder that impedes you from seeing reality, subtle environmental cues, or properly assessing your strengths and weaknesses.[93] People tend to believe that they are much more likely than others to get what they want in life (own a house, for example, or buy a dream car), live longer, and live healthy lives. Yet, when it comes to negative events, such as getting sick, dying early, or having a nightmarish marriage, we tend to think we are less prone to them.[94]

Those who believe in themselves, yet accept that achieving their goals will be challenging, tend to spend more time planning to achieve their goals, exert more effort towards their goals, and are more proactive about taking action.[95]

---

92 Nicholson, N. (1998). How hardwired is human behavior? *Harvard Business Review, 76*(4), 134–47.

93 Ibid.

94 Halvorson, H. G. (2010). *Succeed: How we can reach our goals.* New York, NY: Penguin Publishing Group.

95 Ibid.

Becoming

It is after we dream and believe, and put a lot of effort into achieving our goal (through self-regulation), that we then become.

Becoming is that stage of self-realization in which we acquire a set of skills and competencies that give us complete control over the game. In cognitive terms, becoming is also the process of downloading new habits into the basal ganglia. As new habits are downloaded into our habit-forming system, there is little or no need for cognitive effort or regulation because we have incorporated the new habit.

For example, Jiro does not ponder if he should wake up early, choose the freshest ingredients, or follow the rituals of his craft. He has *become* these habits. These habits are now who he is.

In ancient Chinese philosophy, this concept is known as *wu-wei* (doing without doing). More than 2,000 years ago, Butcher Ding was recognized in his village for conducting a sacrificial ceremony that involved him butchering an ox like no one else. Through a few precise, orchestrated, swift movements with his knife—movements that more closely resembled a dance than the butchering of a massive animal—an entire ox would be swiftly dismembered. The precise position of his feet, his shoulders and the touch of his hands were all part of this elaborate process.[96]

You become *wu-wei* when you are so skilled at doing something that it feels effortless. This effortlessness comes with years of deliberate practice and dedication. The more you do it, the more freely the activity flows through you. At a certain stage of mastery, you and the task become one. Think of a piano player

---

96 Slingerland, E. (2014). *Trying not to try: Ancient China, modern science, and the power of spontaneity.* New York, NY: Broadway Books.

who, when she plays, seems to become one with the instrument being played.

As professional musicians and athletes will tell us, becoming may take years of hard training and dedication to your craft. Becoming is not, however, a stationary stage that, once reached, is automatically maintained. It also requires self-control to keep you there, or you can be quickly overshadowed by changes in the environment.

Next, we will explore the "Ground Zero" of self-control: standards, pre-committing and monitoring.

Strategy #2: Establishing Standards and Pre-Committing

If you are not pre-committed to steering your chariot to any specific direction, your horses—the dark horse, to be more precise—will take you places, oh yes it will, at its will.

Self-control implies that we control our impulses and behaviors to achieve a desired outcome. The desired outcome is typically a personally imposed standard or goal (our idealized self or a dream), or an externally imposed standard or goal. Pre-committing to these standards and goals, and ensuring that our horses are aligned toward them, is a crucial step in our journey toward self-control.

Clear, consistent, and non-conflicting standards and goals is a precondition for achievement.[97] Cognitive dissonance—when your beliefs about yourself, including your standards, values, and

---

97 Baumeister, R. F., & Vohs, K. D. (2007). Self-regulation, ego depletion, and motivation. *Social and Personality Psychology Compass, 1*(1), 115-128.

goals, conflict with reality—can generate an assortment of negative feelings and emotions.

But the good news is that these same negative feelings can actually be used and channeled as motivation through self-regulation.

When we pre-commit to certain standards and goals, we are writing a mental contract between the charioteer, the two horses, and ourselves, holding everyone accountable for carrying out what needs to be done in order to achieve our goals and standards. Although the indulgent dark horse may have a mind of its own and try to sneakily implement its own agenda, and the charioteer may at times be irrational and succumb to the pull of the dark horse, pre-committing to a goal prevents any such last-minute maneuvers from an uncommitted dark horse or potential distractions from the charioteer.

In signing a mental contract, we are limiting our options. We are setting the chariot on a single path with no alternative routes.

One effective way to limit options is by *kicking out the ladder (and burning it).* In other words, giving yourself no alternative but to move towards your desired outcome.

Guy Laliberte, founder of the famous Cirque Du Soleil, provides us with a fascinating example of kicking out the ladder in the business world. In the early 1980s, Laliberte had a vision for a different type of entertainment—one that encompassed physical prowess, music, dance, art, circus acts, and street entertainment. The start of Cirque du Soleil, like with most start-ups, was not smooth sailing. That was when he decided to kick away the ladder and burn it. He booked an opening act at the Los Angeles Arts Festival and told his small troope that if they failed, they would have no money for gas to get back home.

The rest is history. Today Cirque du Soleil has touched millions of people, has more than 20 shows being concurrently performed worldwide, and employs more than 4,000 performers.[98]

One of my students used her own version of kicking out the ladder to focus on her studies. She realized that Facebook was a major distraction, one that was consuming too much time and energy and distracting her from tasks just when she needed to focus the most. So she burned the ladder; she deleted her Facebook profile.

When I share this example in my classes, students will typically roll their eyes as they can't fathom the possibility of a life without social media. But she had given herself no alternative but to be the best student she could possibly be. She had studied her environment, identified what was distracting her, and took a bold move towards her goal. Had she not deleted her Facebook profile, there would always be that lingering thought that it was there, only a hand's reach away, waiting for her whenever she felt tired or in need of some mental relief. Knowing herself, she knew she would probably succumb to the temptation, so she burned the Facebook ladder.

One study involving music students clearly illustrates the power of commitment.[99] Gary McPherson investigated the difference between students who progress quickly at music lessons compared to their not-so-advanced counterparts. In a longitudinal study, he followed students' progress through tests, interviews, and videotaped lessons, from the time the students picked

---

98 Baghai, M., & Quigley, J. (2011). Cirque Du Soleil: A very different vision of teamwork. *FastCompany*. Retrieved from http://www.fastcompany.com/1724123/cirque-du-soleil-very-different-vision-teamwork

99 Coyle, D. (2009). *The talent code: Greatness isn't born. It's grown. Here's how* [Kindle 6.3 version]. Retrieved from http://www.amazon.com.

their instruments (at around the age of seven or eight) all the way through graduation from high school.

Shortly after the students picked their instruments, they started falling into the infamous bell curve of skills development: some developed rapidly, the majority stayed in the middle, while yet others lagged behind. There is nothing new about these findings; experience typically tells us that the bell curve is the natural progression of things. However, McPherson was interested in what caused the bell curve to begin with.

His findings were unexpected and very clear: it was neither intelligence, an acute sense of rhythm, nor social economic status that were the cause.

What he found was that the commitment students vocalized before they started playing explained most of the variance in their skill level. In the beginning of the study, students were asked for how long they intended to play their chosen instrument (through high school, through primary school, or all their lives). The students who declared a long-term commitment to playing, regardless of their level of practice per week, outperformed students who declared a short-term commitment to their instruments.

"Progress was determined not by any measurable aptitude or trait," McPherson concluded, "but by a tiny, powerful idea the child had before even starting lessons. When long-term commitment was combined with high levels of practice, skills skyrockted."[100]

Here are some questions for your personal reflection:

- What is the one goal you are committed to?
- Do you have a short-term or long-term commitment to your goal? How do you know?

---

100 Coyle, D. (2009). *The talent code: Greatness isn't born. It's grown. Here's how* [Kindle 6.3 version]. Retrieved from http://www.amazon.com, p. 104.

- Looking at your past behavior, have you reached similar goals? What makes you think you can achieve this goal? Do you have the skills, time, and competencies required to accomplish the goal?
- Are you willing to burn a ladder to achieve this goal? What ladders can you burn?

Strategy #3: Pre-Committing to Commit

Before pre-committing to specific goals and projects, you can also sign a pre-pre-commitment agreement with yourself. For instance, you may pre-pre-commit to always commit to the things you say you will do and to activities, projects, and ideas that support your larger goal.

In other words, you are pre-committed to committing to only those things that will further support your goal, and to honor your word (if you say you will do it, you will in fact do it!).

The mental contract

Here is a quick exercise: write a mental contract between you and yourself, clearly specifying to all involved (both charioteer and horses) your goal and how you envision achieving it. The contract must include all the steps you will take to achieve the goal. You will not allow any negotiations or rationalizations to creep in.

Then, to demonstrate to your charioteer and horses how committed you are, kick out the ladder and burn it. Here are some ideas to help you do this:

1) Get rid of your social media accounts.
2) Confine yourself to a closed room and only leave after you have tackled the issue.

3) Freeze your smartphone until you get the project done.
4) Move to an expensive hotel room for a week and only leave after you have finished your project. (Why an expensive hotel? Because the nightly cost will hurt your pocket forcing you to stay focused.)
5) Turn off all electronics and media for one week.
6) Take a sabbatical.

Strategy #4: Monitoring

There is a saying in business: "What gets monitored gets done and grows."

Let me tell you a story I remember as if it happened yesterday. I had just gotten a new bicycle for my birthday (which one, I was too young to remember). When the oversized box arrived at home, I was extremely excited. It was the new BMX bike that I had longed for. Filled with excitement, I begin to unwrap the cardboard box that seemed larger than me. I was finally going to be able to ride a real bike. As I opened the box, my jaw fell to the floor. The bike needed to be assembled! This was Brazil in the early '80s, and back then there were no stores where you could buy a ready-to-ride bike.

What?! I thought. I felt utter disbelief. As far as I was concerned, I was never going to ride my bike, *ever* (when you're a kid, having to wait two days to get your bike assembled feels like an eternity).

But life had to continue. That same day I went out with my mom and I can guarantee that everyone in my neighborhood was riding a bike. Everyone! I saw bikes of all colors and shapes. All the kids in my neighborhood looked really happy riding their bikes and I was the only sucker who couldn't join them. The universe was conspiring against me by enticing all those kids to ride their bikes exactly when I was passing by.

Thirty-something years later, I read an article about Zog Sports. I had never heard of them but all of a sudden, I would see the Zog Sports logo on t-shirts and flyers, and people around me were talking about it. Another universal conspiracy?

Of course not. BMX and Zog Sports had become anchor points in my conscious mind; everywhere I went my mind was scanning for them. The bikes and the Zog Sports t-shirts had always been there, they just weren't on my attention radar. As they became, even if unconsciously, part of my focus, I began seeing them.

The book *The 4 Disciplines of Execution* provides a fascinating example that further exemplifies the concept of monitoring—and, better yet, keeping a clear score.[101] The authors of the book report an episode at a high school football game, in an area affected by Hurricane Katrina. The beginning of the game was filled with fanfare and excitement. But interestingly, as the game progressed, no one seemed to be following the game. Katrina had shut down the scoreboard. The people in the stands were following a scoreless game and didn't know how much time was left until the end. Fans quickly lost interest and focused their attention elsewhere. The authors remind us how monitoring and keeping score keep us focused and change our behavior—from a cheering crowd to a chatty, unfocused crowd.

Why are these stories relevant to self-control? Remember that most of the conscious self-control we are discussing in this book has to do with the ability of the pre-frontal cortex to take action. And it so happens that *attention* and *monitoring* are the first steps in cognition and information processing.

101 McChesney, C., Covey, S., & Huling, J. (2012). *The 4 disciplines of execution: Achieving your wildly important goals* [Kindle 6.3 version]. Retrieved from http://www.amazon.com.

You can't make sense of things that you don't notice or monitor. Dieters, exercisers, achievers, and debtors must first pay attention and monitor what they eat, how they exercise, what they want to achieve, and where they spend money, if they hope to make any improvement in these areas.

By the same token, whatever part of our lives we choose to improve, we must pay attention to and monitor where we currently stand in relation to where we want to be (our standards and goals). We must also monitor how much time we spend nurturing and focused on improving our position. In the case of my first BMX, the idea of riding my new bike dominated my attention and my brain automatically started to see everything from that perspective.

Monitoring is the equivalent of keeping score. And when we keep score we are able to make causal connections. When you monitor the number of calories you consume and you notice how it affects your weight, you are now making personal causal inferences. Research by Dr. David Levitsky, from Cornell University's Division of Nutritional Science, suggests that consistent weight monitoring (coupled with visual feedback) is a sufficient condition for weight loss, even without specific diet or exercise plans.[102]

When you monitor the number of client calls you make and the results they bring, you are now able to create causal relationships between calls and results. When you monitor the amount of time you devote to organic chemistry, you can now establish a relationship between hours studied and your GPA. (But be careful about making erroneous causal relationships, such as "BMXs on the street equals a universal conspiracy against me.")

102 Levitsky, D. A., & Pacanowski, C. R. (2011). Free will and the obesity epidemic. *Public Health Nutrition, 15*(1), 126-141.

Today we have a number of monitoring technologies that allow us to quantify calorie consumption, level of activity, where and how we spend our time, where and how we spend our money, the websites we visit, the distances we run, how well we sleep.... and so on. The advantage of such monitoring devices is that they feed us with real-time information, allowing for behavioral change.

I recently downloaded the Nike running app for my iPhone. As my virtual trainer whispered in my ears how many minutes per mile I had run, it fueled my eagerness to beat my own records. One day I went for a long run, and the virtual trainer told me that it was my longest run ever. The next day I beat my previous day's record.

The implications of attention to and monitoring of goal achievement and self-control are substantial. If what we pay attention to grows, then what we *don't* pay attention to either falls away or grows out of control, like a garden overtaken by a parasitic weed.

For instance, you may inadvertently disregard the negative effect that distractions have on your ability to achieve goals. Because you don't monitor these distractions, you fail to recognize the impact they are having in your life. On the other hand, by monitoring them you can pinpoint what is derailing you and how. Then you can take concrete actions to correct it.

Achieving long-term goals is challenging. It requires continuous effort over long periods of time. Often, between now and our distant goals, life happens—and in life we are presented with distractions and urgencies that move our attention away from our long-term goals.

Research confirms that most failures of self-control occur when people shift their attention from distant, larger goals to immediate, more concrete rewards.[103] Meditators, philosophers, and self-help gurus all emphasize the importance of "living in the now." Although I would not disagree with this, we also have to beware that the "now," if not monitored and contrasted against our desired standards and aspirations, can often kill our long-term accomplishments. The now should be lived in relation to our larger goals, values, and concerns. Otherwise, if not properly monitored, attending to the now can and will take away the oxygen needed for your higher accomplishments to grow and thrive.

The dark horse is hungry and constantly looking around for the easy-to-reach pastures. Monitoring allows you to contrast your chariot's intended destination with what is preventing the dark horse and the charioteer from achieving it.

Many of the greatest leaders that I have spoken to are "now-orientated" doers with "future-oriented" minds. They monitor where they are in relation to where they want to be and use the now to get there, without letting distractions derail them.

Critical Output Analysis

One of the most powerful monitoring exercises available is Critical Output Analysis. If we were to develop an objective measure of the value of our lives, this would probably be the most relevant one.

Critical Output Analysis is the objective (thus *critical*) inventory of the actual value we create during our existence. Value,

---

103 Ersner-Hershfield, H., Garton, M. T., Ballard, K., Samanez-Larkin, G. R., & Knutson, B. (2009). Don't stop thinking about the future: Individual differences in future self-continuity account for savings. *Judgment and Decision Making*, 4(4), 280–286.

in this context, can be measured as material goods, implemented ideas, and living by one's values and beliefs. Material goods do not necessarily mean buying and acquiring stuff. It refers to our ability to create real, tangible value. This book is a material good (and an implemented idea). Living by values and beliefs is implementing that which you believe. It is not just about reading the Bible and believing in a life of love—it is actually *living* it.

Think about job interviews. As we mentioned in Chapter 1, at an interview the question no one ever asks you is, "What is the thought you are most proud of?" On the other hand, the question invariably asked of you in some form or other is, "What are the achievements you are most proud of?"

Output analysis is not concerned about what we say we will do or how we say we will live our lives, but what we *actually* do and how we *truly* live our lives. In this model, we are not preoccupied with what goes on inside one's mind, but how we transform thoughts into real action.

Thoughts are cheap and easy to come by; implementing thoughts is a different ball-game.

Committing to one's word is the strategy best suited for Critical Output Analysis: committing to do what you say you will do (and then doing it). Again, the focus here is on the action to get the job done, not the thinking about it. When I had the idea to write this book, I thought to myself, "Gee, I'll have to do it now." So I sat down and started writing it.

This is not to say that words just flowed from my fingertips and I wrote in a state of transcendence. Just the opposite, in fact: I doubted myself. I got tired. I had setbacks. I had to reshuffle my schedule. I had to put in long hours before and after my full-time job. Then I doubted myself a little more. I convinced myself that this was a bad idea—after all, who would read a book from someone whose native language is not even English? My thoughts were running wild. Oh, and let's not forget the effects of blue light: it's said that for a good night of sleep your body has to produce melatonin and the blue light from our computer screens inhibits the production of melatonin. Blue light dupes our brain into thinking it's time to be alert just when we are supposed to be getting ready for a restful night of sleep. I learned the effects of blue light the hard way: every time I wrote until late into the night, I had the most horrible night of sleep (ever!).

But at the end of the day, I would go back to the beginning. I had said I would do it, so I had to just do it.

Critical Output Analysis allows you to critically determine where you are vis-à-vis your goal. The ultimate goal is to use the information emerging from the gap analysis as inspiration to get you going.

But what should you monitor? What are you looking for?

Knowing what to monitor is just as important as monitoring itself. Although the list below is not exhaustive, there are certain things that tend to stand between us and our goals. Above all, look for patterns of behaviors, thoughts, people you encounter, technologies at your disposal, and so on. Remember that a pattern predicts your future. Those elements that create your patterns need to be monitored and, if necessary, changed.

What to monitor	Evidence
Goals	What are our goals and what is the evidence that we are making progress towards them? (Think: Critical Output Analysis!)
Actions	What are the behaviors, conscious or unconscious, that bring you closer to your goals, or that distract you from them?
Results	What is the concrete data that tells you whether or not you are reaching your goals?
Thoughts	What are the thoughts or collections of thoughts that either support or distract you from your goals?
Feelings	What are the emotional states that dictate how you act?
Impulses	What are sudden urges that distance you from your higher goals?
Time	What are the times of the day when you can focus and the times that offer too many distractions?
Desires	What is motivating you towards a certain object, person, or activity that is associated with pleasure or with the avoidance of displeasure?
Technologies	What are the media, entertainment, and/or electronic tools that distract you from your goals?
People	Who are the individuals who support your goal, giving you much-needed support, and who are those who distract and interfere with your goals?

Environments	What are the physical places that ignite certain desired or undesired behaviors? (For instance, while church may ignite calmness and positive thoughts, bars and keg parties may ignite undesired behaviors.)

As you set goals, proactively monitor each of the elements above that conflict with your goals. The objective of this book is to share with you, in the following pages, effective strategies to deal with each of these elements.

CHAPTER 8

The E in EAT (Environment)

THE FIRST STEP IN THE EAT system of self-control is taming the dark horse and focusing the charioteer by manipulating your environment.

Our environment is simply our surroundings: from the physical world to the social surroundings that we are a part of, and from the technology we possess to the route we take to work each day. Everything that does not come from within us can be considered the "environment."

The environment plays a significant role in the way we act. We are situational beings, meaning that our behaviors are controlled to a large extent by the stimuli, cues, situations, and contingencies present at any given environment.

I first learned about the power of designing environments to create behavioral change from a district attorney. She is a passionate advocate for what is called "behavioral change through environmental design." This theory postulates that small changes in the environment can make a huge impact in behavioral change—in this case, crime prevention.

People act according to their environments. Lighting streets, keeping streets clean, or adding neighborhood watch signs are all examples of effective ways to control behavior. I always tell my students the story of a hotel in Honolulu that used this system to put an end to unwanted behavior from overly passionate guests, who would go out at night and invariably find a one-night stand in one of the nearby bars or nightclubs. These individuals would then bring their partners back to the hotel, eventually becoming physically passionate in a dark corner close to the swimming pool. The hotel's solution was to install sensors in that particular dark corner. As the passionate lovers reached it, bright lights went on, announcing that the party was over.

From a more personal perspective, we often fall victim to the "truth-in-context" phenomenon.[104] Our behavior changes considerably depending on the environment in which we find ourselves. A simple change in environment can elicit unexpected behaviors: a supportive environment can elicit the best from us, while an unsupportive environment can elicit uncharacteristic and sometimes maladaptive behavior.

Think, for example, of a team that brings out the best in you, compared to a team that makes you behave in unrecognizable ways. A slight change in context—in this case, team dynamics—can produce either amazing or regrettable behaviors. Each context elicits a different "truth" about you.

One of the seminal studies illustrating how context shapes behavior, as opposed to pure free will, is Professor Milgram's study at Yale University in the mid 1960s. Professor Milgram had scientists wearing white coats (a symbol of authority) tell subjects to administer electrical shocks to a patient placed in another room. The subjects were instructed to increase the intensity of the shock each time it was administered. The subjects could hear

---

104 Ketchum, L. D., & Trist. E. (1992). *All teams are not created equal: How employee empowerment really works.* Newbury Park, CA: Sage Publications.

the patients moaning and screaming in the other room, as the intensity of the shocks increased. Subjects would look at the individual wearing the white coat in despair, waiting for guidance or sympathy, but the white-coated, heartless scientists would not budge. They would insist that the subjects continue to increase the intensity of the shocks. The controversial discovery was that, despite their hesitation, subjects would continue to discharge the shocks.

To relieve you from your angst, the "patients" involved were actually actors and they were not receiving real electrical shocks—they were faking it. Dr. Milgram's conclusion was that very few of us have what it takes to resist authority.

For our larger discussion, I would argue that very few of us can resist various forms of environmental stimuli and that our behavior is often highly influenced by these same stimuli. I always find it amusing that the Our Father prayer ends with "...and lead us not into temptation," a clear indication that we often need Divine intervention to deal with contextual and environmental cues.

When it comes to self-regulation, managing our environment and understanding that it exerts a major influence on our behavior is a low-effort, high-reward strategy. For the most part, changes in our environment require little cognitive effort and control, temporarily relieving the charioteer of their duties and allowing them to allocate energy to other areas that may require executive control.

We have at our disposal the ability to a) select, b) adapt to, and c) change environments.[105] Let's look at each of these in turn.

---

105 Sternberg, R.J. (2007). WICS: A system model of leadership. *The American Psychologist, 62*(1), 34-42.

a) *Environmental selection:* Selection implies we have the freedom, to a certain extent, to choose our environment. When selecting an environment, the focus should be on avoiding those that do not support our goal and, wherever possible, seeking supportive environments. This is easier said than done, as we often find ourselves in situations that we don't have much power to select or change. One of my students, despite her strong desire to succeed, was trapped in a less-than-ideal home environment that turned out to be an enormous obstacle to her goal of becoming a doctor. Her ailing mother needed help running errands and getting things done around the house, leaving her daughter with very little time for herself or her goals and ambitions. In this case, she was not able to select her environment since her mother's condition required her to be at home shortly after school. In the professional world, people often remove themselves from a toxic work environment by quitting, the ultimate form of environmental selection.
b) *Adapting to environments:* Adapting to an environment means trying, to the best of our abilities, to achieve our goals in spite of environmental forces acting against them. If our environment is not conducive to achieving our goals, we can use our ingenuity to re-calibrate our actions, or temporarily re-calibrate our goals until conditions change. We can also meticulously study our current environment in order to find "sweet spots" that can favor us. In the case of the student above, she realized that her mother took an afternoon nap. That was her sweet spot, and she organized most of her study around these naps.
c) *Changing the environment:* Finally, we can make changes to our environment by taking action to make it more

supportive of our goals. Changes to the environment include physical changes, which are usually easier to accomplish, or changes in values, culture and attitudes, which are highly time- and energy-consuming but may offer long-term benefits. Changes in the physical environment may include getting rid of your modem to block your Internet access, turning off audio notifications for your email account, ditching that distracting TV (or moving to a different room), or locking your door to avoid distractions from others. Change in culture, values, and attitudes require unearthing the assumptions and values that drive behavior and creating rewards and punishment systems that sustain the desired behavior.

Managing Environmental Distractions

In August 2011, an emergency medical helicopter crashed, killing all four passengers—the rescued patient, a flight nurse, a paramedic, and the pilot. Four innocent lives were cut short unexpectedly and unnecessarily. The U.S. National Transportation Safety Board officially linked this fatal accident to the pilot texting on his smartphone during the flight, particularly during mandatory pre-flight checks. The pilot was allegedly making dinner plans with one of his co-workers, and in the midst of this distraction, he failed to notice a small but very important detail: the helicopter was low on fuel.

This is indeed an extreme example, as you probably don't fly helicopters. But think about driving. Driving while In*text*icated has become a w orldwide pandemic, dramatically increasing the number of drivers who get involved in accidents which are sometimes fatal, killing both themselves and innocent people.

According to the Texting and Driving Safety website, www.textinganddrivingsafety.com, texting while driving increases the likelihood of an accident by 23 times! This is a staggering statistic.

Environmental distractions eat up our time, divert our attention, and suck our energy into activities that have no major consequence for or impact on our long-term goals. Although they keep our dark horses and present selves satisfied, they can be disastrous to our future.

As established earlier in this book, inhibiting impulses and actions is an energy-driven process, limiting the amount of energy available for other tasks. So when managing our environment, the most effective way to deal with cues that may cause unwanted impulses is to remove ourselves from distractions altogether. By doing so, the dark horse is not tempted and the charioteer is relieved from his duties.

The strategies shared in this chapter are:

- Shielding;
- Getting rid of time and energy leeches;
- The "This 'r Nothing" approach;
- Alone time;
- Managing FOMO;
- Setting defaults;
- Providing structure;
- Setting tripwires.

Strategy #5: Shielding

Our goals are constantly under attack from interferences (interruptions and distractions) from the outside world. The omnipresent quality of interferences, particularly in a highly connected world, means that it will continue to dominate our lives. For instance, a McKinsey & Company article highlights an all-too-common occurrence in today's corporate world: the fact that people multitask on their mobile devices when attending training programs.[106] Multitasking occupies a large portion of the brain's working memory, diminishing our ability to learn.

One way of protecting our goals from coming under attack is by creating a protective casing around them; that is, to shield our goals.

Shielding strategies protect our goals from the "elements," helping us to create focus by deliberately avoiding immanent distractions. Mckinsey reports, for example, that companies are creating immersive learning environments in which attendees have to leave their mobile phones at the door.[107]

Like weasels, distractions find their way into our lives, controlling us without our conscious knowledge. They can be highly deceptive, as once they have found their way in, we tend to assume that they're just part of daily living. They can creep into our lives, lodge themselves within our daily routines, and take control—all without us noticing it.

To make matters worse, distractions come in small sizes, fooling the charioteer who is scanning the environment for major threats. Your dark horse being pulled off course to indulge in a distraction may not feel very relevant, but when we calculate the compounded effect of these countless little tugs, we find ourselves miles away from our intended destination.

---

106 Atabaki, A., Dietsch, S, & Sperling, J. M. (2015, July). How to separate learning myths from reality. *McKinsey Quarterly*. Retrieved from https://www.mckinsey.com/business-functions/organization/our-insights/how-to-separate-learning-myths-from-reality

107 Ibid.

The distraction test

Here is a test to help you identify distractions. The first test everything in your surroundings must pass is: Does it support my goal?

The second test is: does it prevent me from achieving my goal? Beyond my immediate goal, is this environmental force aligned with my larger values and goals in life?

Let's say, for example, that you need to write a proposal for a client, or a term paper. You could be writing it right now, but you are bogged down by small talk with colleagues. Let's put the task to the distraction test. Does the small talk support your immediate goal? It doesn't. Does it prevent you from achieving your goal? It does. Is talking to my colleagues reinforcing deep-seated values and beliefs? You could argue that it feeds your need for bonding and connection, but those opportunities will still be there tomorrow.

Let's take another example: the phone rings and it's your grandmother. Does speaking to grandma support your goal? It doesn't. The difference is that your relationship with your grandmother fulfills your most deep-seated value of cherishing family. Not all distractions are created equal. Grandma passes the distraction test—unless, of course, in the heat of the moment, talking to her is indeed a distraction.

Remember that goals can be long-term, continuous goals (for instance, exercising more frequently), while other goals are short-term or project-based (such as writing a book). Although distractions plague both types of goals, the importance of the distractions may change dramatically depending on the type of goal you are trying to achieve.

For example, I am an avid reader of political news. However, when writing this book I realized that politics was 1) not supporting my goal, and 2) preventing me from achieving my goal (I could be reading articles and books on the subject of self-control instead of reading newspapers). Being acquainted with what is going on in the world is still something I value, but following politics had failed the two first distraction tests and had to be placed on hold until I was done writing.

As you know by now, monitoring is a key step in self-regulation. Let's start by monitoring your surroundings vis-à-vis your goals and identifying the main distractions currently derailing you.

First, determine what type of goals you are trying to achieve and how environmental forces may be affecting these goals.

Use the space below to list everything that distracts you from your goals. After you have identified the environmental forces in your way, ask how you can shape or change your environment to create a shield to ensure that you are not tempted or your attention diverted by these distractions?

Goal: ______________________________

Distractions:	**Change in environment:**
Who in your environment distracts you from your goal (friends, office colleagues)?	1.
What TV shows distract you from your goal?	2.
What sports consume your time, detracting from your goals?	3.
Do you read the news to the point of addiction? Could you be using the same time for other activities that support your goal?	4.

What environments are you immersed in that increase your impulsive behaviors? • Dieters: Are you exposed to environments with abundance of high-calorie foods? Are you meeting clients for lunch and dinner? What kinds of social media are preventing you from fully focusing on your goals (e.g., Facebook, Pinterest, Instagram, Youtube)? Do these distractions pass the first distraction test? (Probably not.) What types of emails are bloating your inbox? Do you feel compelled to answer all of them? Are your answers long-winded and wordy? What are the constant emergencies and ongoing fires that prevent you from focusing on your goal? Who brings them about?	5.

Strategy #6: Getting Rid of Time and Energy Leeches

I once met a woman at a professional conference who testified how her boyfriend was dragging her grades down in college, potentially preventing her from achieving her dream of becoming a medical doctor. In her own words, her boyfriend was worth

32 semester credits. He was consuming a lot of her time and energy on top of her full load of classes.

She came to the realization that she had to choose between the boyfriend or becoming a doctor. She is now a doctor.

When you are traveling fast, you can't allow others to rob you of your two most precious commodities: time and energy. Time and energy leeches are those individuals who will suck your time and energy dry. They divert our allocation of time and energy, preventing us from paying attention to our own goals.

Leeches may be found everywhere, in the form of a partner who demands attention 24/7, a colleague who insists on sharing his daily drama with you during work hours, the office gossiper, or the friend who needs a shoulder to cry on (all the time).

Please don't get me wrong: self-control is not an isolationist strategy that requires us to disregard emotions, feelings, or the need to bond with others. Being available to those in need is an essential part of the human experience. However, we must learn to identify leeches—those who consistently rob your time and energy with their own problems.

As suggested by McKeown, we need to build some fences and keep other people's problems out of our yard. In other words, we need a specific shielding strategy for time and energy leeches.[108]

Step 1*:* Identify leeches. Make an inventory of individuals who persistently require your attention and time.
Step 2: The qualification process. After you have created a preliminary list, make sure they pass the leech test. A leech:

---

108 McKeown, G. (2014). Essentialism: The Disciplined Pursuit of Less. New York, NY: Crown Business.

- Is disrespectful of your time by always being late.
- Engages in small talk/conversations that do not add value to your life and the life of others.
- Is the ultimate drama king/queen and spends substantial time sharing his/her issues with you (issues that you can do little or nothing about)
- Creates emergencies due to their lack of preparation.
- Engages in gossip.
- Does not pay attention to you or your needs when you talk.
- Doesn't know when to stop talking
- Gives long-winded answers and gets off topic easily.
- Texts non-stop.

(Caveat: your grandmother calling to tell you how much she misses you does not qualify. Embrace grandmotherly love.)

Remember that when a leech latches on to you, it is almost impossible to get free of them. That is why they are called leeches: they have been leeching for their entire lives and they need a body to latch onto. A leech without a body is a dead leech. So all leeches that still exist have mastered the art of leeching. Beware.

Step 3: Devise a plan for how to deal with the type of leeches in your life:

- *Gossipers and drama queens*: Avoid the person at all costs; learn how and where the person engages in conversation with you and avoid places where these leeches hang out. Are they always around the watercooler? Bring your own water. When they approach you, look busy and say you have a conference call in five minutes that you need to prepare for. Close your door.

    - If you are the leech: stop! No one wants to know about your gossip or drama. If people are constantly on conference calls or running from the watercooler when you show up… ask yourself why.
- *Emergenciers*: These are people who love an emergency, and everything is due today, now! They leave everything to the last minute and will ask you to drop everything you are doing to attend to their needs. The moment you open the door to their emergencies, there is no going back: you will be enslaved forever. Manage their expectations to the best of your ability. When you know of upcoming deadlines, develop a communication plan with a series of follow-up emails prompting them to act. Try to anticipate potential requests from them and make it clear what you need, and when you need it.
    - If you are the leech: your lack of preparation is not other people's problems. Get organized. Read this book.
- *Disrespectfuls*: These individuals have no respect for you or your schedule. It is all about them. They will schedule and cancel meetings at their will. Be clear about how much time you have available for them; if they cannot see you during the scheduled time, don't sit around and wait—reschedule.
    - If you are the leech: have some respect (not for yourself, but for others). Your lack of planning affects productivity and morale.
- *Long-winders:* These individuals go on and on without stopping. A 5-minute phone call is a 45-minute head-banging experience. Because they don't allow you to speak, you are left to wonder in your head how someone

can have so much to say about so little. Be clear about how much time you have available for them; have a detailed agenda and explain to the person what you intend to cover in that period of time. Schedule short meetings. Always be busy after meetings so you can have an excuse to leave.

  - If you are the leech: Edit your stories. Share just the essentials. Respect the other person.

- *Texters*: No matter where you are or what you're doing, these individuals are texting. They may be in the shower and they're texting. Having a one-on-one conversation is highly frustrating. Establish boundaries. Turn off all push notifications on your phone. Resist the urge to answer every incoming text.
  - If you are the leech: have you no manners? Focus on the person in front of you.

How to effectively manage your emails

Today, managing emails—which includes deleting spam and message strings from listservs, along with answering those that must be answered—consumes a large chunk of our days. To some, answering emails is an art, requiring, a lot of time and effort to craft a beautiful message. Although some messages require more TLC than others, I would argue that most of what is emailed is not high-impact work. Those long emails are eating up your mechanical time and preventing you from focusing on activities with high impact.

Peter Diamandis, a master innovator and entrepreneur, suggests the following tips for managing your email:

1) Three lines—that's what the length of your emails should be. If you need more than three lines, you may want to consider a phone call or a brief meeting.
2) Do spend time on the subject line. It should be a) attention grabbing, b) meaningful, and c) easily searchable.
3) Don't go crazy on the formatting.
4) Your action request should be available in the first line.
5) Make the action/task as simple as possible. Ideally, the responder should answer your request with a "yes" or a "no."
6) Simplify the task in such a way that it is more likely for the person to say "yes."

Each email should follow the three "s" of a request: simple, single, and specific:

- Can I see you for 15 minutes to discuss a proposal?
- Please kindly review and sign the attached document.
- Can we meet for 15 minutes on Wednesday, Oct 14th between 10 a.m. and 1 p.m. in your office?
- I would appreciate it if you could please introduce me to Ms. Smith.

Strategy #7: "This 'R Nothing"

This is probably one of my favorite shielding strategies, and probably the one I struggle with the most. The "This 'r Nothing" strategy allows us to focus exclusively at one task at a time for short periods of time.

Here is how it works:

The goal is to spend a pre-determined period of time, typically 20-60 minutes, focused exclusively in one task. If you don't feel like engaging in the task at hand, then you will do nothing… and I mean *nothing* at all. No texting, cell phones, answering emails, updating social media statuses, watching videos, or taking trips to the refrigerator. (I have seen people go to the refrigerator who are still reported missing. They presumably found Narnia at the back of the refrigerator and are now living in a parallel world.)

Let's suppose that your goal is to study organic chemistry. You bring the book to a quiet place, set the time, and commit to yourself that you will study chemistry, or do nothing. If you just don't feel like it, you will do nothing.

In the beginning, you need to be strong not to reach for that smart phone of yours calling for your attention. You will realize that after 3 minutes (or even 30 seconds) of doing nothing, that chemistry book all of a sudden becomes very attractive.

I have actually created a This 'r Nothing app for the iPhone.[109] The app can be downloaded at the iPhone store (www.thisrnothing.com), and it's very easy to use. You chose a task to work on, set the time you will be working on it, and during that period you either do the task or absolutely nothing. If you decide to play around with your phone, answer calls, or open other apps, you will receive a burnt marshmallow. On the other hand, if you stick to the task, you will be rewarded with two pristine, white marshmallows (remember Mischel's Marshmallow study, discussed earlier?).

By using this technique, you will immediately experience the seductive power of the dark horse. If, at this point, you have not identified the dark horse inside of you, I am positive this exercise will help you. The minute you commit to staying focused,

---

109 https://apple.co/2XmUt9k

the dark horse throws a fit. But the dark horse is subtle—it will convince you to engage in other goals through the power of suggestion. The feedback from one of the users of the app summarizes it well:

> *"I just earned my first marshmallow!! Sixty minutes without blinking! I was tempted to grab a snack; read the incoming mail; check what my daughter was watching on TV; check whose birthday it was today; but I successfully stayed on task. Next time I will focus for one hour and 15 minutes!"*

The most common seductive suggestions from the dark horse are:

- You are hungry!
- You are thirsty!
- You are tired!
- Check what is happening on social media!
- Take a break before you engage in this task, so when you get back you are really ready!

Don't let the dark horse get into your head. Remember... you should focus on the task at hand or nothing else. If you are able to control yourself a few times, your dark horse will immediately understand that you mean business. Eventually, you will become proficient at recognizing the seductive thoughts unleashed by the dark horse and taking them for what they are—pure sweet-talk. Before you know it, you'll be in control.

With this strategy you will probably be (as I was and still am) amazed at how much you can accomplish during an uninterrupted "This 'r Nothing" cycle. You will realize how productive you can be and how much you can accomplish by focusing for 30 minutes on a single task. If you follow through with this strategy, you will have some of the most productive 20-40 minute sessions of your life.

Strategy #8: Alone Time (Put the Dark Horse in Solitary Confinement)

Bad Internet connectivity makes me very productive. I often visit colleges and universities in upstate New York and instead of driving from my Manhattan office (which is a complete waste of time as you can't do anything but drive the car), I take the Amtrak, which offers a wonderful service to its clients - free Internet. Luckily, the connection is bad, so bad, that it gives me no alternative but to work on my favorite projects. In these dire circumstances, browsing the Internet is out of the question, leaving not much else to do besides napping, reading, or writing.

I also love airports and flying for the same reason that I love Amtrak: poor Internet access and lack of distractions. Internet on airplanes is still too expensive and not always available, and I am not the type who strikes up conversations with the person next to me on the plane. As a result, I have the benefit of having some uninterrupted "alone time."

When you are sitting in that narrow middle seat on an airplane, or on a long train ride, with nowhere to go, no one to bother you, and very little distractions, amazing things can happen. Alone time is the equivalent to putting your dark horse in solitary confinement.

One of the most famous executives to fiercely embrace the concept of alone time is Microsoft founder and the head of the Bill and Melinda Gates Foundation, Bill Gates. Once a year, Bill Gates flies to a quiet waterfront cabin in the woods and disconnects from the world he helped create—the hyper-connected world. He also disconnects from family, friends, and the office. He brings to the cabin a lasting supply of Diet Orange Crush and some reading material, including scientific papers and papers by Microsoft engineers, executives, and product managers.[110] He scribbles on the papers, makes annotations, and uses this experience not only to educate himself but also to make decisions about what projects to bet on.[111]

Most of us don't have the luxury of taking two weeks of alone time to reflect and think about life. Very few people do. But what we can do is carve out alone time within our daily routines. As mentioned earlier, arriving at work one hour earlier, for instance, will typically give you a much-needed dose of alone time. Some other ideas are:

1) Arrive at work even earlier.
2) If you take public transportation to and from work, use the time to read, write, and think.
3) Visit the local library to read or write.
4) Work in coffee shops with no distractions (ditch the lure of free Wi-Fi).
5) Block off alone time on your schedule at work and force yourself to work only on new and high-impact projects.

Alone time should be a sacred time in your day, devoted to work that matters. I strongly encourage you to carve out alone time for at least one hour each day and immerse yourself in whatever it is

110 Forrester, D. P. (2011). *Consider: Harnessing the power of reflective thinking in your organization*. New York, NY: Palgrave Macmillan.

111 Yoffie, D. B., & Cusumano, M. A. (2015). *Strategy rules: Five timeless lessons from Bill Gates, Andy Grove, and Steve Jobs*. New York, NY; HarperBusiness.

that you want to accomplish. More than one hour of alone time per day is quite difficult to achieve, but you will be surprised by the exponential effect that a couple of focused minutes in a day will yield in the long term.

Gertrude Stein, a famous American writer, affirmed in her biography that she only wrote 30 minutes per day. In her own words, "If you write a half hour a day it amounts to lot of writing year by year."[112] What we can accomplish in one hour, one half hour, or even on a plane or train ride, compounded over the years, is mesmerizing.

I recently presented a workshop on self-control to a group of enthusiastic and eager-to-learn students. I asked the group to raise their hands if they had any alone time in their day. To my dismay, 90% of the room raised their hands. I was disappointed as it seemed to me that I was sharing a strategy that everyone was already applying in their daily lives. I felt as if my message, that I so eagerly shared, was completely irrelevant.

Then I decided to further investigate my hunch that there was something wrong with that show of hands. When I asked a couple of them to describe their activities during their alone time, the common thread was listening to music, watching TV, or updating social media. Alone time is not merely *time alone.* It is time alone that is focused on your goals, your big goals!

Strategy #9: Managing FOMO (Editing Your Life)

Researchers at MIT have conducted a very interesting study to determine how people act when they have to choose between

112 Currey, M. (2013). *Daily rituals: How artists work* [Kindle 6.3 version]. Retrieved from http://www.amazon.com, Kindle Locations 182–184.

options. Undergraduate students were presented with a computer screen showing three doors—let's call them the blue, pink, and green doors. By clicking on each door, students would get a certain amount of money, the goal of the exercise being to accumulate as much money as possible within a predetermined time period.

Students would click on the blue door and it would yield, let's say, five cents on the first click, seven cents on the second click, and so on. Clicking on the green door they would get seven cents, eight cents, and so on.

Any rational person would be expected to click on the door that offered them the highest yield. When I ask my students, sitting in a comfortable classroom, what they would do in a similar situation, invariably they tell me that they would only click on the doors with the highest yield.

For the most part, my students were right. In this first design of the experiment, the MIT students tended to click on the highest-paying doors. However, some would click on all doors, irrespective of the pay-out.[113]

A second version of the same experiment was presented to students. In the new version, after a certain number of clicks, a door would randomly disappear. How would students react under this new scenario?

My students rationalized that they would click on the door generating the highest yield, and if that door disappeared they would then move on to the door with the second-highest yield. If only reality was that simple. In the actual study, students would frantically click on all doors, regardless of the actual pay-out.

---

113 Ariely, D. (2009). Predictably irrational: The hidden forces that shape our decisions. New York, NY: Harper-Collins Publishers.

This experiment confirms what we have already determined earlier in this book: we can be irrational beings. Although the goal of the exercise was to accumulate as much money as possible, students would act with little regard for the amount of money the doors were yielding.

The MIT study concluded that we have a hard time dealing with the prospect of closing doors on alternatives. We like to keep our options open and have as many alternatives as possible available at our fingertips. Closing a door on a perceived opportunity is anxiety-producing and heats up the emotional system (the dark horse loves open doors).

Extrapolating these finding to our personal experiences, we find that people attempt to keep up with a long list of activities that may have some value, but are not strategically aligned with the achievement of their larger, long-term goals.

In the business world, the desire to keep doors open is pervasive. Marketing strategists will often advise companies to find a niche market and stick with it. Yet I have encountered many professionals who keep bouncing from one market to another, in the hope that one day a dead or low-yield market will finally start producing results. Even when the data clearly indicates that a particular market has never yielded one sale in the past, we keep on going back to it because "it has potential."

Students these days are engaged in endless extra-curricular activities, in order to become well-rounded and hopefully more competitive. They are officers at on-campus clubs, volunteer with humanitarian organizations, they do research, work part-time, play sports, instruments, learn a second (or third) language... and the list goes on. Although some of these activities may have merit in making them more competitive applicants, there are some that are just "busy work" and lack any real value.

An important question to be answered is: why do we continue opening doors that yield no results?

The answer has to do with how we rationalize events in our lives. In the marketing example, although we haven't sold a dollar's worth of goods or services to a client who will probably never buy from us, we still insist on spending time and energy with that client. This is because we rationalize the lack of results not as a failure, but as a *near miss.* We think, "*the client was really close to sealing the deal, I just know it, it almost happened, and because it was so near, I will keep that door open.*" It hasn't happened, it will probably never happen, but we keep that door of opportunity within reach.

In the students' example, doing more makes us feel good about ourselves. We assume causality. More is better; at least we like to think so. It should be clear by now that a central theme of this book is that more is not necessarily better. Focusing on the *right* things is better.

Five minutes ago I took a break from writing this book and was watching Robert Irvine's TV show *Restaurant Impossible* on the Food Network. If you are not familiar with this show, Irvine flips failing restaurants. He is currently trying to save a restaurant in Alabama. As he is approaching the restaurant, he sees a woman dressed up in a hot dog costume trying to lure in customers who drive by the busy highway where the restaurant is located. The woman happens to be the owner of the restaurant. Robert stops his car and asks the talking hot dog why she is dressed up as, of all things, a hot dog, particularly because hers is a steak and seafood restaurant. She answers that she will do whatever is needed to save her business.

Irvine, in his typical brash, TV-like demeanor, asks if she has been successful in bringing in customers by dressing in a hot-dog costume. The response is obvious, "no!" He asks why she does it then. She beautifully summarizes what we have been discussing so far: "On the off chance that it does." On the off chance that a door will yield results, we keep them open.

The Internet and smartphones allow us to open multiple doors at once. We can now incessantly scan our environment seeking information and opportunities, and to stay on top of things. We can scan what our peers, or those whom we admire, are saying or doing. We want to be on top of everything; we want to miss nothing.

This tendency, which has now become a pathology, is called FOMO—the Fear of Missing Out. FOMO is the need to be omniscient, omnipresent, and omnipotent. The anxiety brought about by FOMO makes us want to be everywhere, at every moment. It makes us want to know what our friends and peers are doing at all times, and when and where the next gathering place will be.

Activities that are not aligned with your higher goal will compete for your attention, energy, and focus. By attending to distractions, we divert energy to nonessentials. In short, we must learn how to say no to these nonessentials and strategically focus on activities that leverage our higher goals.

Greg McKeown, author of *Essentialism*, a must-read book for anyone seeking a more productive yet simple life, advocates for massive editing of our lives. Editing, according to him, involves the rigorous elimination of the "trivial, unimportant, or irrelevant."[114]

McKeown reports an encounter with the CEO of Twitter, Jack Dorsey, in which Dorsey said that the role of the CEO is to be the chief editor of a company. He explained that any company could

114 McKeown, G. (2014). *Essentialism: The disciplined pursuit of less* [Kindle 6.3 version]. Retrieved from http://www.amazon.com, p. 156.

be doing hundreds if not thousands of things, when in fact there are only a handful of things that are truly important. There is also a flood of ideas and input from his employees. His job as an editor is to absorb this input and decide on the one thing that they must be doing.

McKeown also reminds us of the advice from one of the most prolific writers, Stephen King, who has sold more than 350 million copies of his books. His advice: leave out the non-essentials, cut to speed up the pace, and to do so you must "kill your darlings."

But which darlings to kill?

The challenge faced by most of us and our charioteers is not that we lack goals, but actually that we may have too many of them. Having a multitude of goals, although it sounds desirable, distracts us from our most important goal by draining much-needed physical and mental energy, time, and other resources from what *really* matters. Multiple goals are often called "competing commitments," meaning any goal you apply productive energy towards that does not help you achieve your *big* goal.

For example, you want to start a blog and a series of podcasts. Each will require different actions that will compete with each other. Eventually one will prevail or both will die.

Think about steering the chariot in multiple directions at once. Your dark horse will absolutely love it. Your white horse will embrace the challenge, but you will probably not get anywhere. Research by Robert Emmons and Laura King has concluded that competing commitments[115]:

---

115 Emmons, R. A., King, L. A., & Sheldon, K. (1993). Goal conflict and the self-regulation of action. In D. M. Wegner & J. W. Pennebaker (Eds.), *Century*

1) Makes you worry more: you have more goals in your life to achieve but only the same amount of mental and physical energy and time. Anxiety increases and so does rumination over what you are not accomplishing.
2) Makes you get less done: your multiple goals drain your energy and time and as a result you get less done.
3) Your physical and mental health suffer: by having competing goals and getting less done, anxiety levels increase, negatively impacting your health.

To uncover the competing commitments sucking your energy and time dry, make a list of the 10-15 goals you are currently trying to achieve:

1) ______________________________
2) ______________________________
3) ______________________________
4) ______________________________
5) ______________________________
6) ______________________________
7) ______________________________
8) ______________________________
9) ______________________________
10) ______________________________

Now mark your three most important goals. After that, mark the goals that conflict with your most important goals.

---

psychology series. Handbook of mental control (pp. 528-551). Englewood Cliffs, NJ, US: Prentice-Hall, Inc.

Success is seldom about doing more. It is often about making the *right* commitments. The question is then: what goals, or commitments, should you keep?

To answer this question, researchers Kegan and Lahey, who also write about competing commitments, propose an excellent question: *What are you doing, or not doing, that is keeping your commitment from being more fully realized?*[116]

I use the following exercise to manage competing commitments.

The Hindu Trinity exercise

In Hinduism, the three major forces of the universe—creation, maintenance and destruction—are personified by three Gods: Brahma, Vishnu, and Shiva. Brahma is known as the keeper of the flame of creation, Vishnu is the keeper of the flame of preservation, and Shiva is the keeper of the flame of destruction. The universe is in a state of dynamic flux under these three flames, as new things are created, some are preserved, and others must be destroyed or transformed.

The Hindu Trinity exercise compels us to look at life, particularly our competing commitments, through the lenses of these three flames.

Shiva: The Flame of Destruction and Transformation:

- What activities are draining your time, energy, and resources, while not yielding results that support your

116 Kegan, R., & Lahey, L. L. (2001). The real reason people won't change. *Harvard Business Review, 79*(10), 84–92.

main goal? What activities can you drop? What activities can you devote less time to?

- Get rid of activities that do not support your goal. Peter Drucker, the renowned management guru, reminds us that highly effective executives do what needs to be done.
- Can you delegate activities that do not add value? Whenever possible, delegate work that can be done by somebody else. Tim Ferriss, author of the *4-hour Workweek*, is known for delegating his work.[117] According to him, he hires armies of intelligent and capable people in developing countries for a fraction of the cost and has them do things that cost him time and energy. After reading about the power of personal outsourcing, I followed suit. I was learning how to develop apps for the iPhone when I decided that I would spend my time more effectively on higher-level projects. I hired a developer through the freelancer website Upwork.com, and a few months later, the "This 'r Nothing" app was born.
- Reduce the number of activities that do not support your goal: eliminating all of them may be difficult as you may derive pleasure, satisfaction, or some much-needed mental relief from them. If that is the case, try to reduce them to a bare minimum and confine them to pre-determined days of the week. For instance, I will allow myself to watch movies and TV shows only on weekends, after I feel I have accomplished enough during the week.

---

117 Ferriss, T. (2007). The 4-Hour Work Week: Escape the 9-5, Live Anywhere and Join the New Rich. New York, NY: Crown Publishers.

Vishnu: Keeper of the Flame of Preservation

- What are the things that you are currently doing that support your goal and that you should keep on doing?

Brahma: Keeper of the Flame of Creation

- What are the things you should start doing to support your goal?
- Can you substitute more productive activities in place of unproductive activities?

After going through this exercise, what does your new list of commitments look like? Remember, your new list should be comprised not of competing commitments, but of stepping-stones to your ultimate goal.

Letting go of things is hard. If you feel anxious, insecure, or afraid that you are missing out by ditching certain activities and projects, McKeown reminds us that we should celebrate our choices.[118]

Celebrate the fact that you chose to focus on your higher goal. Celebrate that you chose to focus on what is essential. Steve Jobs attributed Apple's success to the things they have done and the things they let go of, saying, "I'm as proud of what we don't do as I am of what we do."[119] "A liberating experience" is how Arianna Huffington, author of the book *Thrive*, describes the sensation of dropping unimportant projects.[120] Being the type

---

118 McKeown, G. (2014). *Essentialism: The disciplined pursuit of less* [Kindle 6.3 version]. Retrieved from http://www.amazon.com.

119 Yoffie, D. B., & Cusumano, M. A. (2015). *Strategy rules: Five timeless lessons from Bill Gates, Andy Grove, and Steve Jobs.* New York, NY; HarperBusiness.

120 Huffington, A. (2014). *Thrive: The third metric to redefining success and creating a life of well-being, wisdom, and wonder.* New York, NY: Harmony Books.

A personality and high achiever she is, she had committed to learning German, becoming a good skier, and learning to cook. In her own words, "these countless incomplete projects drained my energy and diffused my attention. [...] Why carry this unnecessary baggage?"[121] She considered these projects completed by dropping them, and it felt good!

Managing FOMO by saying no, delegating, and ditching activities that add little value should not be perceived as losing control or giving up.

To the contrary, they should be perceived as regaining control of the things that really matter. Letting go is part of growing up and pursuing higher aspirations.

Keep in mind that over-committing, not delegating, micromanaging, and engaging in activities that go against your higher aspirations may be a result of hidden commitments that you hold on to in order to protect your self-image. If you have a hard time letting go of unproductive tasks, you will benefit from the hidden commitment strategy outline in Chapter 10. Suffer of FOMO no more!

Strategy #10: Set Defaults (Liberate Yourself From Impulses, Free Yourself From Thinking)

As has been established so far, the dark horse and the charioteer—sometimes unilaterally, and sometimes in cahoots with each other—play an important role derailing us from leading more productive lives.

121 Ibid, p. 155.

Naturally, one way to improve self-control is by removing them from the equation. Goal and task achievement requires volition, willpower, decision-making, and action, activities that deplete the charioteer. It also requires controlling the dark horse... or not. With the help of technology, we can set defaults by manipulating our environment in small ways that free the charioteer from the need to be vigilant and that renders the needs of the dark horse irrelevant.[122] Setting defaults frees us from having to engage in goal achievement while still achieving the goal.

Earlier we discussed how tunnel vision causes us to neglect important areas of our lives. Tunnel vision focuses all our available resources on what is inside the tunnel, typically things that are urgent—the proverbial fires. As a result, the important but not urgent stuff, like saving for your future, or nurturing your body and mind, may be dismissed.

To ensure that the important stuff is not forgotten, you should set defaults that free you from thinking and having to act.

One example is setting up automatic bill payment plans or automatic deposits into a savings account. Saving for the future requires 1) remembering to transfer money from your checking account to a savings account or investment fund; 2) actually making the transfer, which requires opening your computer or phone, signing into your bank account, making the transfer (the dark horse is going crazy by now); and 3) sustaining the habit by repeating these two steps every month.

By setting up an automatic deposit, you free yourself, the dark horse and the charioteer from having to fight over who is going to do what. Without having to think about it, you know your bills will

---

122 Mullainathan, S., & Shafir, E. (2013). *Scarcity: Why having too little means so much.* New York, NY: Times Books.

be paid on time and that money from your paycheck will be automatically transferred to your savings. By setting defaults, you have isolated the dark horse and the charioteer from the equation.

What can you do about it?

- Automate your life as much as possible:
  - Make bills pay themselves
  - Automatically invest money every month
  - Join a meal plan
  - Delegate activities

What other parts of your life can you set defaults?

Strategy #11: SupraMonitoring

How we behave changes drastically when others are watching us. Even mannequins, if we believe they are evaluating us, influence behavior.

Traffic police have used mannequins for years in my old neighborhood to tame people's dark horses. These mannequins, dressed in full traffic officers' paraphernalia, are strategically placed along a busy highway to discourage people from speeding. From a distance, you don't know if the mannequin is a police officer or not. Erring on the side of caution, you reduce your speed. As rational beings (which we are), if we know we are being watched, we will conform to expected norms and standards.

In leadership and group dynamics, the influence of a watcher in shaping behavior has long been documented. Kurt Lewin (yes, the same Lewin from Chapter 2), conducted a study in which preadolescent boys were exposed to leaders with three distinct types of leadership behaviors: autocratic, democratic, and laissez-faire.[123]

Groups under the reigns of an autocratic leader were highly productive, in the short run. There is nothing really surprising about this finding: when we are being observed, we behave according to expectations. Group members were acting out of fear of punishment. The problem was not when the leader was in the room, but when the leader left the room. As soon as the leader was no longer present, productivity plummeted.

Meanwhile, the results clearly indicated that groups under democratic leadership functioned better. Under laissez-faire conditions, with no one in charge, groups were disengaged, uncoordinated, and operated without a sense of direction (supervision is good for us).

Consider this study on procrastination among college students.[124] Students were divided into two groups: one group were given evenly-spaced (externally imposed) deadlines to submit three writing projects, and the second group could choose self-imposed deadlines. More often than not, students chose costly self-imposed deadlines. In other words, while they could set the deadline for all three papers for the end of the semester, most voluntarily selected deadlines before the end of the term, invariably demanding more commitment throughout.

The researchers measured students' performance under these two conditions. Students who were given externally imposed

---

123 Miner, J. B. (2005). *Organizational behavior 1: Essential theories of motivation and leadership.* Armonk, NY: M. E. Sharpe, Inc.

124 Ariely, D., & Wertenbroch, K. (2002). Procrastination, deadlines, and performance: self-control by precommitment. *American Psychological Society, 13*(3), 219-224.

deadlines performed better than those who had the flexibility to choose their own deadlines.

A second study, in which students had to perform a quite uninspiring proofreading task, found similar results. Students who were given evenly-spaced deadlines performed better and spent more time on their assignments than the group with the flexibility to choose their own deadlines.[125]

The important lesson here is that a supervisor (or anyone) breathing down our necks does influence behavior. Research suggests that when that supervision comes from God, then yes, the dark horse certainly gets into shape. Religious people do in fact have higher self-control then the occasional churchgoer.

The perceived presence of an omnipresent, omniscient, all-powerful entity observing and tallying our behavior, and passing judgment and sanctions, is a powerful tool in getting our dark ducks into a straight line. As discussed earlier, a basic premise of Alcoholic Anonymous is accepting that alcohol controls us and that we are not strong enough to control it, only God is. With the help of God, decision-making is deferred to a higher power and we end up more successfully controlling our impulses than if it was up to us alone.

Religion offers a number of other benefits for goal achievement and self-control.[126] Religion influences the goals that people select and the prioritization of these goals. If you have strong religious beliefs, it is likely that you will select and prioritize those goals that are closest to your beliefs. Religion motivates people to achieve goals by sanctifying the goals. If you are aiming for a

---

125 Ibid.

126 McCullough, M. E., & Willoughby, B. L. B. (2009). Religion, self-regulation, and self-control: Associations, explanations, and implications. *Psychological Bulletin, 135*(1), 69–93.

goal of divine proportions, you may have more stamina to diligently pursue it when compared to worldly goals.

Religion and spirituality also create goal integration. In other words, it creates congruency between personal goals, increasing the likelihood that as one goal is achieved, other goals will also be achieved.

But what if your metaphysical worldview does not include God? Then you can count on other external watchers: spouses, friends, and the community at large. Research has shown that the presence of an evaluative audience (not necessarily God alone) heightens self-awareness, which leads us to compare our actions to our self-imposed standards. By publicly stating your goal, you are giving people the opportunity to closely monitor if you have achieved what you set out to achieve.

What can you do about it

Share your goals: share them with those you care strongly about and those with whom you are less connected. Sharing will give you the impetus to strive towards goal completion. There are actually tools available in the market to facilitate goal sharing and monitoring.

With stickK[127], for instance, you set a goal and choose a group of people to monitor that goal. Periodically, you must update your progress towards your goal. As negative reinforcement, you are encouraged to determine how much money you will lose if you fail to reach your goal and where you want that money to go. To make things even more fun, in case of failure, you may choose to fund projects or companies that you abhor or despise—think

127 Available from: http://www.stickk.com/

about donating money to the Democratic National Convention if you are a Republican, and vice-versa.

Strategy #12: Setting Tripwire Systems

The dark horse is a wild and sneaky animal, while the charioteer has only so much energy and attention. Despite our best intentions, the dark horse will eventually wander and get its way, especially when the charioteer is not paying conscious attention.

Tripwires are systems that are deliberately put into place to bring the charioteer's attention back to the dark horse when his or her attention slips. When the horse trips the wire, bells will ring, alerting the charioteer.

Here are some tripwire ideas and tools, most of which are available from the Apple store or Google Play:

- *SelfControl:* A free alarm clock, which acts as a simple yet effective tripwire. If you say you will take a 15-minute break, set your timer for that amount of time. Taking a 30-minute nap? Set your alarm. A 15-minute break and a 30-minute nap can easily get out of your control if you don't do so.
- *This r' Nothing:* The "This r' Nothing" app discussed earlier in this chapter is an effective tripwire, because if you fail to focus, you receive a burnt marshmallow... and who wants a burned marshmallow, right?
- *stickK*: As mentioned above, this app asks you to make a commitment. If you don't reach your goal, the app sends a stipulated amount of money to a charity you dislike—such as the National Rifle Association (NRA), if

you are in favor of gun control or do not support their activities.

- *Anti-Social*: A program that blocks sites for as little as 15 minutes to up to 8 hours. It can't be turned off once you set it, ensuring that you're not wasting time online.
- *LeechBlock*: A Firefox add-on that simply allows you to block those darn time-waster websites.
- *StayFocusd*: A really popular Google Chrome app that limits the amount of time per day you spend on distracting sites. It also has a "nuclear option" that allows you to completely block certain sites for hours at a time.
- *Cold Turkey*: Similar to Anti-Social but has the added function of allowing you to block computer programs like Outlook for a certain amount of time.
- *Clocky*: Probably the most annoying alarm clock to ever be invented, Clocky is an alarm clock on wheels. When the alarm goes off, the wheels start spinning and Clocky starts to move around the room. There is no way around it but to wake up to find Clocky hidden somewhere in your room. For those who have issues waking up on time, Clocky is the perfect tool.

Strategy #13: Feedback Systems (It's Time You Listen)

Monitoring your environment is a distinctive and crucial skill to develop in self-control. How often have leaders and corporations lost their position of leadership because of their inability to read changes in their environment? If the environment is responding to your actions in a positive way, keep doing what you're doing. It's when the system does not respond, or responds negatively, that we need to take new action...immediately.

I often deal with students who fail their classes, only to later tell me that they sensed that something was not going right—but too late.

One quick exercise that I learned from a reporter is to ask: what is *not* happening here that I should be worried about?

If you put a lot of effort into something and the system does not respond, there is something *not* happening. You may be spending thousands of dollars and enormous energy trying to sell your product, but if it's not flying off the shelves, than there's something not happening that you should be worrying about. Or you may be studying on your own and your quiz results are not showing any improvement.

In both cases, there is something not happening that needs your immediate attention. It's time that you listen to the feedback of the system and change your strategies—and fast.

The good news is that there are those who have been through what you're going through and have already tried to take the same course of action that you're planning to take. Those who have "been there and done that" can provide insider tips on how to align your horses toward that specific goal. All you have to do is listen to their feedback.

Linda Rottenberg, goddess of startups and a successful entrepreneur in her own right, advises young entrepreneurs to seek mentors for their valuable feedback and advice. She advises that we listen to all kinds of feedback, from the young to the gray-haired professionals, and that we listen more closely to suggestions with which we disagree.[128]

128 Rottenberg, L. (2014). Crazy Is a compliment: The power of zigging when everyone else zags [Kindle 6.3 version]. Retrieved from http://www.amazon.com/ (p. 162).

Interestingly, we have a hard time embracing feedback from those around us. We often have the sense that we know better and that others don't really "get" us or what we're going through.

In one of my seminars for pre-med students, the advisor approached me afterwards and thanked me for emphasizing how challenging the application process can be. "I tell them the same things but maybe they will hear it coming from you," he said in despair. I realized that this was not the first time I had someone tell me about people not listening to their guidance and feedback, despite the fact that they were experts in their fields. For example, one student of mine wants to be an entrepreneur. He rejects every piece of advice his father offers, even though his father is a successful entrepreneur himself.

It's time we listen. It's time we lower our defensive routines. It's time we listen with open hearts and minds to the feedback we receive from our environment and from those who care about our success.

Take a step, measure the results, learn from it (by analyzing the results or talking to those experts around you), realign your charioteer and your horses according to this feedback, and take a step again. Aligning your chariot towards your desired goals is a continuous cycle.

Questions for reflection:

- What feedback am I receiving from the environment that I may be ignoring?
- Who are those in my immediate surroundings who have experienced what I am going through? How can they assist me?

Strategy #14: Structure and Systems

Strategies such as alone time, "This r' Nothing", managing FOMO by editing one's life, and tripwires all work because they bring structure to a chaotic world. The structure they create around our goals eliminate distractions and interruptions and help us focus. Structure is important because it limits the ability of the dark horse to get out of line.

Marshall Goldsmith is adamant about our need for structuring our environment. After his many years coaching and researching change, he came to one very important conclusion: "we do not get better without structure."[129]

Architects and engineers understand the power of structure. Build a massive edifice without a solid structure, and disaster awaits. Mason Currey, author of *Daily Rituals*, wrote an entire book about how artists and highly accomplished individuals organize their lives around their creative projects. They create a structure that supports their continuous success.

Ludwig van Beethoven, for example, woke up every day at the crack of down and got busy right away. Gertrude Stein wrote for half an hour every day. The poet W. H. Auden was a master of the structured life, waking up at 6 a.m., brewing himself some coffee, and writing when his mind was sharpest, from 7 a.m. until 11:30 a.m. Structure for him was the only way to tame the dark horse: "the surest way to discipline passion [your dark horse] is to discipline time: decide what you want to, or should

129 Goldsmith, M., & Reiter, M. (2015). *Triggers: Creating behaviors that lasts-becoming the person you want to be.* New York, NY: Crown Publishing, p. 169.

do, during the day, then always do it at exactly the same moment every day, and passion will give you no trouble."[130]

This is true for successful or struggling organizations (and particularly for struggling organizations) and for successful or struggling individuals (and particularly for struggling individuals). The current structure, or lack thereof, in your daily routine is a major force against change, and a considerable factor in making you regress towards mediocrity (as discussed in Chapter 2).

To create new results, a new structure is necessary. When you create a structure with set routines within your daily schedule, you create a *system* for success.

The creator of the widely successful cartoon *Dilbert*, Scott Adams, is a major proponent of building systems.[131] According to him, having a system for success is wildly more important than just setting goals. Goals are something you are waiting to achieve in the future; they have deadlines, may or may not be achieved, and don't inspire action after they have been achieved.

The activities within a system, in contrast, are: 1) something you do every day, 2) are expected to work more often than not, and 3) have no deadlines.

Adams created a system built around an important uncompromising pillar—no matter what day of the week it is, at 7 a.m. you can find him at his desk doing what he does: drawing cartoons.

In an attempt to put the *Dilbert* structure to the test in my own life, I asked myself: if it is Monday at 7:15 a.m.; if it is Thursday

---

130 Currey, M. (2013). *Daily rituals: How artists work* [Kindle 6.3 version]. Retrieved from http://www.amazon.com, Kindle Locations 182-184.

131 Adams, S. (2013). *How to fail at almost anything and still win big: Kind of the story of my life.* New York, NY: Penguin Publishing Group.

after a major snowstorm (and the trains are still running); if it is raining cats and dogs; if I went out the night before and had one drink too many… where can you find me at 7:15 a.m.?

The answer is always the same: I am in my office, sipping a cup of coffee, listening to trance music on Spotify (search for the Dark Horse Tamed playlist) and working on my pet projects. I passed the Scott Adams test. I realized I have a structure, a system, not just goals.

Reflecting on my own system, I came up with the following graph:

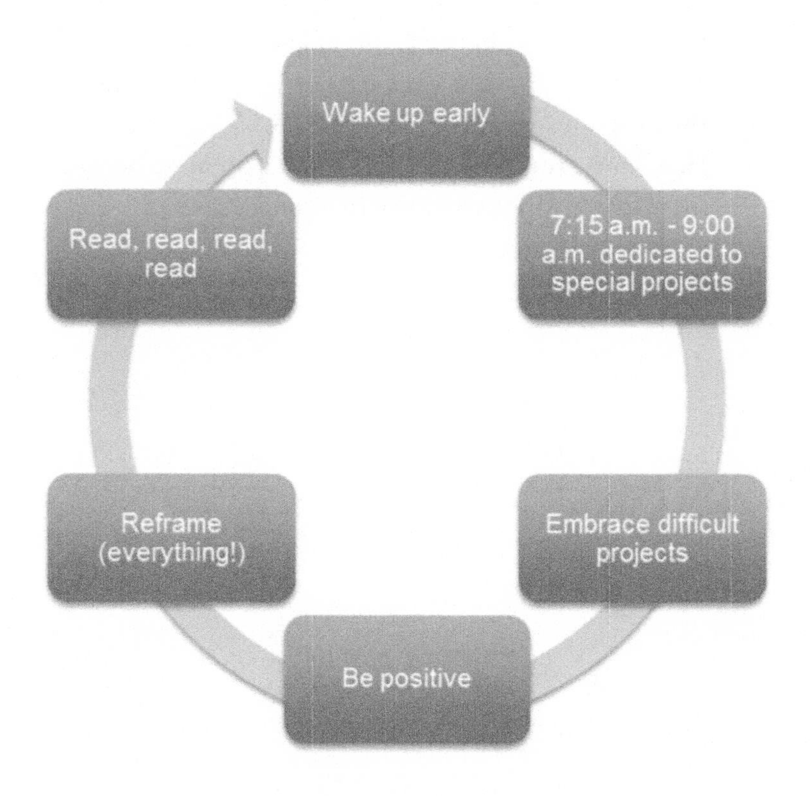

Reinventing a structure requires brutally honest reflective thinking to help you identify the pillars of your current structure that are not conducive to creating an environment that fosters successful outcomes.

We, particularly our dark horses, need clear routines, boundaries, and limitations. Having structure and a system in place will give us just that.

Questions for reflection:

- What is your system for achievement?
- How do you know it works? How is your current structure/system supporting your goal?
- How can you restructure your system/structure to increase the odds of goal achievement?

CHAPTER 9

The A in EAT (Act)

THIS CHAPTER FOCUSES ON THE things we do—the actual steps we take in order to fulfill our goals. You measure the value of a person's life not by how he or she thinks, but by results.

Setting goals do not create results, actions do. I became interested in the topic of self-control early on in life when I noticed a major disconnect between what was inside my head (my thoughts, aspirations, and goals) and my actions. For a long time I had to live with the harsh reality of having two "me"s—the thinker and the doer—which were not connected. I experienced a split between what I wanted for myself in my heart/mind and what I was actually doing to get there.

I later learned that I was not alone. As I spoke to people struggling with self-control issues, I learned that often people know *what* to do, and *how* to do it, but they fail to take action.

Researchers call this the "knowing–doing" gap. The charioteer is aware that it needs to control the horses and steer the chariot in a different direction, yet fails to do so.

We know that we should take our vitamins, yet we fail to do so. We know we should avoid sweets, yet I am munching on a Dove dark chocolate bar as I write. We know we should stop binge-watching, yet last night I watched two episodes of *Dateline NBC*. We know we should ditch distractions, yet we can't stop answering WhatsApp messages. It is as if the charioteer were the audience in a bad movie, in which he, the bright and dark horses were the protagonists.

We want different results, yet we are trapped in old habits wondering why we can't achieve our goals. The book *The 4 Disciplines of Execution* translates it well: "To achieve a goal you have never achieved before, you must start *doing* things you have never done before" [emphasis added].[132]

The word *doing* in the quote above deserves attention. The authors deliberately chose that word and not *thinking* or *dreaming* or *envisioning*, because in the end it is our ability to act that matters.

Talk is cheap. Knowing what to do is useless, unless you take action. Action diminishes and potentially eliminates the knowing–doing gap. And without being over simplistic and stating the obvious (but at the great risk of doing so), nothing known to the human species has ever been created without good old action.

Moreover, there is a strong body of evidence that suggests that when trying to self-regulate, we focus too much on our cognitive capacities. We think through problems. We go to talk therapy. We strategize solutions in our heads. We try to self-regulate using the rational charioteer. But research tells us that action and movement—that is, allowing the body to have experiences that reinforce or contradict our beliefs—is as important, if not more important, in successful self-regulation.

---

132 McChesney, C., Covey, S., Huling, J. (2012). *The 4 disciplines of execution: Achieving your wildly important goals* [Kindle 6.3 version]. Retrieved from http://www.amazon.com, p. 4.

The strategies included in this chapter include:

- Breaking old habits and creating new habits
- The no-thinking zone
- Flossing your teeth
- Doing Less to Accomplish More: Winning a War by Fighting Fewer Battles
- To Do; In Progress; Done!
- Checklists
- Eat a Frog Early in the Morning
- Archetypes
- Delaying Action
- Acting strategically

Strategy #15: Breaking Old Habits, Creating New Habits

If you have taken any psychology course, you'll have learned about behaviorism. The behaviorist is not interested in what goes inside a person's mind; instead he or she is interested in how people act. According to the behaviorist, a person may *say* that he acts in a certain way, but in real life will *act* in the exact opposite manner.

Behavior is the observable and measurable expression of cognition.[133] Think of the athlete who publicly criticizes the use of steroids in sports, but then injects them while in the locker room when no one is watching. What goes on inside our heads

133 Strack, F., Deutsch, R., & Krieglmeyer, R. (2009). The two horses of behavior: Reflection and impulse. In E. Morsella, J. Bargh & P. Gollwitzer (Eds.), *Oxford handbook of human action* (pp. 104-117). New York, NY: Oxford University Press.

and the things we say are subjective, while behavior and actions are measurable and objective. Although behaviorists have been vehemently criticized for their disregard for what goes on inside the individual, they offer an interesting and effective way to think about and manage behavior.

Behaviorism posits that future behavior is dictated by the consequences that follow any given behavior in a certain environment. Individuals are active agents in controlling and negotiating their behaviors, depending on the environmental response to that behavior. In other words, people do not behave monolithically and consistently across the board—they act according to environmental conditions.

So what determines how people will behave? The behaviorist claims that the contingencies of punishment and reinforcement (rewards) in the person's immediate environment determine their future actions. By nature, people (and their horses) avoid pain and seek pleasure. Behaviors that bring about undesirable consequences tend to die off, while behaviors that are rewarded tend to continue. Therefore, to manipulate behavior, or create expected behavior, requires a manipulation of the consequences.[134]

For behavior to be reinforced, the consequences (reward or punishment) need to fulfill three criteria[135]. The consequences need to be:

1) Immediate.
2) Proportionate.
3) Probable.

---

134 Duhigg, C. (2014). *The power of habit: Why we do what we do in life and business.* New York, NY: Random House.

135 Marlott, M. E. (2003). Paradox of organizational change: Engineering organizations with behavior systems analysis. Nevo, NV: Context Press.

Let's use the common example of the hangover to illustrate how rewards and punishments shape behavior. (If you have never experienced a hangover, I can assure you, you're not missing anything.) The question that must be asked is: why do we engage in behavior (that is, heavy drinking) we know is going to make us feel sick and miserable? When we are truly sick, we take medicine hoping (and praying) to get better. But with heavy drinking and drug use, people know that these activities will make them feel sick the next day and they do it anyway.

So why do we engage in this irrational behavior that goes against our well-being and any reason? Consider the 'immediate, proportionate, and probable" test: the immediate rewards for drinking are quite high. There is a sense of euphoria, our self-editing mechanisms are turned off, we become "smarter," more eloquent, better looking, more assertive—or so we would like to think. The consequences of drinking meet all three criteria. It is proportionate (the more you drink the more euphoric and more assertive you become). It is immediate (we become euphoric soon after a couple of glasses). And it is probable (if you drink, it will affect your thinking processes).

On the other hand, hangovers, as a punishment for your behavior, only meet two of the criteria: proportionality and probability. If you drink heavily it is very probable that you will have a hangover; and the more you drink, the more your head will ache the next morning.

However, hangovers fail in one important criterion: immediacy. When you drink, you will not get a hangover right away; it comes with an in-built delay that allows us to engage in drinking as if there is no tomorrow. Imagine the euphoria of drinking and the misery of a hangover kicking in at the same time—probably impossible, as these are feelings are polar opposites. But you get the idea.

Besides the consequences, behavior is context dependent and are triggered by what behaviorists call "antecedents" or "cues." A cue is what triggers a behavior. It can be a location, an emotional state, a time of day, a person, or anything in the environment that triggers behavior.

For instance, your goal may be to become more focused at work. However, every time you hear the *bling!* sound of your email, you feel that burning urge to check your inbox, distracting you from what you were working on. The bling sound is the cue to look at your email. It is the antecedent of unfocused behavior.

Or, imagine you decide to focus on your studies by going to the library every day at 3 p.m. It just so happens that the cute guy you have a crush on also studies at the library at that time. You spend most of your time talking to him at the expense of your studies. There are several cues in this situation: the library (place), 3 p.m. (time), and the cute guy (person).

You may be wondering how this applies to self-control. Behaviorism helps us identify behaviors that we want to change and decide how to change them by reassessing the rewards and punishments and understanding their antecedents. There are a few important points that we must understand and embrace to use this method effectively:

1) We behave the way we do because we get something out of it—we either get a reward or we avoid punishment. (There are also other motivations for behavior, but for the purposes of this exercise we have to assume that we choose behaviors according to their consequences.)

2) For (almost) every behavior, there is an antecedent or a cue. We do not operate in a vacuum. There are often elements in the environment (people, emotional states, sounds, time of the day, smells) that ignite particular behaviors. To change a routine, we first need to understand what the cues are.

Then new behaviors and habits can be created and reshaped by the implementation of a four step process:

1) Identify the behavior you want to change;
2) Identify the cues associated with the undesired behavior;
3) Identify the rewards associated with the undesired behavior;
4) Manipulate the rewards and cues until you find what is causing the undesired behavior.

Let me give you a personal example to illustrate how this process works.

At a certain point in my career, I was struggling to find focus and work on my pet projects. By the time I got to work, I was swamped with emails, people wanting to see me, meetings, and phone calls. At the end of the day, I had done none of the things that I truly liked about my job. I decided to try this concept to change my behavior.

Step 1: Identify the behavior you want to change: I wanted to become more focused, increasing the time available to work on "fun" stuff.
Step 2: Identify the cues associated with the behavior: Remember that a cue can be a time, a place, people, or an emotional state. I realized that 9 a.m. is when everyone arrives at

work, and that is when I would get distracted, by emails, my colleagues, and phone calls.

Step 3: Identify the rewards associated with the undesired behavior: Thinking about it, I realized that the reward that I was getting from my lack of focus was "being sociable." My colleagues would arrive at 9 a.m., and living in New York City, we always had a subway story to share. It was either a miserable rider giving you a hard time because you looked at him unintentionally in the "wrong way," or someone who got sick meaning everyone had to evacuate. Also, I didn't want to be that unsociable person who locks himself up in his office and doesn't engage in small talk with colleagues.

Step 4: Manipulate rewards and cues until you find what is causing the undesired behavior: Having identified the rewards and the cues, I decided to make a change in my schedule and beat the office traffic by getting to work every day at 7 a.m. For that, I had to wake up every morning at 6 a.m., which in the beginning I was no fan of. However, I also identified new rewards. By getting to work earlier, I would be rewarded with the ability to work on creative work. There were also unintended rewards—by taking the subway early in the morning, I could usually find a place to sit and rarely had to deal with subway cars filled with angry people.

A new routine was established and I successfully changed my behavior from unfocused to very focused. I also made a commitment that I would only work on creative work or special projects from 7 a.m. to 9 a.m.; after that I would live a normal office life.

It is said that after 21 days of any given repeated action, the action becomes a habit. Did it take me 21 days? Probably not... most likely less. But it indeed became a habit.

Now, just thinking about not waking up at 6 a.m. gives me the chills. To think that I won't be able to spend two hours of my day doing the projects I choose is highly anxiety-producing. (Imagining the high volume of people in the subway at a later hour is equally anxiety-producing). I am not sure how life existed before this change. I feel much more satisfied and fulfilled, as I am now in control of my schedule.

There are scores of articles available about what successful people do early in the morning. Laura Vanderkam, a journalist and author, wrote a lovely short book on this topic: *What the Most Successful People Do Before Breakfast.*[136] When you analyze the cases of these very successful people who start their day early, you typically find that early in the morning, cues are reduced to a minimum, and most of the distracting cues that do exist are self-generated. Early in the morning there are rarely any people in the office, the phone will not ring, there are no scheduled meetings, and better yet, there will rarely be notifications that a new email has just arrived in your inbox. Yes, one can choose to surf the web aimlessly—but again, that is a self-inflicted wound, and not a distraction generated by the surrounding environment.

The old adage goes: the early bird gets the worm. Yes, and why? The late bird, on his way to the worm, meets a friend, and they talk for a while. As it continues on its journey

136 Vanderkam, L. (2012). *Short guide to making over your mornings—and life* [Kindle 6.3 version]. Retrieved from http://www.amazon.com.

towards the worm, it receives a call from a family member, and then an email, and then it decides to grab a cup of coffee, and then comes the text messages and then it is noon and the bird still hasn't gotten to the damn worm yet. The early bird, on his way to the worm, finds no distractions—and has time to eat it too.

I would like to take this moment to formally request the abolition of the 9 a.m. to 5 p.m. work schedule. If you decide to keep it, do so at your own peril. From 9-5, everyone else is in control of your schedule—everyone but you. It is time that we regain control over our own schedules.

As discussed earlier in this book, we often underestimate the effect of unknown situational factors on our ability to achieve. The early bird purposefully controls its environment, avoiding situational factors that may interfere with its goals at all cost.

Here is how you can create new, healthy habits of your own. Follow the four step process we just learned about by filling out the chart below. Start with step 1, which is to identify the behavior or habit you want to change. Write this down on the center block of the first line. Then follow steps 2 and 3: identifying cues and rewards probably causing the undesired behavior. I use the word "probably" here deliberately, as there could be confounding cues that are causing the behavior. Identifying the real cue is crucial. Remember, cues could be a mental state, a person, location, or time of day.

When you are done with steps 1 through 3, identify the new behavior you wish to create and the rewards and cues associated with it, and fill them in on the second line.

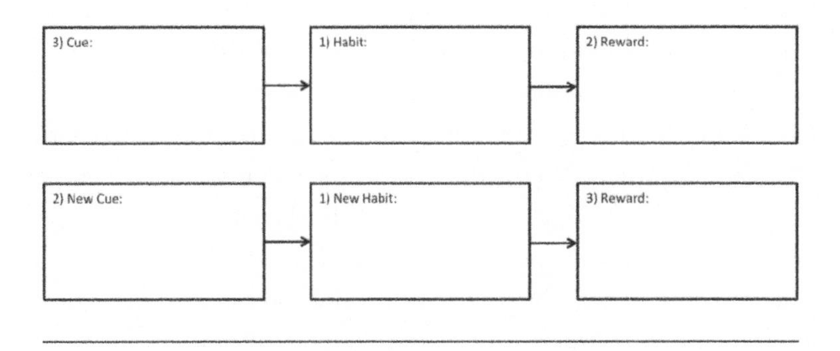

Strategy #16: The No-Thinking Zone

Thinking is highly regarded in our society; after all, we are rational beings who have conquered the natural world with the power of thought.

Thinking, however, does get in the way of getting things done, especially thinking that is muddled by too much noise (typically triggered by emotions and our dark horse).

I learned about the "no-thinking zone" from a friend of mine who is a serial entrepreneur and is second-to-none in getting things done. When jogging with him some time ago, I asked him what his secret was for managing so many different projects and getting so much done. He first acknowledged that he was busy from the moment he woke up to the moment he went to bed, with no idle time for unimportant distractions. He then dropped a bombshell: "I just do it. If I know something needs to get done, I don't think about it. I do it."

What an elegant concept, I thought to myself. In those days, when I thought about all the things I needed to do, I often felt as if the weight of the universe was on my shoulders. Just to think about endless To Do lists made me want to take a nap. But my friend's comment had an interesting effect on my thinking: it brought concepts together, and made things connect. I did not need to *think* about the things that had to be done, I just had to *do* them.

This is quite a liberating idea. Also, it explained why my friend was always in good spirits and displayed a disposition for life that I secretly envied. He did all he needed to do, without thinking much about it. It's the equivalent of placing the chatter between the dark horse and the charioteer in mute mode.

Peter Drucker has argued that the different between very successful leaders and their not-so-successful counterparts is that the first group does what needs to be done.[137] What Drucker says here is just as important as what he *doesn't* say. He doesn't say that these successful CEOs think about what needs to be done and then think some more, or that they strategize about the future like no one else. Successful people *do* what needs to be done. Period.

Our mind can be highly discriminatory, choosing likes and dislikes along the way. However, the world, the environment, reality, which is where things happen, cares less about what we think. For us to change circumstances in our favor, there are things that need to be done. And the best way to do it is by avoiding judgment and simply doing it.

In my last class with my students, on the last slide of my presentation on self-discipline and self-control, I always leave the audience with this final thought: "Liking is irrelevant."

---

137 Drucker, P. F. (2004). What makes and Effective Executive? *Harvard Business Review, 82*(6), 58–63.

We encountered this idea in Chapter 3. Liking is a highly personal judgement. We usually like something over something else. Now, there is nothing wrong with having likes and dislikes—the problem is that the world doesn't care, and achievements happen in the world out there, not in our minds.

Take for instance a student trying to gain admission into a competitive medical program. She may "like" physics over organic chemistry, but the truth of the matter is that the competitive reality of medical school admissions doesn't care about her likes. If she wants to stand a fair chance, she needs to prove herself in various courses. So she is left with little option but to apply herself to all courses equally, without discriminating. She needs to just do it, without judgment.

The same is true in the business world. When launching a business, a person may prefer the product development process to the sales and marketing aspect, including the endless hours that one needs to spend contacting, schmoozing, persuading and cajoling potential clients. While you might hate this part of the business, the business does not care. If you fail to do it, your business will fail. You either just do it, or hire someone to do it for you—either way, it has to be done.

This chapter has focused on the importance of suppressing thoughts and focusing on actions. I also suggest that the foundation of Eastern philosophies, including Buddhism, revolves around the concept of non-attachment to thoughts, emotions and objects.

When asked what one should do before gaining enlightenment, a Buddhist monk replied that one must chop wood and haul water. When asked about what one should do after enlightenment, his answer was "chop wood and haul water." This tale reinforces the need to engage in action towards an ultimate goal.

There is another Buddhist anecdote that illustrates the need for mindlessness when acting. The Buddha is quoted as saying: "Those who practice the Way might well follow the example of an ox that marches through the deep mire carrying a heavy load. He is tired, but his steady gaze, looking forward, will never relax until he comes out of the mire, and it is only then that he takes a respite."

A steady gaze, pulling the heavy load, in complete state of mindlessness. Have you ever seen the gaze of a working ox? It is stoic, infinite, almost empty. The ox does not show any signs of pain nor does it balk. It gazes toward where it needs to go and it steadily makes progress in that direction.

I always thought this to be a highly inspirational passage. I later found a real-life example of this parable in Linda Rottenberg's book *Crazy is a Compliment* (if you are an aspiring entrepreneur, you should get a copy of this book today). She tells the story of Mark Chang, an entrepreneur who sits on the board of a company she co-founded. Chang created Jobstreet.com, a recruitment website in Malaysia. This website—which, according to Chang, was supposed to be a mom-and-pop version of Monster.com—survived the dot-com bubble and the 2008 recession. Jobstreet.com is considered one of the most successful companies in Southeast Asia, and was acquired in 2014 for a mere $524 million. Chang has told the media that in his company they "only know the 'kerbau way,'" referring to the Indonesian water buffalo, which has similarities to the ox. Chang summed up this approach as: "Work hard and wait for the rain."[138]

---

138 Rottenberg, L. (2014). *Crazy is a compliment: The power of zigging when everyone else zags* [Kindle 6.3 version]. Retrieved from http://www.amazon.com, p. 131.

We are often in situations where a lot is demanded of us, and the weight of the world is heavy on our shoulders. But in these cases, we should fix our gaze on what needs to be accomplished and just do it.

What can you do about it?

- What are things that you just need to do, for which you must adopt the posture of the ox—put your head down and just do it?
- Can you try doing it right now?
- Can you carve out time in your schedule to focus solely on doing what needs to be done, mindlessly, without thinking too much about it?

Strategy #17: Floss Your Teeth Every Day to Improve Self-Control

Self-control has a cascading effect. Just as athletes hit the gym for cross-training and muscle-strengthening that may not necessarily be directly related to their sport, working out your self-control muscles in areas not related to your core goals can increase your overall self-control fitness score.

Self-control is like a muscle. The more you exercise it, the better you get at it. But just like with any muscle, you have to work it for it to grow strong. Research on self-control shows that one way of building the self-control muscle is by creating small habits that may have nothing to do with your ultimate goal: for instance, flossing once a day.[139]

This is not about flossing your teeth. It is not about hygiene. It is about developing good habits, committing yourself to them, and increasing your sense of self-control, and that sense of self-control then overflowing to other parts of your life—for example, controlling your thoughts or writing.

By creating the habit of flossing, you learn that you can commit to goals. This feeling increases your sense of self-efficacy—the belief that you can achieve the goals you set for yourself—which in turn increases your chances of actually achieving your goals.

When you floss, it is important that you are doing so not only because it is the right thing to do, but also because it is a means of proving to yourself that you are on the path to something greater.

My wife and I have a habit of cutting alcohol or red meat from our diets for 40 days, at least once a year. Going out for happy hour and only ordering a glass of water is not that much fun. But what you will find is that it is not *bad,* either. At the end of the day, we are reminding ourselves that we can do what we set our minds to, that we can resist the impulses of the dark horse, increasing our sense of self-efficacy.

139 Baumeister, R. F., & Tierney, J. (2011). *Willpower: Rediscovering the greatest human strength.* New York, NY: Penguin Books.

Questions for reflection

What are three small changes in your daily routine that you can implement right now? Can you cut carbs, sugar, alcohol, or red meat from your diet? Can you temporarily adopt an all raw food diet? Can you take a different mode of transportation to school/work? Can you wake up one hour earlier? Can you start your day meditating or working for one hour in important projects?

Strategy #18: Do Less to Accomplish More (Winning a War by Fighting Fewer Battles)

Earlier in this book, we discussed how the charioteer is often fighting competing priorities, pulling the horses in different directions, ultimately impeding them from achieving higher goals.

Doing less to accomplish more is a strategy that helps you apply time and energy towards fewer goals. This strategy is adapted from the book *The 4 Disciplines of Execution* (I strongly recommend you get a copy of this book; it is worth every cent). According to the authors, the law of diminishing returns is as real as the law of gravity when it comes to achievement.[140]

In short, your ability to achieve is inversely proportional to the number of goals you have.

First, you must clearly define the goal that is of greatest importance to you. Ask yourself: if everything else in my life remains constant, what is the one goal that would have the

140 McChesney, C., Covey, S., & Huling, J. (2012). *The 4 disciplines of execution: Achieving your wildly important goals* [Kindle 6.3 version]. Retrieved from http://www.amazon.com.

highest impact in my future? What is the one goal that would considerably increase my future prospects?

After you have selected your goal, you must determine what to do to achieve it by asking: "What are the fewest battles I must win in order to win the war?"

Once these battles have been identified, you must then find measures or targets to determine whether you are successfully progressing towards winning the battle. Carefully crafting and choosing the correct measures is key.

We often make the mistake of setting after-the-fact measurements, measurements that can only be taken and reported after an activity has taken place.

For instance, my students' war is to get into competitive professional programs. When asked to think about the battles they must win in order to win the overall war, and how to measure their progress, they respond: 1) Securing a 3.5 GPA; 2) securing a standardized test score in the 90th percentile; and 3) volunteer 200 hours.

But these are all after-the-fact measurements. In themselves, these measurements can't inform the person whether she or he will actually achieve that goal.

What we need instead are measures that on a weekly or monthly basis will inform us if we are on track to achieve that goal. The authors of *The 4 Disciplines of Execution* call these "lead measures." Lead measures are behaviors that taken over a period of time will lead you to your goal. These measures are predictive and influenceable. Simply stating that you "must get a 3.5 GPA by your junior year" won't cut it, because this is an outcome measure, something that is only measurable after the fact, instead of a predictive or influenceable measure.

On the other hand, we know that time spent on tasks, attending tutoring sessions, and attending review sessions are all predictive of success. Crucially, these are also all things the student can control. Now the student has a list of behaviors that are both predictive of success and influenceable.

A student's list of lead measures might look something like this:

Lead Measures	**Battles**	**War**
• Review my notes every day • Attend weekly review session • Attend weekly tutoring sessions • Study 5 hours a week for each subject	Science GPA above 3.5	Get admitted into medical school
• Answer one "MCAT Question of the Day" every day • Take 1 mock test every month for the next 4 months • Study 400 hours for the test • Review 2 prep books from cover to cover	MCAT above a 32	
• Contact 5 people a day in local hospitals, until I am granted a volunteering opportunity	300 Hours of Volunteering	
• Write 2 pages of a research paper per week • Read and discuss with my professor 2 scientific articles per week	Research	

All of the measures mentioned above have the quality of being predictive (that is, they help determine the results of the battle), and are influenceable (you and you alone can do something about them).

Jack Canfield, co-author of *Chicken Soup for the Soul,* offers insightful advice for aspiring authors who want to publish their first book. He calls it the "Five Things" strategy.[141] He basically urges novice (and not-so-novice) authors to do five things every day that will directly have an impact on their book. This is a lead measure at its best. If every day you put an effort into five actions towards your goal, then however small they may seem, you will soon have something solid in hand.

Prolific suspense writer James Scott Bell offers a similar piece of advice. The advice he was given early on his writing career was to set quotas for the number words he had to write in a certain week (setting daily quotas was too stifling, he says). Why is this a good lead measure? First, it is predictive: if you write a certain number of words day after day, month after month, year after year, you will eventually have a book (or more) to your name. It is also influenceable: you and you alone can do something about it. Interestingly, Scott Bell sets weekly word quotas, which he then breaks down into daily quotas. If he fails to achieve a daily quota, he knows he has until the end of the week to catch up.

When choosing activities to focus on, be as pragmatic as you can about them. Focus on those activities that are actually linked to results, and forget about the "nice to have" activities. When you are travelling fast, you just don't have the resources to focus on anything that is not going to contribute to your overall goal.

Remember Steve Jobs' advice that choosing the things you *won't* do are as important as choosing the things that you *will* do.

---

141 Harrison, S. Personal Communication. March 8, 2017.

We all know that Apple went through some ups and downs over the course of its history—during one of its "down" periods, it was making dozens of different computers that were in fact confusing customers. When Jobs was rehired by Apple to revamp its operations, he announced at a company meeting that it was time to do less. It was time to focus on what they did well and pay full attention to it. Today, Apple reports billions of dollars in revenue with a line of products that fits on a single coffee table.

What can you do about it?

- Identify the war you want to win.
- Identify the battles you need to fight to win the war.
- Identify the lead measures, actions, and behaviors that are both predictive of achieving the goal and influenceable.
- Implement them!

Strategy #19: To Do; In Progress; Done!

This next strategy is inspired by Jeff Sutherland, the inventor of SCRUM[142], a method of getting things done that has deeply transformed how software is designed.[143] Dr. Sutherland created a system of work, based on how things actually get done and not on how we think they do. Forget about fancy charts, schedules and reports—SCRUM is a framework for managing projects based on accountability and progress monitoring towards a well-defined goal.

142 In the game of Rugby, Scrum refers to the formation of player on a game restart, in which player in interlocked arms and head down, press forward in unison against their opponents. The ball is thrown in the middle of the formation and the teams try to capture the ball and kick it to their side.
143 Sutherland, J. (2014). *Scrum: The art of doing twice the work in half the time.* New York, NY: Crown Business.

SCRUM involves the following steps:

- Pick a project and a team to implement the project.
- Create a prioritized To Do list of actions that must be accomplished in order to successfully implement your project. This must be a very comprehensive and detailed list. You have probably encountered the pasta making exercise in school, in which you are asked to describe the process of making pasta. It is not enough to say "dump the pasta into boiling water." No, first you have to find the pasta, open it, grab a pot, fill the pot with water, light the fire... in the same way, be as detailed as possible, and prioritize!
- List each task into three different columns: Backlog (To do), In Progress, and Done. In the beginning, all tasks will be in the backlog column. As you progress with the implementation of each task, you can move them to the other two columns.
- The team leader must ensure that every team member understands what needs to be done and how it will get done, and remembers that everything on this list is part of the overall road map that will guide all efforts, without deviation.
- Estimate how much time and energy it will take to complete each task. Remember that we are horrible guesstimators—if you think it will take a week, it is more likely it will take two.
- Plan for "sprints," which are periods of less than a month when the team works with full focus on the implementation of items on the To Do list. The name says it all—you are not walking or jogging towards goal completion, you

are sprinting! Measure how much you are accomplishing during each sprint to determine your team's velocity.

- If your team's velocity is below ideal, further effort should be made to determine what barriers needs to be removed and how the team can be further supported.
- Make progress visible by creating a SCRUM board. The goal is to visually represent the status of each task (backlog, in progress, done), and to move as many items as possible from backlog to the other two columns.
- During sprints, organize 15-minutes daily progress meetings. These should not be progress report meetings, but rather opportunities for team members to share ideas and ask for help.
- Demonstrate: as the project comes to life, demo what is being created as early as possible so that the team and users can provide real-time feedback.
- Reflect on the process.

SCRUM eliminates several major issues in goal achievement.

1) The first issue in personal goal achievement is the lack of clarity in terms of what needs to be accomplished for a goal to be achieved. I did a short SCRUM exercise to finalize this book, and when I outlined the backlog (or the To Do list) I thought to myself, "holy S@#%!, there's a lot to be done!" Visualizing what had to be done, however, created focus and I was able to move two tasks from "To Do" to "In Progress" in a couple of hours.
2) The SCRUM process forces us to deliver, no matter how perfect (or imperfect) the final product. By releasing

products into the world, the world has the ability to test it and you gain instant feedback on how to improve it.

3) SCRUM forces a shared understanding of what needs to be accomplished and an understanding of what it means to get something done. In his book, *Competing Against Time,* George Stalk Jr. makes a compelling case as to why projects within organizations are often over budget and behind schedule.[144] Imagine that you are working for a multidisciplinary team to develop a new online training program. Your marketing manager is focused on creating something that is appealing to consumers, engaging the feelings and emotions of your audience. The content team wants to add value by delivering as much knowledge as possible on that particular topic. The tech team focuses on creating a sophisticated platform for sharing content and allowing for as much interaction as possible between learners and facilitators, including synchronous and asynchronous communication tools.

   In searching for perfection and trying to meet their own individual standards and goals, each team member had little or no incentive to compromise. After many delays, and a significant increase in costs, the team is ready to deliver a product that has not yet been tested by the audience it is supposed to serve. All the additional bells and whistles, developed by the tech team, is not what students want in terms of interacting with the content, the facilitators, or each other. The training is too content-heavy and impractical.

144 Stalk, Jr., G, & Hout, T. M. (1990). *Competing against time: How time-based competition is reshaping global markets.* New York, NY: The Free Press.

In this example, the teams have no clear direction, do not share a unified definition of "done," are not pressed to deliver a pilot for testing, and are working independently, each in its own little universe with very specific and unilateral definitions about what needs to be done.

Sample SCRUM template for creating the cover of this book:

Action	Backlog	In progress	Done
Identify designer			X
Contact designer			X
Negotiate rates		X	
Submit draft	X		
Approve draft	X		

Strategy #20: Checklists

"Too much airplane for one man to fly."[145] That was one newspaper's conclusion about the Boeing Model 299 crash. It happened on October 30, 1935, at the Wright Air Field in Dayton, Ohio, when airplane manufacturers gathered for a flight competition organized by the U.S. Army Air Corps. The goal of the competition was to select which manufacturer would build the next generation of bombers for the Air Corps.

At first, the Boeing 299 seemed to have a distinctive advantage. The aircraft was much faster, could fly much further, and could carry much more weight in bombs than any other bomber—a military dream come true. The new model had one

145 Gawande, A. (2007). The checklist. *New Yorker*. Retrieved from http://www.newyorker.com/magazine/2007/12/10/the-checklist

issue, however: it was considerably more difficult to fly than other aircrafts. The pilot for this new, massive flying machine had to control multiple functions to get the aircraft airborne, including controlling four engines, a retractable landing gear, the wing flaps, the hydraulic controls that regulated the pitch of constant-speed propellers... and the list went on.

It happened right in front of their eyes. As engineers and the high-ranking officers rubbed shoulders to watch this symbol of military might take off, the aircraft taxied down the airstrip, then smoothly took off to reach three hundred feet. That's when it stalled, twisted, fell, and crashed into the ground.

Further investigation into the accident found that it was caused by human error. This accident did not deter the Army from buying some aircrafts, and it became one of their major advantages during World War II, by which time Model 299 had become known as the B-17.

But how did an aircraft that was considerably more complex to fly and had crashed on one of its first test flights become an icon of military force?

The answer is checklists. A specific and detailed checklist for each step of the flying experience was created for that aircraft: taxiing, takeoff, flight, and landing.

Checklists rule. They keep us focused. They keep us on task. With the unbelievable amount of distractions we face nowadays, checklists keep our horses aligned and directed towards our goal, and eliminate the need for the charioteer to be involved in decision-making. Each box on the checklist is a stepping stone that the charioteer and the horses must achieve in order to realize your goal. By transferring what is in your mind to paper in the form of a checklist, you open up mental space for other more important tasks—or simply give your brain a much-needed rest.

When creating checklists, especially in the form of To Do lists, it is important to follow some basic principles:

- If it can be done immediately, don't put it on your list. Follow the two-minute rule: if it can be finished in two minutes, take care of it now!
- Be as specific as possible. Goals often involved a number of smaller sub-steps, which must first be fulfilled for the goal to be achieved. For instance, to fix dinner you must find a good recipe, drive to the store, buy the ingredients, and cook. Stay away from stating your goal as simply: "Fix Dinner." Instead, list all the sub-steps required, to the maximum level of detail possible.
- "This 'r Nothing" your To Do list. Use the This 'r Nothing strategy on every item of your To Do list.

Strategy #21: Eat a Frog Early in the Morning

The expression to *eat a frog* has bad connotations, which it does not in fact deserve. "Eating a frog" is typically associated with a distasteful or unpleasant activity. The dark horse—with its inherent need to seek immediate gratification—abhors such activities.

But I would argue that eating frogs is good for you. Better yet, my recommendation is that frogs should be eaten in the crack of dawn, early in the morning.

Frogs are those activities we avoid at all costs because they cause us little pleasure—or, to be more precise, they cause us sheer displeasure. But remember, in this game, success is determined by doing what the game requires. And the game often requires that you do things you would rather not do voluntarily. So eat that frog early in the morning and be done with it for the rest of the day.

As part of my job I am required to answer a lot of emails. Emails are my daily frogs. I eat them early in the morning, sometimes when I am on the train on my way to work, so that I can move on to more interesting things. I often revisit them later in the day to keep up to speed.

What can you do about it?

Identify one or two things you don't like to do but that must be done on a daily basis. Get rid of them first thing in the morning. By doing that, not only you will get something off of your To Do list, you will feel a sense of accomplishment which will cascade down into other, more relevant tasks.

Strategy #22: Archetypes (or How Thinking Like Other People Can Help Us Achieve Our Goals)

"Students have never been very good at listening to their elders, but have never failed to imitate them."

—*James Baldwin*

Dr. Robert Sternberg is one of the most renowned and respected psychologists in the world, a true household name in the field. He is highly published, with more than 1,500 papers, book chapters, and books to his name. His most significant contributions to psychology lie in the theories of intelligence, wisdom, and creativity. Several years ago, he was invited to run for president of the American Psychological Association.

In the beginning, he was inclined to refuse the offer. But after much thought, he decided to embrace the challenge. In his own words: "My first reaction was not to do it: I did not feel that I was extroverted enough. But the more I thought about it, the more I thought I had a useful mission for the organization—unity. My goal was to unify a diverse and sometimes fractious organization. So I decided on a plan. I would act the role of someone running for APA President. I would do what such a person would do, knowing that I was no such person. After enacting the role for a few months, I became that person. I forgot I was acting. I decided for leadership."[146]

In his book *The Talent Code*, Daniel Coyle discusses how talent hotbeds are created. After visiting known hotbeds of talent all over the world, he concluded that the igniting spark for talent is not necessarily an inner-grown passion; rather, it is often ignited by the outside world.

Take, for instance, the number of South Koreans on the Ladies Professional Golf Association (LPGA) Tours and of Russians in the Women's Tennis Association (WTA) top 100. In 1998, there was only 1 Korean and 3 Russians, respectively. A mere ten years later (and remember that mastery theory suggests that talent takes about ten years to develop), there are 33 South Koreans in the LPGA and 15 Russians on the top 100 list of the WTA. What happened at the end of the '90s that ignited

146 Stenberg, R. J. (2005). Producing tomorrow's leaders in psychology and everything else. *Eye on Psi Chi, 10(*14-15), 32-33.

a flood of talented golfers in South Korea and tennis players in Russia?

According to Coyle's hypothesis, breakthrough successes follow an explosion of talent. South Korea's explosion in golf came in May 1998 when Se Ri Pak, a twenty-year-old female, won the McDonald's LPGA Championship. As for the Russians, during that same summer, Anna Kournikova gained prominence by reaching the semifinals at Wimbledon.

People started watching these athletes and thinking to themselves, "this is who I want to be" and, "if she/he can do it, so can I." Christina Kim, a South Korean-American golfer, remembers watching Se Ri Pak on TV and thinking to herself, "She wasn't blond or blue-eyed, and we were of the same blood ... you say to yourself, 'If she can do it, why can't I?'"[147] Such thoughts sparked the motivation for these individuals to invest the necessary energy and time into becoming successful athletes themselves.

But most critical to our discussion is not the self-efficacy that these individuals felt, but how they saw in others who they could become—and in some instances, like in Dr. Sternberg's story, incorporated the mannerisms of their idols as their own. As stated by a tennis couch at Spartak Tennis Club in Moscow, a veritable hotbed of talent according to Coyle: "All the little girls started wearing their hair in ponytails and grunting when they hit. They were all little Annas."[148]

As pointed out by Dr. Heidi Grant Halvorson in her book, *Succeed: How We Can Reach Our Goals,* "the sight of someone

---

147 Coyle, D. (2009). *The talent code: Greatness isn't born. It's grown. Here's how.* New York, NY: Bantam Dell, p. 101.

148 Ibid.

pursuing a particular goal is one of the more potent triggers of unconscious goal pursuit psychologists have discovered."[149]

Dr. Sternberg embraced the archetype of an APA president, the little Annas embraced Anna Kournikova's archetype, while female South Korean golfers made the success of their idol their own. An archetype is someone that others want to aspire to be like. In other words, an archetype is a stereotypical character we can emulate.

For instance, one may use the archetype of a Buddhist deity, by focusing on this deity's primary qualities (such as compassion). By building a closer relationship with this archetype, one consciously begins to identify with it. Finding the correct archetype promotes physical and psychological integration and gives us the feeling that we have achieved the same qualities promoted by the archetype.[150]

For instance, think of a mission you want to accomplish or a problem you have to solve. Now think of someone who you have the ultimate respect for having solved a similar problem. What are the qualities that this person posses that you admire? What qualities made this person achieve the goal you want to achieve? What qualities you can emulate? If you were this person, how would she or he act at this very moment?

Sternberg's mentor at Stanford University, Gordon Bower, was a major influence on him—an archetype of sorts. According to Sternberg, what was great about his mentor was that he showed him what could be possible by emulating him.

Sternberg adds a note of caution, however: "You don't want to become the archetype. You want to find as much in yourself as

149 Halvorson, H. G. (2010) *Succeed: How we can reach our goals.* New York, NY: Penguin Publishing Group.

150 Nelson, A. (2007). The spacious mind: Using archetypes for transformation towards wisdom. *The Humanistic Psychologist, 35*(3), 235–245.

the archetype found in herself, to become as much of you as the archetype became of her."[151]

This is important to bear in mind. As much as we may emulate the qualities of our archetype, we are not the archetype—nor should we want to be them. There are a number of factors that have led this person to think, react, and act how they do, which are just not part of our upbringing.

Simply embracing the archetype of Kasparov will not make you a master chess player. The challenge, and the fun, is to try to think like Kasparov thinks, to love the game as much as he does, and to dedicate the same number of hours as he does.

What can you do about it?

1) Identify a person or entity you admire.
2) Isolate the qualities you admire in that person or entity.
3) Act as if you were them—at least for a short period of time, or until you solve the problem you are trying to solve.

Strategy #23: Delaying Action (Distancing)

Napoleon Bonaparte allegedly had a curious strategy to manage incoming mail. He simply let it sit in his inbox. If no one followed up on it, he would deem the correspondence to be unimportant and not worthy of his time.

Today we are bombarded with incoming messages, encouraging us to exist in a never-ending state of alert. I am not suggesting

151 Morgeson, F. P., Seligman, M. E. P., Sternberg, R. J., Taylor, S. E., & Manning, C. M. (1999). Lessons learned from a life in psychological science: Implications for young scientists. *American Psychologist*, 54(2), 106–116.

that you don't answer your emails—but in some cases, particularly when you are being nudged into action by base impulses, distancing yourself from the situation can be a very effective self-control strategy.

The dark horse is always on high alert and will react to the slightest impulses. The intervention of the charioteer, on the other hand, depends on your available resources. When acting, you want to make sure that the charioteer is in full control instead of succumbing to dark horse's urge to react.

Let's suppose you receive a nasty email from a work colleague and it hits a nerve. You just can't take it anymore. You immediately start writing a reply, which is fueled by rage. In other words, your message contains one or two expletives and words that shouldn't be spelled out. Acting in the heat of the moment often leads us to kneejerk reactions that we later regret. The consequences of this kind of action can be costly.

Now imagine that before hitting the send bottom, you leave your desk and go for a walk around the block to let off some steam. Upon returning to your desk, you read over your email again and realize that your previously chosen language was too strong. You reread the original email from your colleague and now realize that the email wasn't that bad and maybe you even misinterpreted what he was trying to say.

In this example, creating a lag between the impulse (the pull of the dark horse) and a response has given you some much-needed time to reflect upon the event, reframe the information in your mind, and respond to the situation with professionalism and courtesy. You can now craft your response using cold cognition, instead of reacting with the hot, emotional center of your brain.

Consider the shopaholic who can't control himself. I have to confess that when it comes to books, I am a compulsive buyer—much to my wife's dismay. Amazon has made it ridiculously easy to buy not one but multiple related books at once. At first, when I would hear the name of a newly released book that might be of interest to me, I would immediately act on my instincts. My dark horse screamed, "you need this, you need this!" With so much screaming inside my head, how could I you not act upon my instincts?

But I now have a distancing rule. Every time I feel the urge to buy a book, I will wait until the next day to act upon my urge. Typically, by then I will have forgotten about it. I also joined a public library and now borrow the book first, before making a commitment to buy it.

We live in an action-based society. We are taught that we need to act and that we need to act *now*. Delaying a decision to ponder, reflect on, and analyze alternative routes or consequences is perceived to be a sign of weakness. In executive boardrooms, those who are swift in making decisions are seen as powerful, intelligent, and having the necessary decision-making chops. Those who don't are instead chopped.[152]

Delaying action gives us time to tinker with ideas and look at the situation from different perspectives, despite of our immediate urge to act upon our impulses.

Think about the power of Twitter in damaging and scarring people's reputation and careers. Never in the history of humanity have people, particularly the famous, had to so often and so publicly apologize for the unfortunate comments they have uttered. Twitter, metaphorically speaking, is a connection between our hot system (the dark horse) and the world out there, with no

---

152 Dweck, C. S. (2006). *Mindset: The new psychology of success*. New York, NY: Random House, p. 135.

filtering applied by the cold system (the charioteer). A Tweet is a 280-character hot reaction to something we are passionate about and want to express our raw opinion on, or an impulse to share a thought or idea. To add to the problem, in a world where speed rules, the faster you publish that thought, opinion or idea, the better.

This gives little time for cold cognition to kick in. If you were writing the same message in an email, you would probably be more verbose and would have more time to think about what you were saying and how you were saying it.

As a result, people say things they later regret. If only they had distanced themselves from the message for five minutes before pressing that send button.

Gazzaley and Rosen, whom we met in our discussion on information foragers in Chapter 2, argue that a critical time delay between impulse and response is a gift from our evolutionary history, separating us from our lizard friends who act purely on reflexive impulses.[153] This time delay separating impulse or stimuli from action opens up a space for evaluating alternatives and making better decisions. Unfortunately, technology—Twitter being a perfect case in point—has diminished and continuous to diminish that space.

What can you do about it:

Don't act now. If a problem presents itself, look it in the face, try to understand it as much as you can... and then get away from it—go for a walk, or sleep on it. In the meantime, isolate

153 Gazzaley, A., & Rosen, L. D. (2016). *The distracted mind: Ancient brains in a high-tech world*. Boston, MA: MIT Press.

your immediate answer to the issue and ask: what are the consequences if I take this action? Did similar actions work in the past? What could I be missing? Do I need to speak with someone about this? Your brain will inevitably ruminate over it and provide you with various alternative solutions to the issue. Sometimes your initial gut reaction will be the correct one. Sometimes it will not.

Before crucial decisions, stop and ask yourself:

- Do I have enough information to act in a well-informed manner?
- Could my instincts be misleading, or even outright wrong?
- Can I sleep on it and make a decision later?

Putting your "can do" attitude to sleep

I often have the hardest time sleeping. As soon as I lay down on my pillow, my head starts to run through a list of unfinished business. This is total torture, as in that moment, lying in bed, there is absolutely nothing I can do about it. I toss and turn. I agonize. And the more I toss and turn, the more relentless I become.

However, that has changed after a mental exercise I learned not long ago. Author Geronimo Theml, a productivity expert, proposes a simple yet effective concept for dealing with unresolved business that keeps us awake.[154] In his own words, "The

154 Theml, G. (2016). *Produtividade para quem quer tempo: aprenda a produzir mais sem ter que trabalhar mais.* Sao Paulo, Brazil: Editora Gente.

biggest energy drag is to think about something in a moment you can't solve it."

This simple concept hit me like a lightning bolt. Here I was, processing not one thing but lists of things in a moment when I could do absolutely nothing about them. Interestingly, after a poor night's sleep, I would only feel good again after sitting down in my chair at work. I was then in control. I learned that I had to let go of the need to be in control and to relax in those moments when I couldn't do anything about a particular problem. I will not go as far as to say that I now sleep soundly every single night, but I will say that when I start tossing and turning, I remind myself that my can-do attitude in that moment is really not helpful, as there is nothing I can do about anything right then. A sense of calm usually ensues.

Strategy #24: Act Strategically (Acting Today to Build and Free Tomorrow)

My current To Do list contains the following items:

- Answer emails.
- Answer calls.
- Schedule trips.
- Sign agreement with University X.
- Finish performance evaluations.
- Write strategic plan.

There is no doubt that writing a departmental strategic plan is the most important task on this list. Writing a well-thought out plan will potentially have a ripple effect for my department and maybe even for my career—I will learn tremendously from it. It will give direction to the future of my department and it will generate results!

Conversely, I will not make a name for myself or achieve professional success through the number of emails, phone calls, trips, and performance evaluations I conduct. Although all these other tasks are relevant and need to get done, clearly they don't qualify as major career enhancers.

Career-enhancing tasks take time, energy, focus, and forethought. They require us to push our intellectual efforts to the limit. They can rarely be completed in one sitting. They make you doubt you can actually achieve them.

Having a clear understanding of the difference between career enhancers and "busywork" is at the crux of effective decision-making. Productivity experts often encourage people to focus on no more than three tasks every day. These tasks are typically career enhancers, which with the right amount of focus and energy will grow and evolve, taking on forms superior to the initial task itself.

There are also tasks that if taken care of today will free up space for you tomorrow, so that you can then focus on developing your big ideas. Before I leave work each day, I create a list of things I need to get done to resolve quick problems or complete trivial tasks, such as returning phone calls, answering emails, or booking trips. I also focus on trigger actions—trivial tasks that will trigger and assist in the implementation of my career-enhancing tasks.

By acting quickly and swiftly on these trivial tasks today, I free up time to accomplish career-enhancing tasks tomorrow. The following day, when I arrive at work, I will first focus on these career enhancers, knowing that yesterday's must-get-out-of-the-way tasks have been taken care of. If I have failed to take care of them the day before, I will then only get back to them after spending at least two hours on my career-enhancing tasks.

What can you do about it:

- Set aside 15-30 minutes at the end of each day to think. In the first 5 minutes, write down every open task that demands your attention. Identify those that are career enhancers, and those that are trivial but must-do tasks. In your leftover time, try to get as many trivial tasks done as possible. Cross them off of your list. Save the tasks you cannot deal with for the next day. Now you are free to enjoy some quality time as everything is written down.

  First thing in the next morning, work on your career-enhancing tasks. Don't feel compelled to start with any tasks from the day before. After spending a good hour and a half on career enhancers, you will now be feeling good about your progress. You'll feel in total control and ready to start tackling the rest of your day.

Keep in mind that sometimes action alone is not sufficient. If you are taking action but you keep getting the same, undesirable results, then it may be an indication that you must first change how you think. We act based on a software that has been programmed over our lifespan and this program may need some updating, patching, or even a good old reformatting. Changing how you think is the topic of our next chapter, when we will look at this step in more detail.

CHAPTER 10

The T in EAT (Think)

In previous chapters, we discussed how to achieve self-control by managing our environmental conditions and by acting towards our goals. In this chapter we will discuss how to increase self-control by thinking—or, to be more precise, by thinking about thinking.

In the previous chapter I made a strong point that actions matter more than words, desires, and thinking. They do.

Thoughts and feelings, however, in a sense precede action. And in the triad, action is a result of the coordinated effort of the three elements, including the charioteer and his or her ability to outsmart the dark horse. For that reason, this chapter will focus on sharing important tools for the charioteer.

Thinking is often attributed to cognitive processing. I would like to expand this definition by embracing a concept developed by Chinese philosophers millennia ago: the concept of the combined heart/mind. Although cognitive processing does take part in our brains, it is also deeply influenced by our emotions, which have long been associated with the heart.

In other words, thinking is as much a product of our rational minds as it is a product of emotions, our hearts. And so changing the state of both is critical in developing self-control. By understanding that our most logical thinking and our emotions are engaged in a seesawing relationship, where one continually influences the other, can help us better regulate the self.

The strategies shared in this chapter are:

- Developing a growth mindset
- Reappraising thoughts and situations
- In the beginning: A very short meditation
- Think big, Think why, Think values
- Mental contrasting
- If-Then
- Labeling
- Hidden commitments
- Thinking future self
- Self-reflection
- Understanding (and accepting) the pluralistic self

Strategy #25: Develop a Growth Mindset

Mindsets are sets of beliefs and assumptions that shape how we see, interpret, and interact with the world around us. Mindsets are the lenses through which we see; they dictate what we pay attention to and how we react to things.

In other words, mindsets determine our reality. They can be a truthful representation of the world—and yet, for the most part, they are faulty and incomplete. They can be limiting or liberating.

External vs. internal loci of control

There are two predominant mindsets in the human psyche that color our views of reality: either an external or internal locus of control. A person with an *external* locus of control believes that their fate depends on external factors such as the weather, their boss, traffic, or luck (your chariot and your horses are controlled by environmental forces).[155] Conversely, a person with an *internal* locus of control believes that they control whatever happens in their lives (you are in control of your chariot and your horses).

These two very different set of beliefs about who is in control have major implications for self-regulation.

Needless to say, an external locus of control is not very helpful if you are trying to orient your life; after all, based on this mindset, external forces are in control of your life. What happens to you has nothing to do with what you do, but with some worldly conspiracy, either for or against you. This can often lead to a sense of helplessness—no matter what you do, you have no control over the outcomes. Helplessness can lead to inactivity, anxiety, and even depression.

An internal locus of control, on the other hand, reinforces the metaphor used throughout this book: you are in charge of the charioteer and of your horses. Although, as discussed in Chapter 8, the charioteer and the horses are affected by external conditions (the environment), there are a number of strategies that we can adopt to control external forces and to increase our effectiveness in moving the chariot towards the desired direction.

Shifting from an external to an internal mindset also has major implications for productivity and motivation. Experiments have shown that increasing how "in control" you feel about your circumstances (that is, increasing your internal locus), the more

155 Lefcourt, H. M. (2014). *Locus of Control: Current trends in theory and research* (2nd Ed.). New York, NY: Psychology Press.

productive you will be.[156] This happens because the act of taking control triggers the parts of our neurology where self-motivation resides.

How can you improve your internal locus of control mindset?

1) Think that you are in control (even if everything suggests otherwise). Think about the small decisions you can make right now that will remind you that you are, in fact, in control. For instance, it is in your control to choose how much sugar you pour into your coffee, or how to respond to certain situations.
2) Choose to do something, even if it is something small, and then do it. Show your horses who's in charge!

GROWTH VS. FIXED MINDSETS

Another important mindset has to do with how well we set our cognitive structure to accept that we can, in fact, change. How we structure our beliefs and assumptions about the world and ourselves sets the foundation for what we deem possible.

According to a series of studies conducted by Dr. Dweck, a leading psychologist from Princeton University, each of us possesses one of two mindsets: a growth mindset or a fixed mindset.[157] Both mindsets carry very large, and very specific, assumptions about our capacity to learn, change, grow, and develop. People in these different groups also differ when it comes to how they interpret learning, growth, and development.

---

156 Duhigg, C. (2016). *Smarter faster better: The secrets of being productive in life and business.* New York, NY: Random House.

157 Dweck, C. S. (2006). *Mindset: The new psychology of success.* New York, NY: Random House.

Individuals with a "growth mindset" believe that ability, intelligence, and even personality are malleable constructs—not constructs you were born with and have no control over, but rather something that if worked on long enough can grow and develop. A growth-oriented individual operates under the assumption that, with enough nourishment and training, any undesirable part of the self (your dark horse, for instance) can be shaped and one day generate positive outcomes. The focus of growth-oriented individuals is to learn and develop.

On the other hand, "fixed mindset" individuals see personal characteristics as something rigid, that either one has or does not. In this view, intelligence, for instance, is a trait that a person either possesses or doesn't—and shouldn't bother trying to develop it. Because they believe that intelligence is an either/or preposition, they want to look smart, sound smart, and act smart. In this case, the focus of fixed-mindset individuals is to maintain and protect their smarts.

The mindsets we adopt have major psychological, behavioral, and physiological consequences for various parts of our lives. Studies have shown that individuals who have a negative fixed mindset about aging are less likely to visit the doctor, eat well, and exercise. They may even die sooner in comparison to those who have a positive mindset about aging.[158] Students who have a growth mindset, as opposed to a fixed mindset, displayed greater appreciation for academic pursuits, better attitudes towards their studies, improved GPAs, and increased effort. Hotel housekeeping workers who adopted a growth mindset perceived their jobs as an opportunity for physical exercise. As a

158 Crum, A. J., Salovey, P., & Achor, S. (2013). Rethinking stress: The role of mindsets in determining the stress response. *Journal of Personality and Social Psychology, 104*(4), 716–733.

result, they lost weight and experienced a lower body-mass index and lower systolic blood pressure. The thought that cleaning rooms represented good exercise made them engage in their work with more vigor and a sense of purpose.[159]

Stress is enhancing vs. stress is debilitating mindsets

Mindsets have also been connected with how we perceive and react to stress. Stress has long been considered a modern plague of sorts, with undesirable consequences for our mental and physical health, in many cases even leading to death.

But stress, on the other hand, can also be seen an adaptive response to prepare us psychologically and physiologically to meet the demands of changing circumstances. In stress-inducing situations, our blood pressure rises, we release hormones that make us more attentive, and we become mentally and physically ready to take action. However, to remain in a state of constant alert is believed to be detrimental to our health.

Just like Dweck proposed an intelligence-is-malleable mindset (growth mindset), researchers tested the hypothesis of the existence of two stress-related mindsets: stress-is-enhancing and stress-is-debilitating. Those who displayed a stress-is-enhancing mindset reported being less prone to the negative effects of stress. They reported being in better health, having fewer symptoms of anxiety and depression, and having more energy when compared to stress-is-debilitating individuals. They also reported higher levels of satisfaction with life and performance at work.

---

159 Ibid.

Results follows the mindset

A fixed mindset works well when events confirm your beliefs and work in your favor. If you believe that a science-oriented mind is something fixed and you happen to be doing well in your science courses, then you're in a sweet spot. Or if you think that speaking in public or writing is a fixed trait, and you write and speak well, then life is good.

The problem occurs when you're not doing well in your science courses, or need extra help with public speaking and writing. According to the fixed mindset, there is a good reason you are failing: you were not meant to be a science major, a speaker, or a writer. You may logically conclude that "I'm not a science person" and in the next test you just won't try hard enough, inevitably creating a self-fulfilling prophecy.

The consequences of this type of mindset can be quite limiting. Science may come naturally to some and require more effort from others. The fact is that struggling and failing are part of learning and growth. A fixed mindset portrays struggle and failure as a personal failure and an indication that the person is not cut out for the task. Giving up prematurely could be the end of a fruitful career.

For instance, I struggled with statistics my entire life. I still vividly remember my statistic class in college, because it was such a painful experience. I had to sit in lectures that sounded to me like they were being given in a foreign language. They made my stomach churn. I could not relate what was being explained to my own life, or to anyone's life for that matter.

It was only when later I started using statistics in my job to understand matters I cared about that I became quite interested in the subject. Although I still wouldn't say I am good at statistics, I now understand it to a degree I never thought possible.

Growth-oriented individuals focus on cultivating their intelligence or skills. Not understanding statistics, for example, is simply a matter of not putting enough effort into it.

Dweck's work tells us that we need to be very careful how we label behavior, as these labels create our mindsets (and our destinies). If I have been labeled my entire life as the smartest person on the planet, I may well start believing it. When any disconfirming evidence arises and I fail that statistics test, the natural tendency is to reject the subject and to conclude that it's not meant for me.

On the other hand, If I was labeled as a disciplined, hard worker, who will think through a problem until I can solve it, then I will create a very different mindset (and different results will follow).

What can you do about it?

Avoid labeling yourself (and others) with labels typical of fixed mindsets, such as: "You're an intelligent student," "I'm not good in math," "I can't control my dark horse," "you're a talented athlete," or "you're a superstar." (By now you should know how I feel about the superstar mentality).

Instead, use labels that imply a growth-mindset, such as: "you work hard," "you are diligent," or "you are self-disciplined."

Monitor your thinking. What kind of mindset do you typically revert to, growth or fixed? If you tend to revert to a fixed mindset, given the new evidence that's just been presented to you, what will you do to challenge it?

Mindsets are created through experiences and our conclusions about the results of our experiences. To change your mindset, it's important to have experiences that challenge your preconceived notions. Try to engage in something small that will do this. For instance, if you believe you can't learn a certain subject, try to learn it over the next few weeks using a growth mindset: "If I invest the necessary time and energy in learning this subject, I too can do it."

If you face obstacles, spend enough time trying to understand the root of the problem and then spend enough time trying to solve it. If time alone does not help you solve the problem, change strategies. It's important to keep an open mind and to remind yourself that even the hardest problem can be solved if you just pay continued attention to it and try different strategies to solve it.

Strategy #26: Reappraising Thoughts and Situations (Dealing with Setbacks, Boring and Uninteresting Tasks, or Very Exciting Distractions)

> *If an optimist was to have his arm bitten off by an alligator, he might say "Oh boy, half-price manicures for life." Whereas the rest of us would say, "Ah, my arm."*
>
> — *Lemony Snicket, A Series of Unfortunate Events*

Often when we think (in our minds and hearts), our stream of thoughts and feelings aren't necessarily in sync with our goals. You may know that you need to engage in a certain activity but your mind is muddled by a concoction of fuzzy thoughts and feelings about it.

Yesterday I had pre-committed to commit to writing. My mind immediately got muddled by suggestions to go and watch another episode of a Coursera course, clean my house, or run some stats on a project I am working on. Writing can be draining. Writing can be difficult. Writing takes time and the results are often uncertain—at least for me.

So what can we do when our thoughts are hijacked by this kind of negative thinking? Reappraise!

I am fascinated with mixed martial arts (MMA). I never thought I would be, as it's a somewhat barbaric and violent sport more fitting for a 14th century culture than the 21st century. But sure enough, every Sunday, I would spend a good amount of time online reading about the results of Saturday night's cards and trying to find videos of the knockouts. While I spent time on the results of a sport I had mixed feelings about, I was getting distracted from more important tasks that could actually have a real impact in my life, such as writing this book.

Mixed martial arts, like sports in general and most other distractions that we tend to succumb to, are like sugar to the dark horse. They are filled with excitement, action, and jolts of energy. They make us react at an emotional level, delivering an addictive dose of instant gratification. Our brains value these experiences in the sense that it satisfies the brain's need to seek pleasure, avoid pain, and conserve energy.

On the other hand, writing this book is costly to my brain in the short term—it requires a lot of energy and effort, and the rewards are distant, abstract, and uncertain (maybe only my wife and my mother will ever read this far). Writing a report, in the short-term, is costly. Studying a difficult subject is costly. The long-term benefits are distant and our dark horse will pull us towards pleasure.

Beware—our dark horses constantly pester us about things they think we need. The dark horse will make suggestions: you need to watch this show; you need to rest, you need caffeine, you need a drink.

The reality is that most of the time, we don't need these things. We can live without the drink, the caffeine, the show, and we can work a little longer.

A medical doctor once approached me after one of my talks and shared a quote he uses when delivering orientation sessions for students attending a medical mission he helps run in Honduras. He tells his students: "If there is anything you need, let me know… and I will teach you how to get along without it." Brilliant! This is him speaking to his students' dark horses. Tell me what you need, and I will tell you that you actually don't.

One of the most successful strategies in dealing with the urges of the dark horse to veer towards instantly gratifying activities is a strategy called "reappraisal."[160]

Reappraisal is the process of consciously and voluntarily rewriting your thoughts about a particular task or situation. It involves a conscious effort to deliberately replace feelings, thoughts, and values that our brains assign to a certain object with something else. This "something else" will typically be a thought or feeling that supports, and will further, your goal and your mission.

In my case, for example, I used to associate MMA with entertainment, fun, and excitement. It is as if MMA spoke to a primal need of my basic human nature. By reappraising the situation, I had to come up with a new way to define it, a new way to talk about it. My reappraised thought was that MMA is a waste of my (very) valuable and limited time.

---

160 Meeks, T. W., & Jeste, D. V. (2009). Neurobiology of wisdom: A literature overview. *Archives of General Psychiatry*, 66(4), 355–365.

Another way that I reappraised the situation was to think, "while those fighters were making hundreds of thousands of dollars, if not millions, I was actually using my time unproductively on something that would have no impact whatsoever on my future."

Reappraisal is a very effective tool for addressing boring, unappealing, and difficult tasks, or tasks that you just don't feel like doing. By reappraising the task, your goal is to make the reappraised version look as sexy and appealing as possible. A boring organic chemistry class now becomes the "key to your future"; that project you have been dreading writing is now what will make you earn brownie points with your boss or the door to a better future. That dreadful workout session that you couldn't get motivated about now becomes "me time" or "nurturing my physical self"; that dreadful lab report is a blank canvas and you are the artist.

It is also an effective tool for reconsidering impulses, urges, and primal desires. These are typically built into our systems as sources of pleasure as well as psychological and physical relief. They can also get us into trouble. The goal of reappraisal in this case is to associate psychological states and actions that are pleasure-producing with negative outcomes.

For instance, binge-watching shows on Netflix is pleasurable and disconnects our minds from a very busy world. It also consumes enormous amount of time that anyone on a mission just can't afford to waste. You can reappraise binge-watching by associating it with negative feelings and outcomes: "binge-watching is for people with time to waste," or "binge watching is for losers."

Research shows that reappraising our emotions diminishes brain activity in the amygdale (where the dark horse resides) and increases brain activity in the prefrontal cortex (the charioteer).[161]

In other words, simply reappraising a situation shifts control from the dark horse to the charioteer.

Reappraisal is the equivalent of convincing yourself that the opposite to what you are thinking, feeling, and valuing at a given moment is actually true, even if that requires telling yourself some small, harmless lies. It is the process of duping the dark horse. When your desirous and indulgent mind is looking in one direction, you force it to look in another, as if what's over there is actually better for you. And the mind will actually buy into it.

For instance, you may be craving that tenth cup of coffee of the day, which you know will keep you awake at night and mess with your sleep pattern. As the dark horse is convincing you to reach for it, you show it a glass of juice or water: "Look! having this glass of water instead will be much better for you."

Reappraisal is identifying something that is attracting and exciting the dark horse and telling it "look here, you'll like this even more!", thus changing the direction of its focus. The truth of the matter is that the dark horse may not like it better, but you make it *believe* that it will.

Research on how we appraise stress shows that individuals who report high levels of stress and appraise stress as being debilitating to their health actually also report more health issues and an increased risk of premature death when compared

---

161 Meeks, T. W., & Jeste, D. V. (2009). Neurobiology of wisdom: A literature overview. *Archives of General Psychiatry*, 66(4), 355–365. Also: Lieberman, M. D, Eisenberger, N. I., Crockett, M. J., Tom, S. M., Pfeifer, J. H., & Way, B. M. (2007). Putting feelings into words: Affect labeling disrupts amygdala activity in response to affective stimuli. *Psychological Science*, 18(5), 421–428.

to those who were stressed but did not see stress as debilitating.[162] The simple act of reappraising stress, from debilitating to enhancing, has psychological, behavioral, and physiological consequences. This can be influenced by the simple act of watching short videos portraying the effects of stress as enhancing instead of debilitating.

It is actually amusing how easy it is to fool our brain and our horses. Either watching short videos that change our perception of a situation or simply forcing ourselves to interpret an event in a different light has major implications, not only for our psychology but also for our physiology. In reappraisal, when a thought is produced or a belief emerges in the mind, all we need to do is suggest something else—often the opposite of what the mind came up with. The results are actually fascinating.[163]

What can you do about it?

The process of using reappraisal is quite simple:

1) Identify and isolate the unproductive behavior or thought.
2) Think of a thought or reward to substitute the present thought.
3) Mentally state the reappraised thought.

162 Keller, A., Litzelman, K., Wisk, L. E., Maddox, T., Cheng, E. R., Creswell, P.D., & Witt, W. P. (2012). Does the Perception that Stress Affects Health Matter? The Association with Health and Mortality. *Health Psychology*, 31(5): 677–684.

163 While this works in general, it is important to note however that there are certain beliefs, dependencies, and traumas that are deeply ingrained and may require the help of a professional and perhaps years of intense treatment to shift.

Let's put this into practice. Imagine your boss asks you to write a long industry report. You are dreading it and just can't find the energy to get it started.

The first step is to isolate the thought. To jump-start the process, you may ask yourself why you are dreading it. Let's suppose that your mind responds that you "absolutely hate writing reports."

Now that you have isolated the root of your indifference, substitute that thought with a thought that will generate momentum for you to get started. For instance:

1) When I dedicate myself to writing, I can be very good at it.
2) This report, if well-written, could be a stepping stone in my career.
3) How can I put my mark on this report?

Now let's suppose that you have to engage in a very difficult task that makes you drowsy just to think about it, such as studying for organic chemistry. You know you have to study for it, but the mere thought of it makes your stomach churn.

My first recommendation would be to set a "This 'r Nothing" cycle: setting aside a pre-determined period of time to focus exclusively on the task at hand. The next step would be to reappraise the task following the three-step process:

1) *Isolate the thought:* "Organic chemistry is boring and I will never understand it."
2) *Substitute the current thought with a thought that will help you achieve your goal*: "Organic chemistry is an interesting subject and the key to my future. If I apply myself, I will make it."
3) *State the reappraised thought.*

Here are some examples of reappraised thoughts:

Original Thought	Reappraised Thought
Subject X is hard.	Subject X is the key to my future.
I need caffeine.	I am fine with a glass of water.
Professor X is boring.	Professor X teaches a class that will be important for my future.
I hate X.	I love X.
I despise Y.	Y is my stepping stone to a better life.
I love [insert name of your favorite TV show that demands insurmountable amounts of time].	TV show X is for the weak.
I don't feel like doing X.	X is a career builder.
I don't see the point of Y.	Y will be useful for me in the future, although I can't clearly see the value of it now.
I am a loser.	If I apply myself, I can do it.
I am too old (or too young).	I am the perfect age/ in my prime.

Strategy # 27: *In the Beginning* (A Very short Meditation)

The *In the Beginning* meditation is a very quick and easy reappraisal exercise. It takes seconds and is highly effective in eliminating distractions and reducing mental noise.

I don't know about you, but witnessing people answer their phones in the middle of a movie drives me absolutely nuts! People texting while having an in-person, one-on-one conversation drives me insane.

I'm aware that I sound like a grumpy old man when I say this, but years ago texting was not as prevalent as it is today and people still survived to live another day. Critics will say that times have changed and now people are expected to answer their text messages, phone calls, and emails immediately. Is this really the case? I doubt it. We are more than ever emotionally and physically attached to our technological devices.

Another phenomena that controls our lives and distances us from our goals is on-demand, 24/7, wherever-we-are entertainment. Binge watching a favorite TV series has never been easier. I don't have cable TV at home and would rarely watch shows on the Internet before a friend introduced me *Walking Dead.* I became quickly addicted to it.

The truth is that it is becoming harder and harder for us to control the urge to respond to the massive amount of immediate gratification available to us.

So here is the easiest and quickest meditation you will ever do in your life.

When I feel the urge to watch the *Walking Dead,* I think to myself: "In the beginning there was no *Walking Dead.*" When I feel the urge to watch MMA, I think: "In the beginning there was no MMA." It's that simple!

You must be asking yourself, what does "in the beginning" even mean? The answer is the beginning of everything in this universe, the beginning of life, the beginning of the universe itself. Think of the time when the universe had just been created and what existed at that moment. There were no TVs, smartphones, or soap operas. The universe just was. And then we created our human extensions, our cultural artifacts, and addictive TV series.

What I am telling myself during this brief meditation is that these distractions are human creations and that because they were created by us, they should be controlled by us. We create, we control. Not the other way around.

Cognitively, in this exercise we are rationalizing an impulse, switching cognition from the limbic system to the prefrontal cortex; in other words, taking control away from the dark horse and giving it back to the charioteer.

You will be surprised by how easily your mind is redirected.

Strategy #28: Creativity and Reappraisal

My first boss taught me a lesson that I still carry today and that I apply to as many projects as possible. He taught me that I should "never take a project as given to me."

Working for him was a highly energetic endeavor. Creativity abounded, and we worked very long hours, without complaining, as we were excited and proud of the work we were producing. Every time a new project was given to me, following his advice, I would think of ways to make it exciting, different, and creative. I would, in essence, reappraise the given project.

A dull budgeting spreadsheet all of a sudden became something that could be turned into something unique—maybe I could add filters or macros that others had never used before, or maybe I could design it in a way that was more visually appealing. Every project that was reappraised released a burst of creative energy, making work more interesting, engaging, and worthwhile.

A quick exercise

How can you reappraise a project that was recently given to you? What features can you change, improve upon, or get rid of that will make it unique and memorable?

Strategy #29: Think Big, Think Why, Think Values.

There are times when we are exhausted, our egos are depleted, and it seems like there's little we can do to pull ourselves up. We make every possible effort to keep the chariot airborne and to conduct it to our desired destination, but regardless of how well we've played the game, we just can't keep going. We're ready to throw in the towel.

Although ego depletion can substantially diminish our ability to exert control over future tasks, the science of self-control tells us that a depleted ego does not need to be the end of the journey. When the going gets tough, we have a visceral weapon that can give us that last drop of self-control that we so much need in order to cross the finish line: our deep-seated values.

Restating one's values is an effective strategy to overcome depletion and regain self-control. By restating values, you are reminding yourself of what is most important to you, thereby finding a new source of energy and stamina to keep on pressing forward.

Let's say that you've been working hard to save money but now feel the urge to spend it on frivolous things. This is when thinking values comes into play. If you place a high value on family, for example, and you are saving money with the intention of improving your family's wellbeing, then bringing that value to mind deflects your urge to buy something unnecessary since now your decision-making is now based on higher-order needs.

Thinking values is a form of reappraisal, in which you are able to devalue the temptation at hand and value a higher-order goal: a deep-seated value.

Research conducted by Dr. Kentaro Fujita and colleagues proposes that abstract thinking and how we construe and interpret events in our minds is essential to self-control.[164] When people are encouraged to think about *why* they should engage in desirable actions as opposed to *how* or *what*, they display increased self-control.

For instance, thinking about why you should exercise is more effective than thinking about how and what you should do. Think about it. The *how* of exercising includes: I have to go to the gym, park my car, change my clothes, lift weights. The *what* includes lifting weights, running, squatting. Not very inspiring!

The *why*, on the other hand, forces us to consider the overall benefits of exercising: it improves my overall health, which can spill into other areas of my life, including increased energy for playing with my kids or doing my work. Abstract, higher-level thinking is the equivalent of seeing the forest from the trees.

Values are thinking of the highest order, allowing us to shift attention from the dreary of details of the situation at hand to a larger framework that speaks to our reason d'etre (our reason for being). Thinking why, and of our values, transforms a mundane action into something you care deeply about.

---

164 Fujita, K., Trope, Y., Liberman, N., & Levin-Sagi, M. (2006). Construal levels and self-control. *Journal of Personality and* Social Psychology, *90*(3):351–67.

As beautifully described by Duhigg in his book *Smarter, Faster, Better*, our actions should be affirmations of our values.[165]

In your next project, at work, home, or at school, think about how the activity at hand fits into your larger value framework.

Task requiring self-control	Value framework
Exercising	I am getting into excellent health, and will have additional energy to play with my kids.
Boring tasks	These are a path for me towards quality and accomplishment.
Writing this book	I am doing it for my family and for my students.
Carrying a heavy bag of groceries through the streets of New York during winter	I am providing nutrition for my family and getting much-needed exercise. If I already exercised today, even better—I am getting that extra dose that makes all the difference (I am also exercising different muscles).

Strategy #30: Mental Contrasting (Envision Preferred Futures, Prepare for the Worst)

Personal goals are mental creations. It is common for us to fantasize about a project we would like to work on, or a product, business, or website we would like to create, or perhaps a life-changing trip we would like to take.

165 Duhigg, C. (2016). *Smarter, faster, better: The secrets of being productive in life and business.* New York, NY: Random House.

As we discussed in Chapter 7, fantasizing about future accomplishments is energizing and motivating. But then there is life as we live it.

Life presents us with obstacles, challenges, distractions, and competing goals. Projects that we were once highly excited about become mere fantasies, never to be realized.

One of the issues with getting things done is that we tend to be good at fantasizing about a desired future, but not so good at assessing our capabilities and the challenges of getting there. According to Gabriele Oettingen, a psychologist who studies the psychology of achievement, there are people who indulge in fantasies about future accomplishments with complete disregard for what it takes to actually implement them. Conversely, there are those who dwell on the obstacles along the way without creating a compelling view of the future.[166]

These "indulgers" and "dwellers" are at two opposites on the goal achievement spectrum. They are one-sided views of achievement; but both are important for successful goal achievement. If brought together in a systematic way, Dr. Oettingen's research suggests that significant results can be achieved.[167]

166 Gollwitzer, P. M., & Oettingen, G. (2013). Implementation intentions. In M. Gellman & J. R. Turner (Eds.), *Encyclopedia of behavioral medicine* (pp. 1043-1048). New York, NY: Springer-Verlag.

167 Ibid. Also: Duckworth, A. L., Grant, H., Loew, B., Oettingen, G., & Gollwitzer, P. M. (2011) Self-regulation strategies improve self-discipline in adolescents: Benefits of mental contrasting and implementation intentions. *Educational Psychology, 31*(1), 17-26.

The strategy for bringing both the need to fantasize about the future and the need to ponder the obstacles that stand in the way is called "mental contrasting," which is the mental exercise of contrasting a vision of the future with reality.

When thinking about reality (or what is standing on our way), it is important for you to be as self-reflective and critical as possible. The first step is to begin with the assumption that the biggest obstacle between you and your goal may in fact be you (your dark horse and its need to indulge or an inattentive charioteer).

As we also learned in Chapter 7, humans have a tendency to considerably overrate their abilities, skills, capacities, and fail to critically evaluate what it actually takes to accomplish goals. We have a tendency to rate ourselves as above average, from driving cars to our ability to foresee problems in the future. Experts in the area of self-assessment state that people tend to "overestimate the likelihood that they will engage in desirable behaviors and achieve favorable outcomes, furnish overly optimistic estimates of when they will complete future projects, and reach judgments with too much confidence."[168] We also tend to think that we are entitled to all good things in life and believe that negative things are less likely to happen to us.[169]

Take for instance project management. Projects are often stubbornly over budget and behind schedule. Part of the problem is our inability to accurately predict the amount of time,

---

168 Dunning, D., Heath, C., & Suls, J. (2004). Flawed self-assessment: Implications for health, education, and the workplace. *Psychological Science in the Public Interest, 5*(3), 69 106: p 60.

169 Halvorson, H. G. (2010). *Succeed: How we can reach our goals.* New York, NY: Penguin Publishing Group.

energy, resources, personal skills, and knowledge needed to implement a given project, and the potential environmental disturbances that may push the most carefully created plan off track. Yet, we tend to be overconfident about our ability to make accurate predictions.[170]

Believing that you will succeed is important, and so is believing that it won't be easy. It rarely is. When we believe that pursuing our goals won't be a breeze, we tend to expend more effort, energy, and resources, while also taking more action to achieve our goals.[171] When we expect that we will have to fight many battles before accomplishing our goals, we prepare ourselves better for action. On the other hand, if we overate our abilities and underestimate the challenges ahead, we can be overwhelmed by reality and disengage from our goals or invest less energy than the situation requires.

As Dr. Halvorson explains, the latest empirical evidence supports the claim that expecting the best and preparing for the worst is a good proposition. One of the studies reported on her book found that women who enrolled in a weight-loss program and believed they would successfully lose weight lost on average 26 pounds more than those who believed that they would fail. Interestingly, those who believed that they could lose weight but that it would be a difficult, uphill battle—for instance, that resisting temptation was going to be a struggle—lost 24 pounds more than those who thought it would be a breeze.[172]

170 Hammond, J. S., Keeney, R. J., & Raiffa, H. (2006). The hidden traps in decision making. *Harvard Business Review, 84*(1), 118–126.

171 Halvorson, H. G. (2010). *Succeed: How we can reach our goals.* New York, NY: Penguin Publishing Group.

172 Ibid.

In one study on job seekers, those who thought that job hunting would be a breeze sent out fewer applications than those who thought it would be a challenging proposition.[173]

Yet another study suggests that sedentary individuals who have a high sense of self-efficacy (the belief that they can achieve their goals), are three times more likely to continue exercising after one year than those who have low self-efficacy. Self-efficacy alone, however, is not sufficient. One must also account for the potential distractions along the way.

When engaging in mental contrasting, try and remember the following principles of reality:

- The world is messy. The plans you have created in your mind will be challenged every step of the way, as you move from idealization to implementation.
- The plans you have created in your mind are probably overly optimistic in terms of the time, money, and energy required to accomplish them.
- Your mental immune system will kick in as you try to implement your goal. You, the person who creates the goal, will eventually turn on yourself in an attempt to maintain balance.
- The emotional state you are in when you create the goal is not the same as the various emotional states you will find yourself in when implementing it. Know that emotional states are temporal, they come and go, and must be monitored and controlled.

173 Ibid.

- The outside world may be indifferent, against, in favor, or even supportive of your idea. Don't expect much from the world.
- As soon as you engage in new behaviors, old habits will reassert themselves and remind you why they existed in the first place.

So, how to successfully implement mental contrasting? I suggest a two-step process:

1) *Envision future ideal scenarios in your mind*: For example, think of an ideal meeting with your staff. In this meeting everyone is collaborating, ideas are being shared and discussed, decisions are being made, and the meeting is over fifteen minutes before the scheduled time.
2) *Treat goals always as an uphill battle:* This does not mean you see them negatively, as otherwise even before you begin you will be discouraged. Instead, prepare yourself mentally for the battles that you will potentially come across. In the meeting example, you know for a fact based on experience that someone will try to veer off on a tangent, that so-and-so will be late and uncooperative, that someone else will play the contrarian.

Now that you have anticipated the challenges, we will discuss solutions in the next section. Before we do so, I want to share a laundry list of potential obstacles to think about:

- Lack of time and energy;
- Distractions;

- Other people standing in your way;
- Lack of support;
- Changes in strategy;
- Lack of human resources;
- Bad organizational culture;
- Internal politics;
- Wrong timing;
- Lack of skills/competencies/knowledge.

Contrasting your future goals with the present reality is an effective strategy in itself for goal achievement. However, studies suggest that coupling mental contrasting with other types of implementation strategies can substantially improve our ability to follow through with our plans. The following strategy, when combined with mental contrasting, is proven to enhance our potential for achievement.

Strategy #31: If-Then Strategies

Researchers have empirically tested a successful strategy for dealing with obstacles standing between us and our goals. This strategy requires active mental engagement in anticipating both barriers that you know may be in your way (largely due to past personal experience), as well as imagined barriers, and then actively devising an alternative strategy to deal with these potential barriers. This strategy is called the "If-Then" strategy.

First, think of a goal you want to achieve. We typically think in terms of "I want to achieve Y." For instance, "I want to write a book."

At this point, such a statement is a one-sided, indulgent statement. To make it whole, we also need to think about reality and anticipate the potential barriers standing between us and our goals. We then can apply the if-then strategy to every potential barrier. If-then clauses are framed in the form of "If [barrier], then I will [solution]."[174]

For example: "I want to write a book, and if I realize that I don't have time during the day to write it, then I will wake up one hour earlier to write."

Now, think about the major barriers that exists between you and your goals and try to develop if-then strategies to deal with them. For instance:

- "I want to focus on my study/work, and if someone interrupts me, then I will move to a quiet location."
- "If my friends invite me to go out, then I will tell them that I will go out next weekend for sure but that I have to focus on my work this weekend."
- "I am on a diet and if I go out to eat, then I will ask for a salad."
- "If Robert goes off on a tangent, then I will politely interrupt the meeting and suggest we focus on the task at hand; if Mary becomes non-cooperative, then I will ask for solutions and not problems."

To improve customer service, Starbucks adopted self-control strategies in their training program, particularly for situations that get out of control (when self-control is actually called for). Employees are encouraged to imagine possible scenarios where

174 Duckworth, A. L., Grant, H., Loew, B., Oettingen, G., & Gollwitzer, P. M. (2011) Self-regulation strategies improve self-discipline in adolescents: Benefits of mental contrasting and implementation intentions. *Educational Psychology, 31*(1),17–26.

service could be derailed (mental contrasting), such as having to deal with an angry customer, and then develop implementation intentions for when the time comes. For each potential scenario, employees develop "If-Then" strategies. For example, "If a customer is unhappy, then I will ..." or "if a customer starts yelling, then I will..." Employees rehearse their response until it becomes a habit.

I use If-Then thinking quite often in my personal life with a great deal of success. Once in a while, my wife and I like to eliminate something from our diets for a pre-determined number of days. I have already mentioned that at least once a year I abstain from drinking alcohol for 40 consecutive days. Not drinking during social events can be quite a challenging feat. That is when I will say to myself, "If I feel tempted to break my fast or if a friend offers me a drink, then I will ask for a glass of water or juice."

Having this rule helps me to think out in advance what I will do when the problem arises, releasing me from the obligation to have to make an on-the-spot decision. I have already made the decision beforehand, so when the temptation arises all I need to do is to follow through with my plan. It might not seem like much but it is one less step that I need to implement and means that I know exactly how to respond to the situation.

Also, notice that I don't suppress the urge to have something to drink. Just like we looked at in our reappraisal strategies, I substitute what I *can't* drink with something I *can* drink. I can also choose to ignore the cue or say no to the offer. Substitution and ignoring are more effective goal implementation strategies than having a negative response to the situation.[175]

175 Gollwitzer, P. M., & Oettingen, G. (2013). Implementation intentions. In M. Gellman & J. R. Turner (Eds.), *Encyclopedia of behavioral medicine* (pp. 1043–1048). New York, NY: Springer-Verlag.

If-Then strategies alleviate the burden on the charioteer, as you are not forcing him or her to make instant decisions. On some occasions, you are even pleasing the dark horse by offering a substitute alternative.

Think about potential substitutions for barriers that we face on a daily basis:

- If I am offered dessert, then I will ask for fresh fruit.
- If I am asked to go out today, then I will ask to go out on a different day.
- If I don't feel like going to the gym, then I will go jogging in the park.
- If I am asked to commit to something I know I will regret, then I will ask to sleep on it.

As mentioned before, the effectiveness of coupling metal contrasting with the if-then strategy is supported by empirical evidence.

In one study, high school students studying for a high-stakes standardized test completed 60% more practice questions than students in a placebo control condition.[176] A group of randomly selected high school students who were preparing to take the preparatory SAT (the PSAT), were instructed to think vividly and write about two positive outcomes of preparing for the test by answering all the questions in the preparatory workbook. Students were also asked to think and write about potential barriers that could prevent them from answering all questions. They were then asked to

176 Duckworth, A. L., Grant, H., Loew, B., Oettingen, G., & Gollwitzer, P. M. (2011) Self-regulation strategies improve self-discipline in adolescents: Benefits of mental contrasting and implementation intentions. *Educational Psychology, 31*(1), 17-26.

propose solutions to the obstacles by writing if-then propositions. The control group, on the other hand, was asked to only think about positive outcomes and potential barriers.

On average, students who engaged in the mental contrasting and if-then strategies responded to 140 questions, compared to 84 questions answered by the control group.

In the exercise below, state your goal and anticipate every possible obstacle that could possibly stand on your way. Think of challenges that are both unique to this situation and those that you typically struggle with. For instance, if you have to work on a major proposal at work, a unique challenge for this project might be your team members not providing information in a timely manner, while a typical struggle may be dealing with time leeches in the office. You then devise a strategy for each of these challenges in advance.

My goal: ________________________________	
Potential challenges ahead of you (mental contrasting):	If-Then strategies to deal with each challenge
1. Friend will invite me to the hookah bar.	If my friend invites me to the hookah bar, then I will promise to go out with her after my project is completed.
2. Happy hour with office staff when I am not drinking.	If I am invited to attend a happy hour, then I will only order water.
3. No motivation to do work.	I am not motivated to finish a project, then I will remind myself of the positive future consequences this project can bring me.

4. Information not provided in a timely manner	If information is not provided in a timely manner, then I will send daily reminder email.
5. Time leeches	If there are time leeches lurking around, then I will do whatever possible to avoid them.
6.	

Strategy #32: Labeling

An acquaintance recently became very sick with what was believed to be a bad case of the flu. After weeks of being sick, it became obvious that it wasn't the flu. It was some other "thing" that could not be named that was causing his sickness. After intense batteries of tests, doctors finally diagnosed him with Lyme disease—a virus infection transmitted by a tiny deer tick.

His predicament ended when the disease was correctly labeled. Before the virus was labeled, the doctors were unsuccessful in providing him with the correct diagnosis and treatment, causing a great deal of additional pain and suffering.

Take wine tasting as another example of labeling. If you are an unsophisticated consumer of wine like me, you probably have a very limited language for classifying wine. I, for instance, tend to classify wine as either good or bad. When the sommelier describes the wine I am about to drink as being "fruity with hints of peach, blueberry and raspberry," my typical reactions is *Okay, whatever you say.* Without having developed a comprehensive classificatory system and language to describe the different aromas, bouquet, mouth feel, acidity levels, and texture of different wines, I have to resort to my broad categories or labels (that is, good or bad), hampering my ability to fully explore and appreciate the depth and breadth of wine tasting.

Behavioral economics suggests that developing a sophisticated preference vocabulary (or consumption vocabulary) can significantly impact our ability to not only better appreciate wine (or other things in life), but also make better decisions when choosing in the future—decisions that are grounded on facts instead of emotions.

The truth is that there are many things in life that we enjoy and appreciate or dislike and reject, but we don't have the vocabulary to describe them. You enjoy (or don't) a glass of wine, without fully understanding why you approve of it or decide to never buy that bottle again.

Wine, like many things in life, is multidimensional. A preference vocabulary, a label, allows us to tap into the multidimensionality of things, opening up new levels of awareness and understanding.

Labeling is the process of categorizing an object using language. Labeling is a major part of the human experience in making sense of the world around us. In the Bible, when Adam was made responsible for the animal kingdom, his first job consisted of naming every living creature. David Rock, author of *Your Brain at Work,* suggests that developing language to describe things involves the prefrontal cortex, giving us more power over the labeled object as a result.[177]

---

177 Rock, D. (2009). *Your brain at work: Strategies for overcoming distractions, regaining focus, and working smarter all day long* [Kindle 6.3 version]. Retrieved from http://www.amazon.com, pp. 113-114.

For instance, once my acquaintance's disease was correctly labeled as Lyme disease, he entered a treatment routine that brought him back to good health. Likewise, having a more sophisticated set of labels to distinguish different types of wine allows us to make better choices.

Controlling our impulses and emotions is an essential part of self-control. Impulses and emotions can make or break us. Positive emotions get us elated, energized, and enthusiastic about life and living. Negative emotions, on the other hand, may have a devastating effect on how we perceive reality—including other people, situations, and ourselves.

Emotions, when not identified and labeled correctly, can be as devastating as the virus carried by the Lyme disease tick: slowly corroding our resolve and deflating the ego. Labeling, as it so happens, is a powerful strategy in dealing with impulses and emotions. Because it involves prefrontal cortex activity, it increases our veto power over negative emotions.

Labeling is nothing more than giving a name to the unnamed. It's that simple. And it works beautifully.

By identifying an emotion, you are transferring the emotion from the more primitive parts of the brain, such as the amygdale, to the executive, rational, decision-making part of your brain.[178]

As described by Dr. Van der Kolk, a psychiatrist who specializes in patients suffering from post traumatic stress disorder:

> "If you've been hurt, you need to acknowledge and name what happened to you. [...] Feeling that we have been

---

178 Lieberman, M. D., Eisenberger, N. I., Crockett, M. J., Tom, S. M., Pfeifer, J. H., & Way, B. M. (2007). Putting feelings into words: Affect labeling disrupts amygdala activity in response to affective stimuli. *Psychological Science, 18*(5), 421–8.

heard, and understood, changes our physiology; being able to articulate a complex feeling, and having our feelings recognized, lights up our limbic brain and creates an 'aha moment.' In contrast, being met by silence and incomprehension kills the spirit."[179]

In a study by Dr. Lieberman, a neuroscientist at UCLA, and colleagues, participants were asked to look at pictures of people with angry, scared, or happy faces. In one half of cases, the participants were asked to match the faces with other, similar-looking faces. The second half was asked to match the faces to words that correctly described the emotions on the faces—in other words, labeling emotions by attaching words to them.

The subjects were hooked up to a Functional Magnetic Resonance Imaging machine, which showed which part of the brain was most active while the subjects matched pictures or labeled them. The group that labeled the emotions showed significantly less activity in the amygdale and increased activity in the ventrolateral prefrontal cortex, the part of our anatomy responsible for inhibition of the limbic system.[180]

In other words, labeling allows the charioteer to determine what the dark horse was getting worked up about. By identifying and labeling the root of the trouble, the charioteer could develop strategies to address it.

---

179 Van der Kolk, B. A. (2014). *The body keeps the score: Brain, mind, and body in the healing of trauma.* New York, NY: Penguin Publishing Group, p. 232.

180 Rock, D. (2009). *Your brain at work: Strategies for overcoming distractions, regaining focus, and working smarter all day long* [Kindle 6.3 version]. Retrieved from http://www.amazon.com,

What can you do about it?

Below is an adapted version of a labeling exercise developed by Dr. Eugene Gendlin (the original exercise can be found in his book *Focusing*[181]). I have been using this adaptation for years now and it helps me tremendously in gaining a better understanding of what I am going through and how to deal with it.

1) Find a quiet place and a comfortable position to rest in. It can be lying down or sitting comfortably on a chair.
2) Close your eyes for about two minutes and relax all parts of your body.
3) After you are completely relaxed, ask yourself: "What am I feeling? There is something not right, what is bothering me?" Thoughts will immediately start rushing through your mind. The key here is to identify the problem that has the most significant impact on the way you feel.
4) Isolate one feeling, or a sensation, that is associated with the problem at stake. For instance, you may feel overwhelmed, irritated, cheated, jealous, or envious. Or you may feel as if you were inside a tightly closed box or jailed.
5) After you have identified a feeling or emotion, ask yourself: "Why am I feeling this emotion? What is it about this problem that makes me feel...irate?"
6) After you come up with one answer, keep on asking why, until you feel that you have the right answer.

Here is how it works:

I have an uneasy, uncomfortable feeling that needs to be addressed. I sit down, relax, and ask: "What is going on?"

181 Gendlin, E. T. (1978). *Focusing*. New York, NY: Batam Dell.

The answer pops up: "I am worried about what is happening at work."

I then try to isolate a word that describes my feelings by asking a question: "What am I feeling?" or "How do I feel?"

"Anxiety," pops up in my mind.

I will then ask myself: "Why am I anxious?"

My brain answers: "There are too many things to get done and I am losing control."

I will then ask "why" again: "Why are there too many things to get done?"

The answer: "Because on top of your work, you committed yourself to present at a conference. There won't be enough time to get everything done."

I ask: "Why did I commit myself to speak on top of my busy agenda?"

The answer: "Because I like to speak at conferences."

I am now at peace… I feel anxious but it is because I chose an additional activity that I love. I did so out of love for my profession. My brain calms down. I calm down.

Here is another real example, from when I helped a colleague after he had an argument with a coworker:

"What is happening?"

"I just had a heated argument with a coworker that is consuming my energy."

"What are you feeling?"

"Threatened."

"Why?"

"Because he is making accusations that aren't true."

"Why is he making accusations?"

"Because he's an idiot."

I asked why again: "Why is he making accusations?"

"Because he doesn't know what he is talking about."

"Why?"

"Because he does not have the facts."

"Can you give him the facts?"

"Yes."

As a result, my friend wrote an email to his co-worker explaining the facts. Problem solved.

A student of mine went through this process and her process developed as follows:

"What is going on?"

"I am feeling worthless."

"Try to think of one word to describe your feelings."

Without hesitation she replied, "empty."

"Why?"

"Because I am feel that I am not using my talents at work."

"Why?"

"Because I am not in a job that is deserving of me."

"Why?"

"Because I have to stay in this job until I finish my studies."

"Why?"

"Because I received a scholarship from my employer."

She suddenly realized that her feelings were temporary and that her life was not defined by this one job! After she was done with her studies, she could find new ways to express her talent. The exercise gave her enough impetus to fast-track her studies and graduate sooner.

There is an important caveat to labeling, however. In the exercise proposed above, we label the one emotion that is causing us discomfort, we find the source of that emotion, and we typically find a resolution. Labeling, to reduce arousal, must be done using one or two words to describe the emotion or maybe using symbolic language such as metaphors and analogies. A study discussed by Rock confirms that describing emotions in few words dampened arousal. However, opening a conversation about deep-seated emotions can indeed cause more harm than good as it increases limbic activity.[182]

Strategy #33: Hidden Commitments and Intentions

Earlier, we discussed how competing commitments derail us. For instance, reading the news every morning takes time away from my writing.

These types of competing commitments are easy to identify and to correct. But there are other types of commitments that can be much harder to identify and that may be controlling the direction of our chariots more than we would like to believe. These are hidden commitments.

Scholars Kegan and Lahey suggest that there are goals that we have, and then there are goals that have us. Hidden commitments are goals that have us.[183] They control our lives without our conscious knowledge. They operate in the background of our conscious decision-making, quietly controlling our every move.

The purpose of hidden commitments is to form a self-protective layer for our deep-seated beliefs about ourselves and the world. Just like our skulls protect our soft brain tissue and the

---

182 Rock, D. (2009). *Your brain at work: Strategies for overcoming distractions, regaining focus, and working smarter all day long* [Kindle 6.3 version]. Retrieved from http://www.amazon.com,

183 Kegan, R. & Lahey, L. L. (2001, November). The real reason people won't change. *Harvard Business Review, 79*(10), 84–92.

womb protects the fetus, a hidden commitment shelters our most valued beliefs about who we are. These deep-seated beliefs, although highly important in defining how we see and interact with the world, often go unexamined and unquestioned. Whenever external forces potentially threaten our beliefs, our hidden commitments kick in, protecting the order of the world as we construct it in our heads.

Take, for example, a person who despite his best intentions always finds an excuse not to launch his business idea. Or the novice writer who has never published one piece of writing.

In both cases, these individuals had goals: to launch a business and to write. But they also had goals that had them. Both had a fear and were terrified of criticism. Because of this aversion to having their ideas or work scrutinized by others, they kept waiting for "the right moment" to launch the business, or waiting for the right idea to write about. The goals that had them were stronger than their willpower to succeed.

INTENTIONS

When we act, we act based on intentions. We have an aim, a purpose, and a goal that needs to be fulfilled. The goal could be a stated goal that you want to achieve (goals we have) or an unconscious goal that serves to protect our egos (goals that have us).

If we don't reflect upon the goal that is driving our behavior, it is difficult to truly know whether we are acting on goals we have or goals that have us. Thus, creating a space between an impulse to act and the action itself, by identifying the intention of our actions, is a powerful step toward self-regulation.

Let's engage in a mental exercise. Think of the last time you received constructive feedback from someone and you were a bit defensive. Your chosen reaction was defensiveness. What was the intended goal you were trying to achieve? (Remember we are assuming that every action fulfills a purpose.) The intent of a defensive response is often to protect the ego, to save face, or to justify previous actions.

Now, what if you switched your intention from one of protection to one of learning and growth? How different would your actions be?

My wife is probably one of the most patient people I have known when it comes to child rearing. In fact, she is the one who taught me the power of intention. Before losing her control when our daughter misbehaves, she reminds herself of her intention. Is her intention to simply punish our daughter for being naughty or is it her intention to educate? These two distinctive intentions bring about very different subsequent actions, including the tone of voice used to address our daughter, the quality of the conversation my wife has with her, and the overall outcome of the ordeal.

I use this strategy when dealing with distractions and it has proven to be very effective. When I am about to open my browser to check the news or browse for the sake of browsing, I will ask myself: "What is my intention here?"

The answer is usually not very appealing. Half of the time I am escaping writing; the other half… I don't even have a justification for the other half (in other words, I am still escaping writing). The majority of the time, you will find that the urge to do something else is pure escapism.

The beauty of the intention technique is that when you ask yourself your intention for engaging in an activity, the answer to this rhetorical question usually proves to be either disappointing or embarrassing, or it forces us to engage in higher thinking before choosing a course of action.

To use this strategy effectively, ask:

1) What is my true intention by engaging in this action?
2) How do my intentions in engaging in this action promote my goals?
3) How do my intentions in engaging in this action promote my values?
4) Will engaging in this action truly promote my intended intention? How do I know?

Kegan and Lahey offer us a structured way to unearth the major assumptions that may be holding us back.[184] Below is a very brief outline of their process. I encourage the reader to buy their book *Immunity to Change*, in which the process is described in great detail and using vivid examples.[185]

Step 1. Define your big improvement goal: what is it that you want to get better at?

Example: I want to publish an article a week

Step 2. Make a list of things that you are not doing, or the things that you are doing instead of focusing on your goal, which end up sabotaging the goal. You should focus on specific behaviors that sabotage your

184 Kegan, R., & Lahey, L. L. (2001, November). The real reason people won't change. *Harvard Business Review, 79*(10), 84–92.

185 Kegan, R. & Lahey, L. L. (2009). *Immunity to change: How to overcome it and unlock the potential in yourself and your organization.* Boston, MA: Harvard Business Press.

goals—not mental states or feelings, but actual behaviors.

Example: I watch TV instead of writing; I call my mom, I cook a meal, or I find things to fill up the time that should be dedicated to writing.

Step 3. Identify what you are worried about. What worries you if you did the opposite of the activities in step 2? What is the worst that could happen if you did the opposite of the behavior in step 2?

Example: I am worried that if I write, I will be judged; I will be criticized; I will be in the spotlight; I will stand out; I will be ashamed to show who I really am. If I focus on my goal, then I may fail.

Step 4. Based on the results of step 3, determine what your hidden commitments are. Hidden commitments are the goals that have us, that we embrace to help protect us from the worries in step 3. Write these commitments in the form of a statement, such as: "I am committed to..."

Example: I am committed to not being judged. I am committed to not failing.

Step 5. Identify the big assumption you carry about yourself, life, and other people.

Example: People will always judge my work in a negative way.

Step 6. Observe the big assumption at play. Commit yourself to observe, for a week or so, how and when these assumptions play out in your life. At this stage, you should restrain your motivation to act on your assumptions. Can you instead identify specific situations or patterns of when the big assumption plays out?

Step 6a. Look for opposing information. We often look for information that confirms our assumptions and biases. Here you will do the opposite and look for information that challenges or contradicts your big assumption.

Example: I received positive reviews for my writing when....

Step 6b. Explore the origins of your assumption. Reflect upon your personal history and identify when, how, and why your big assumption came into being. Were there people who influenced you in embracing your big assumption? Is there any evidence that you interpreted these experiences correctly?

Step 7. Test the big assumption. How can you make sure that your big assumption is actually true? Create small experiments to test your big assumption.

Example: Publish one article on LinkedIn and monitor the comments.

Step 8. Rewrite your assumptions. Use the observations and small experimentation to measure results and either keep or rewrite your assumptions.

As you progress through this exercise, you will see that the hidden commitments unearthed in step 4 make sense and explain to a large degree why we act the way we do.

We act this way to honor our hidden commitments, and often these commitments are in juxtaposition to our big goals, impeding us from achieving them. We want to take our chariot in a certain direction but there are forces imposed by ourselves that are taking it in a different direction. The fact that we are the source of these forces is what makes this process both revealing and liberating.

Big assumptions are mental representations of the world out there and of how and where we fit into it. Big assumptions are like a piece of software code that dictates how we should act.

As seen above, the code is an intrinsic part of us as it has run the show for quite some time, and for the most part, it has been successful in doing so. However, as circumstances change, it may be advisable to rethink the code and write a code that is better adapted to the present situation. Running outdated codes can cause major negative consequences in the long run.[186]

Permission to sin

Human beings have an impressive capacity to rationalize events. We work away at a given task and all of a sudden the dark horse is whispering into our ear: "You've worked hard. Take a much-needed break. Indulge in your favorite food. You deserve it." The inattentive charioteer listens to the reasoning of the dark horse and ends up succumbing to its seductive proposition.

In other words, your dark horse and your charioteer are giving you permission to sin. The rationalization is that they are working so hard that goofing off is permissible.

Think about the last time you gave yourself permission to sin. What were your surroundings? Were you tired and depleted from exerting self-control in prior tasks? What were the consequences of your actions?

186 There are some codes, also called implicit theories, that shape our assumptions—assumptions about learning, intelligence, or motivation. These are very big assumptions: assumptions about assumptions. To explore how implicit theories affect our ability to self-regulate, I suggest you read more about the work of world-renowned psychologist, Carol Dweck, including his book *Mindset: The new psychology of success* mentioned in the beginning of this chapter.

What can you do about it?

The dark horse will insist that you indulge after long periods of exerting self-control. There are a number of things you can do to control the urge to give yourself a permission slip:

1) Stay alert. Knowing that the dark horse will try to seduce you is the first step towards self-control.
2) Focus on the forest as opposed to the trees by reminding yourself of your deep-seated values.
3) Consider the aggregated consequences of indulging. If you give yourself permission to sin every time you accomplish something positive, think about the aggregated consequences of this decision in the long-term.
4) Finally, talk back. As the horse tries to implant thoughts in your mind that you "deserve" to indulge because you work so hard, talk back by restating your values, goal, and mission.

Strategy #35: Think Future Self

We are all amazing... in the future. In the future we will exercise more, tidy our room, clean our houses, study more, start projects on time, indulge less, eat better, and be more positive. In the future, or so we think today, our dark horse will be tamed and our bright horse and charioteer will be in full control.

There is just one small issue with this thinking. As I tell my students, your future-self is simply your current-self tomorrow. Your past and your present will most likely become your future.

Think about it this way: if you have achieved less-than-ideal performance in the past and achieve less-than-ideal performance now, it is very unlikely that your performance will improve dramatically in the near future. We are all somewhat stuck in well-established patterns and these patterns tend to repeat themselves, shaping our future.

Unless—and I purposefully emphasize unless here—you change these life-defining patterns.

Most of us are creatures of habit. To a large extent, we do today what we did yesterday, from ordering coffee to the chair we sit in during each class at school, and from the time we wake up at each morning to where we choose to spend our money. And yet we want our lives to be different: we want to achieve more, we want to improve our competitiveness, we want to save money, we want to change.

In the science of self-control, this phenomenon is called "future self-continuity."[187] There are some people who treat their future self as being the same person as their present self. And there are others who treat their present and future selves as if they were two completely different people, as if their future self were a complete stranger to them.

This is an important finding, since there are things you would do to yourself that you wouldn't do to a stranger and vice versa. For instance, saving money is an irrational act if you perceive your future self to be a stranger. Why give money to someone I don't know if I can use it to satisfy the needs of my present self? And as far as your diet is concerned, you may choose to eat now with no regard to the consequences that your future self will have to deal with, including negative health consequences associated with a poor diet.

A study by the Department of Psychology at Stanford University looked at this difference in our perceptions of the

---

187 Ersner-Hershfield, H., Garton, M. T., Ballard, K., Samanez-Larkin, G. R., & Knutson, B. (2009). Don't stop thinking about tomorrow: Individual differences in future self-continuity account for saving. *Judgment and Decision Making*, 4(4), 280–286.

continuity between our present and future selves.[188] These views, in both laboratory tests and real-life decisions, have proven to determine how we value future rewards and how much we save for the future. For instance, those who experience a disconnect between their present and future selves may indulge in short-term gratification, while those who feel more connected to their future selves are more able to delay gratification.

The future self-continuity effect is aggravated by when and how we think about the future. We tend to make assumptions about how we will feel and act in the future based on how we feel today. Estimating our future feeling and actions is always difficult, but for those with a present/future self split, it is a near impossibility. This is because we infer future behavior based on our cognition processes now, which could be either hot (emotional) or cold (rational), with little regard for how we will feel when the time comes to implement our actions in the future.

For instance, you may think now that on Monday you will start that exercise program you have been putting off for months. Today, you are probably basing your intentions for future action on cold cognition: the rational view of the charioteer and the bright horse that exercising is good for you. You might also be basing your intentions for future action on hot cognition: a sense of arousal when you think about having the body you always dreamed of. You imagine an energized-self hitting the gym with enthusiasm.

But of course, your future self is not who you are today. When Monday evening arrives, after a long day at work, you

188 Ibid.

feel tired, depleted, and you just want to go home and take a warm shower and rest. Your charioteer is tired and inattentive and succumbs easily to the dark horse. The plan to begin your exercise regimen goes down the drain once again.

Students with very low GPAs often come to seek my advice, swearing that their grades do not reflect their true potential. Can I trust their word? Unfortunately, most of the time, I cannot.

Yes, I understand that there are those who may have faced extraneous life circumstances that have derailed them. But for the most part, struggling students have a present/future self disconnect. Their transcripts are mirrors of their present self, clearly indicating that their level of effort and commitment is close to zero. However, they bet all their chips on their future self. What they are telling me is: "my present self has nothing to show for my efforts, but do not worry, my future self will take care of everything."

Again, when they make inferences about future behavior, it is generally based on today's cognition. They may be either aroused by enthusiasm about their future prospects or basing their future predictions on cold, rational cognition. When the future arrives, the same issues that haunted them in the past—be it procrastination, lack of organization, or their desire to indulge in instant gratification—will invariably kick in. The odds are that your future self will be your present self tomorrow and nothing much will change.

The research is conclusive: those who restrain their desires in favor of their future selves do much better in various aspects of life, including saving, dieting, and performance in school.

So far, I have emphases the point that our future self is not dramatically different to our present self. Now I will argue, somewhat paradoxically, that our future self is *not* our present self.

Preferences do change over time. The things I value today are not the same things I valued when I was in my twenties. Changes in values, however, are progressive and gradual.

You may be too young to appreciate this, but as we age, our perspective starts to shift.

But the general rule of thumb is that when it comes to the short- to medium-term wins we hope to achieve, we can't rely on changing much from our current form.

What can you do about it?

1) *Acknowledge:* The most important favor we can do for our future self is to acknowledge that it will be a modified version of our present self. Not a completely different, better, improved version, but a somewhat similar version. In fact, depending on your age, your future self might as well be a less-than-ideal version of your present self. As we age, we burn less calories, our cognitive functions decline, our body mass diminishes, and so on—this is just extra motivation for you to take better care of your present self!
2) *Think future self:* Determine how you want your future self to look, act and live. Be a steward of your future self. Ask yourself the question: Are my current decisions empowering/improving/benefiting my future self? If the answer is no, go back to the Hindu Trinity exercise in Chapter 8 and determine what you must *start, stop,* and *continue* doing to ensure a better future for yourself.
3) *Meet your future self:* I sometimes show my students a picture of myself thirty years from now, compliments of

> the Aging Booth app. Research shows that people who meet their future self using digital aging software are more generous towards their future self by putting more money aside in a retirement account, compared to individuals who haven't met their future selves. Try to imagine yourself 30 years from now. Where do you want to be positioned personally and professionally? What do you look like? Are your current decisions conducive of the lifestyle you imagine for your future?

You need to realize that, to a large degree, the person you see in the future is your present self, tomorrow. Many of the decisions you make today will determine who that person will be, how they will feel, and the quality of life they will enjoy. Above all, remember that you will eventually meet your future self. Treat your future self as they deserve to be treated: with loving care.

Strategy #36: Self-Reflection

I wanted to understand the difference between students who were highly praised by faculty for their clinical skills and their less successful peers. As I began interviewing successful student-clinicians, one pattern quickly became clear: student-clinicians deemed by faculty to be highly competent were exceedingly reflective about their clinical experiences. They also scored high on a reflection scale.

This was a very interesting finding. Success wasn't about how intelligent they were or how well they performed in standardized tests, but their ability to take feedback, listen to advice, and incorporate what they had learned into how they practiced.

I also asked these high-performers how they compared themselves with their less-successful peers. Again a pattern emerged. One after the other, they would tell me that those who were less successful would typically get defensive when criticized and would do very little to incorporate new learning into their practice.

In other words, high performers had a growth mindset and the poor performers had a fixed mindset.

Although that seems like a natural conclusion, there is more to it. These individuals told me that although they not always agreed with the feedback given by faculty, either in terms of content and style—they may have disagreed with the comments or deemed the professor to be rude —they would often reflect upon why faculty were saying what they were saying and would ask themselves what they could have been missing. They also controlled their sense of self-aggrandizement by reminding themselves that these were experienced faculty members and that they, as students, had been doing clinical work for no more than three years. They also understood, at a deeper level, that they had to pass the class and to do so they had to dance to the beat of each faculty member. Their less successful peers were dancing to their own beats.

Reflection is the act of putting a virtual mirror in front of you and observing your behavior with an open mind. It is the act of critically analyzing the dynamics between the charioteer, the bright horse, and the dark horse and determining who is calling the shots. It is asking questions about what you can see in that mirror, without being afraid to hear the answer and having the courage to correct any wrongdoing.

This goes back to an earlier discussion in this book. In Chapter 3, we looked at how self-control often involves suppressing the demands of the ego and understanding the rules of the game. In the case of clinical experience, a figure of authority imposed the rules and the successful individuals listened to the rules, learned the rules, abided by the rules and, as a consequence, received flying remarks. They were also great students and clinicians, but their ability to reflect upon the feedback and their experiences made them that much more successful.

It is important to note that this has nothing to do with becoming "yes" men and women. In certain domains of life, including skilled and technical training, or domains that have specific standards to be achieved, the more you abide by the standards without deviation, the more likely you are to succeed.

In the business world it is no different. Businesses have value statements depicting what behaviors are expected of employees. For example, Whole Foods, the giant food supermarket specializing in organic foods, values employee excellence and happiness. To that end, they commit to having "open and timely information" available to employees. A manager with tendencies to operate in the dark, without making information available to employees (and there are many of these out there, believe me), and who can't adapt, will likely not fit in at Whole Foods. Without going through the self-reflection loop and looking at what the environment is asking of them, then examining their own reflection and making the necessary adjustments, they will not succeed.

Reflection works best as a series of questions you ask yourself with the goal of attaining a better understanding of your position vis-à-vis your goals. For instance, the good clinicians asked such questions: What am I doing right/wrong? Although I feel I am right, could I be wrong since I don't have nearly a fraction of the experience of the faculty member who is giving me feedback? What can I do to correct my course of action? What are the knowledge areas that I need to develop?

Benjamin Franklin, in his autobiography, stated that he began and ended his day with two short meditative questions: "What good shall I do this day?" and later, "What good have I done to-day?"[189]

Marshal Goldsmith, recognized as the number one executive coach in the United States, offers an extremely useful set of reflective of questions to harness action toward a goal.[190]

Before we get to these questions, let's explore how Goldsmith came up with them. As a talented corporate trainer and coach, Goldsmith did a lot of work with organizations on employee engagement, or lack thereof. He categorized some of the worst customer service providers as either cynical (those who are passive and negative) or hostile (active and negative). He reminded organizations that employees required continuous feedback to improve their behaviors. His daughter—his personal mirror—reminded him that he was putting too much emphasis on the organization's role in creating engaged employees. She reminded him that employees also have a personal responsibility for their choices and actions.

Goldsmith then devised a study to determine the effectiveness of active questions with employees who undergo training. This study divided employees into three groups. The first group was a no-treatment group: they received no training and received questions on happiness, meaning, building positive

---

189 Franklin, B. (2012). *The autobiography of Benjamin Franklin* [Kindle 6.3 version]. Retrieved from https://www.amazon.com.

190 Goldsmith, M., & Reiter, M. (2015). *Triggers: Creating behaviors that lasts-becoming the person you want to be.* New York, NY: Crown Publishing.

relationships, and engagement both before the experiment and two weeks later. The second group received two hours of training on engagement and were followed up with for ten working days with passive questions, such as: How happy are you? How meaningful was your day? How positive were your relationships with people? How engaged were you? The third, and last, group received the same training but with active questions for ten working days. These included: Did you do your best to be happy? Did you do your best to find meaning? Did you do your best to build positive relationships with people? Did you do your best to be fully engaged?

At the end of the experiment, participants were asked to rate themselves on the items measured by the questions: levels of happiness, meaning, relationship, and engagement.

As expected, the group who held the reflective mirror in front of themselves—that is, who answered the active questions—reported double the improvement on all items. Follow-up also proved to be better than no follow-up.

What can you do about it?

Goldsmith proposes that we mull over the following daily questions:

- Did I do my best to set clear goals today?
- Did I do my best to make progress toward my goals today?
- Did I do my best to find meaning today?
- Did I do my best to be happy today?
- Did I do my best to build positive relationships today?
- Did I do my best to be fully engaged today?

I would also add two more questions:

- Did I do my best to serve others today?
- Did I do my best to be grateful today?

These questions, although helpful, are quite broad. You may want to refine them for your own specific needs. For instance, if you have a goal to improve your eating habits, you can ask yourself: "Did I do my best to eat healthily today?"

Stopping in the middle of the day to ask these questions can be quite energizing, as it helps you align your horses and charioteer while on the go.

Reflection and anxiety

Earlier in this book, we discussed how anxiety is now prevalent in our society. We also explained that anxiety is natural reaction to both real and imagined threats in the environment. Threats can be overestimated, while our ability to manage threats can be underestimated.

There are important cognitive distortions that can lead to the overestimation of threats and underestimation of our coping abilities.[191] The most common cognitive distortions include:

- **All-or-nothing thinking**: You see things as absolutes, with no space for gray areas. This type of thinking encourages extreme views that can be counterproductive. The

191 Burns, D. D. (2012). *Feeling good: The new mood therapy*. NewYork, NY: Avon Books.

nuances of reality get lost and you may feel you are trapped in one way of thinking.

- **Overgeneralizing:** You make conclusions based on an isolated event. For instance, if someone broke their word, then no one is to be trusted. This type of thinking leads to erroneous assumptions about people and events.
- **Blaming:** You tend to blame external factors for your own fate. This type of thinking prevents you from taking responsibility for your own actions while promoting anger directed at others. After all, your failures are caused by everyone else and by external events, not by you.
- **Negative filtering:** You only see the negative while discounting the positive. Positives don't matter. This thinking fosters negativity and makes positives disappear, even when they exist.
- **Jumping to conclusions:**
  - *Mind reading*: You think you know what other people are thinking about you or about a given situation. This thinking makes you jump to conclusions and leads to distrust and a false grasp on reality. As a rule of thumb, there is no way to know what other people are thinking. Many of us like to believe we are great at 'reading' people, when in fact we are absolutely terrible at it.
  - *Fortune-telling/clairvoyance*: You think you know how people will act and how things will unfold. It is very common for people who engage in this kind of thinking to escalate situations by always expecting the worst.
- **Emotional reasoning:** You mistake emotions for facts. If you feel it, after all, then it must be true. This thinking

leads you to believe in feelings without evidence, when in fact the only evidence is that you felt a certain way.

- **Labeling:** You label yourself, others, and situations negatively. This thinking is deflating for your spirit. When we think, "I am a failure," we use a very powerful label to overgeneralize a situation. Yes, we may fail now and again, but that does not mean we are overall failures, as in fact we have succeeded in many other areas.
- **Personalization:** You take things personally and blame yourself for things that aren't entirely your fault.

What can we do about it?

- Identify and isolate each distorted thought.
- Label the type of cognitive distortion causing the anxiety.
- Analyze the distortion. In this step you may ask: "What is the evidence supporting my thinking? What evidence am I overlooking?"
- Finally, you should correct the thinking with a broader, more nuanced view of reality.

Here is a very personal example of the above.

Throughout this book, I have been plagued with issues of anxiety caused by distortions of thinking. Here are just a few:

Step 1. Identify each distorted thought	Step 2. Label cognitive distortion
English is my second language—how can I dare to write a book?	Labeling, Negative filtering
I am a poor writer.	Labeling, Negative filtering
No one will want to read this.	Mindreading, Fortune-telling
How will my boss react to it? He will probably think this is not good enough.	Mindreading
What if no one buys a copy?	Fortune-telling
If I self-publish, people will think that the material here is not good enough to be picked up by a traditional publishing company.	Fortune-telling
What if I only receive negative reviews on Amazon?	Negative filtering, Fortune-telling

This exercise gives you a clear picture of the cognitive distortions clouding your judgment. As seen above, I am an amazing clairvoyant with a negative tilt. If I were to rethink my career, I should open a fortune-telling center. The book has not even been written and my dark horse is already thinking about who is or is not going to read it and whether people will like it.

Luckily, these thoughts did not stop me from writing it anyway. By understanding their limitations and appreciating the fact that they are natural responses from our anxious brains, all I needed to do was identify, accept, and deal with them.

Reframing your cognitive distortions in an important step.

Distorted Thought	**Step 3. Analysis, and 4. resolution**
English is my second language—how can I dare to write a book?	There are many other authors writing in English as a second language. *Resolution: Shut up and write!*
I am a poor writer.	What is the evidence? You have written good pieces in the past that were well received by your community. What are you going to do about it? *Resolution: Avoid labeling. Hire a good editor. Re-read your work as many times as possible.*
No one will want to read this.	How do you know this to be true? I have many people who respect my work. *Resolution: Shut up and write.*

Distorted Thought	**Step 3. Analysis, and 4. resolution**
How will my boss react to it? He will probably think this is not good enough.	How do you know this to be true? You are transposing a thought onto someone. This is mindreading and in the past you have proven to be wildly wrong when mindreading. Oh, and have I reminded you that the book is not even written and you are already anticipating how your boss will react to it? *Resolution: Don't assume to know what people will think. Shut up and write.*
What if no one buys a copy?	That is just not true. I know my mom, my dad, my wife, and my siblings will probably buy a copy. *Resolution: shut up and write.*
If I self-publish, people will think that the material here is not good enough to be picked up by a traditional publishing company.	This is still your desire to predict the future and what people will think about your work. *Resolution: shut up and write.*
What if I only receive negative reviews on Amazon?	Really? No comment. After all we have discussed above, let's not go there. *Resolution: shut up and write.*

Dr. Burns, who popularized the concept of cognitive distortions, encourages us to speak with ourselves as if we were speaking with a good friend. Telling myself to "shut up" like I did in the table above is probably not the tone Dr. Burns had in mind, but sometimes friends have to be brutally honest with each other. We can choose between being a gentle friend who smooths things over or that friend that gives us blunt, hard to swallow advice. I prefer bluntness.

Strategy #37: Understand (and Accept) the Pluralistic Self

Think of a family sitting down for Thanksgiving dinner. As you look around the table, you are surprised by the different personalities and characters. There is the loud uncle who typically has one drink too many, the insecure cousin who barely opens his mouth and at the first chance will hide behind a computer screen, the neurotic father who is always concerned about everything and everyone, the righteous mother, and the straight-talking uncle who thinks he can say whatever he wants because he made it big in life (or not).

As a thought experiment, imagine that Thanksgiving dinner we just described happening inside your head, with your many selves having a feast. Your worried self does what it does best, worries; your risky self desires to embrace new opportunities, only to be reminded by your cautious self that you should not move so fast. Your planning self sets goals and standards, while your lazy self encourages you to watch the next episode of your favorite Netflix show. At this very moment, as you read this book, there is probably a part of yourself that is interested in learning and another part wanting to go for a walk or take a nap.

Although it is comforting to think of the self as a unified, monolithic force, you have probably experienced the scenario above playing out in your mind. We house a number of factions of ourselves inside our heads, with different individual roles, goals, and agendas.[192] In fact, the whole premise of this book is that we live with a dark horse, a charioteer, and a bright horse inside our minds, all calling the shots independently and simultaneously of one another, with little or no cohesion between them.

Based on this recognition, psychotherapist Richard Schwartz developed the Internal Family System to deal with patients suffering from posttraumatic stress disorder (PTSD). Patients with PTSD live as if they were constantly reliving the situation that originated the trauma. A part of their self is in constant alert and fear.

Schwartz suggests that the self is divided into four main parts:

- Managers, the part of our self that protects our internal systems from disappointment and pain by making us control situations and relationships.
- Exiles, who hold strong emotions and tend to act out or engage in self-destructive behavior when the system is threatened.
- Firefighters, who try to calm the actions of exiles by often engaging in maladaptive behavior such as compulsion, isolation, obsession, or fantasy.
- The core self, who when in control of the entire system does so with an aura of confidence, calmness and ease.

192 Van der Kolk, B. A. (2014). *The body keeps the score: Brain, mind, and body in the healing of trauma.* New York, NY: Penguin Publishing Group.

The problem begins when we take a part to be the whole. When we say, "I am lazy" or "I am unfocused," we are referring to one part of the self that may be lazy or unfocused, at the risk of believing that the whole is lazy and unfocused.

When we confound the part with the whole, the parts are "blended." Being in a blended state is the equivalent of thinking that the voice of our neurotic self represents all the voices at the dinner table. The solution is to "unblend" the voices and recognize each of them individually.[193]

What can you do about it?

First, take a relaxed position. Try to image all the voices in your head and identify the voices present. Who is speaking louder? Is it your confident self or your insecure self? What voices are not present? For instance, the dominant voice at this moment may be your insecure self but you know you have a very secure voice inside of you who may just not be at the table (invite that secure voice to join the party). Realize that the dominant voice does not speak for all the voices you have.

To unblend these voices, we need to:

1) Recognize the many selves at play—all those around the mental dinner table.
2) Listen to each of their concerns, neurosis, and worries.
3) Acknowledge the input of each.
4) Thank them for existing and for their perspectives, with the understanding that they were created to protect the system, even if their behavior may at times seem counterproductive and destructive.
5) Ask them to temporarily step aside.

193 Ibid, p. 284.

An important part of this strategy is to determine who you want to be in control and make that part of the self the most assertive part. If you are a well-adapted individual, you will probably choose the core self, the planner, the self that helps you achieve your goals.

CHAPTER 11

Boot Camp—All in

THE JOURNEY TO ACHIEVING SELF-CONTROL is long. It requires incredible amounts of energy and effort, exerted over extended periods of time. It also requires dealing with unintended consequences, fallouts, small wins, naysayers, and setbacks.

But when everything else is equal, self-control is the one strength that keeps our horses and the chariot aligned towards the goals worth achieving.

The dark horse is unruly, and the charioteer gets tired, distracted, and may eventually give in to its demands. However, we have the power to tame the dark horse by exercising our self-control muscle.

In the beginning, particularly if your self-control muscle is weak, it will not be easy. It never is. The dark horse will rear and buck. The charioteer will lack the strength, stamina as well as the right methods to tame the horse. But with the EAT method of self-control, you can make significant strides towards keeping the chariot airborne and under control.

Your Personalized Boot Camp

The best way to acquire any skill, including self-control, is to fully immerse yourself in intensive training. I invite you to create your own self-control boot camp, using the strategies proposed in this book as a guiding manual.

The following steps summarize most of the strategies discussed in this book, in a simple framework for your own use:

Step1. Define a goal you want to achieve: Set a 20-day self-control challenge. Remember that different types of goals will require different strategies. Give your goal an exciting title. This title should be inspirational and a source of motivation.
Step 2. Pre-commit to commit: Make a pact with yourself that you will see this project through its completion.
Step 3. Define all the sub-goals or lead measures you must achieve in order to achieve your big goal: Remember that lead measures are predictive and influenceable. Outcome measures won't do. For instance, if your goal is to lose weight, a lead measure is the number of calories you will consume every day and how much you will exercise each week. Losing five pounds is an outcome measure that depends on good lead measures. Build a SCRUM grid for your goal with each lead measure.
Step 4. Clearly define how you will measure your progress toward your goal: Build metrics that will inform you if you are on the right track or veering away from your goal.
Step 5. Identify areas of conflict between your dark horse's desires and your ultimate goal: Identify the nature of the conflict using the EAT method—is the conflict related to your environment, actions, or thinking? Predict, based on your experiences, what environmental factors, habits, and internal factors (thoughts and emotions) will likely prevent you from achieving your goal.

Apply the strategies of the EAT method of self-control according to the nature of the conflict.

Here is your personal self-control worksheet, for you to fill in and begin mapping out your path to achievement.

1. **Goal:** ________________ (remember to make it exciting)
2. **Pre-commit to commit:** ________________ (make a pact with yourself to see this through)
3. **Sub-Goals/Lead Measure:** 4. **Monitoring:**

What actions are essential, under your control and will create the most impact toward your big goal?	How will you measure/ monitor your progress?
Sub-Goal A:	
Sub-Goal B:	
Sub-Goal C:	
Sub-Goal D:	

5. **Areas of conflict and how to address them:**

E: Environment	A: Act	T: Think
Shielding: Our goals are under attack! Shield them from environmental forces that might derail them!	**Breaking bad habits**: Create new habits by understanding the cues and rewards of current habits that are not serving you well.	**Labeling**: Identify the feeling or behavior that is causing a loss of self-control. Isolate it and deal with it.

E: Environment	A: Act	T: Think
Structure: Create a daily system or structure that is guaranteed to help you reach your goal. **Time leeches**: Identify time leeches, both human and non-human, that may be diverting time and energy from your goals. **Manage FOMO**: Goal achievement involves sacrifice. Let go of FOMO by editing your life and focusing on the things that really matter. **This 'r Nothing**: Break your time down into 20-40 minutes chunks of focused work. During that time, everything else must wait—and that means *everything* else. **Alone time**: Create alone time—time just between you and your goal.	**Eat a frog**: Don't delay difficult tasks! Get them done early in the day. **No-thinking zone**: Don't think. Just do it! **Checklists & to-do lists**: Set up checklists and to-do lists to keep you on track and in check. **Floss your teeth**: Self-control is contagious. Change habits in your life that are unrelated to your goal, as a way to increase your sense of self-efficacy. **Fight fewer battles**: Identify the lead measures, actions, and behaviors that are both predictive of achieving your goal and influenceable. Get rid of low-yield, unnecessary tasks. **Archetype**: Think about others who have reached similar goals. How did they go about it? How did they approach the same problem?	**Mental contrasting**: Dream of you desired outcome, and anticipate potential challenges. **"If, Then"**: Create "if, then" clauses for each of the challenges you have anticipated above. For instance, "If I feel the urge to eat desert, then I will ask for a fruit salad"; or "If I don't feel like writing a report, then I will just start typing words regardless of my feelings." **Think values**: Engage in abstract or higher-order thinking (e.g., "I am writing this report because it will help hundreds of people.") **Reappraisal**: Look at things from a different angle; turn negative affirmations into positive affirmations.

E: Environment	A: Act	T: Think
Set defaults: Automate certain activities in order to free time for your goal. **Set tripwires**: Set alarms, booby-traps, and other devices to inform you when you are deviating from your goal.	**Delay action**: Take a rest. Take a break. Distance yourself from your goal for a short period of time. This will recharge your batteries and give you new perspective. **Act strategically**: Do the things that will create the largest return on investment. Reconsider tasks that yield little results (e.g., keep your emails short and objective).	**Growth mindset**: When in doubt, remind yourself that you can accomplish many things if you spend enough time and energy on them. **Future self**: Invest on your future self by putting some of the burden on your present self. By doing so, your future self will collect the fruits of your present diligence. Think of who you want your future self to be and what you need to do today in order to get there. **Hidden commitments**: are there hidden commitments and intentions that are holding you back? What are they? What are the big assumptions driving them and how can they be neutralized?

E: Environment	A: Act	T: Think
		Pluralistic self: There are many voices inside our heads—voices of encouragement, doubt, anxiety, courage, fear, etc. Which voice is most prominent? Which voice is calling the shots? Bring the positive voices to the surface and allow them to be in control. **Self-reflection**: Engage in some honest internal dialogue about what you hoped to achieve and where you actually stand in relation to your goal. Are you engaging is distorted thinking? How can these distorted thoughts be corrected?

Real Life Examples

Here are two examples of the boot camp in action, demonstrating how to apply the EAT method.

Example 1

Step 1. Goal: To write a diversity report within two months to be distributed to all employees.

As written, this goal is not bad. It is specific, has a time frame, and is accomplishable. Yet it lacks some pizzazz. Let's reframe the goal to make it more exciting in itself:

Reframed Goal: to write a data-driven, comprehensive, well-designed and well-written report within two months that will awe all those who read it.

Step 2. Pre-commit to commit: Come rain or thunder, I will make sure this report is all I wish it to be.

Step 3. Sub-Goals/Lead Measure **Step 4. Monitoring**

SCRUM grid:

Sub-Goal/Lead measure	Backlog	In progress	Done	Week 1	Week 2	Week 3	Week 4	Week 5	Week 6	Week 7	Week 8
Sub-Goal 1. Collect Data		X									
1a. Create Survey		X									
1b. Contact IT dept. to get email from all employees			X								
1c. Send survey	X										
1d. Download results	X										
1e. Analyze results	X										
Sub-Goal 2. Write report											
2a. Write every morning, 7–9 a.m. and on train ride home	X										
2b. Share writing with editors	X										
2c. Incorporate edits											
Sub-Goal 3. Create design											
3a. Contact designer											
3b. Gather pictures and images											
Project completed											

Legend:

	Needs immediate attention
	Time frame for subgoal completion
	Deadline for each subgoal

5. Areas of conflict and how to address them:

E: Environment	A: Act	T:Think
Shielding: There are too many distractions in my day-to-day life. I will write early in the mornings and during my train ride home when I have no distractions. **Structure**: I will write every day for two hours a day; take two days off to focus solely on writing; answer emails three times a day during these two months.	**Breaking bad habits:** I need to break the habit of waking up at 7 a.m. to go to work and start waking up at 5:45 a.m., allowing me to have free time in the morning (the train ride early morning is an additional plus). **Eat a frog**: My dark horse suggests I write when I feel like it, yet the urge to write never comes naturally. Writing every morning will be my daily frog.	**Labeling**: When unfocused, anxious, having doubts or fears, I will label what is causing these feelings and confront the root cause. **Mental contrasting**: I have identified numerous barriers between me and my goal: distractions, lack of confidence, interruptions by colleagues, variations in energy levels. Now that these barriers have been identified, I will come up with a plan to overcome each of them.

E: Environment	A: Act	T:Think
Time leeches: Meetings are consuming precious time that I could be using for productive writing. I will keep meetings to a minimum during these two months. **Manage FOMO:** My need to get involved in many different projects is diverting time and energy away from this project. Some pet projects and other goals will be placed on hold until this report is finalized. **This 'r Nothing**: As soon as I start to write, my dark horse starts suggesting other, more interesting things to do. When I am writing, I will use the "This 'r Nothing" strategy. If I don't feel like writing, I will just stare at the screen.	**No-thinking zone**: Don't think, just do it! When I start doubting or questioning, I will keep on charging. **Checklists & to-do lists**: With so many things to manage on my daily job, it becomes easy to lose oneself on the demands of the job. Every morning I will write down what I want to accomplish that day related to the report. The SCRUM board above is my checklist.	**"If, Then":** Strategies to deal with the barriers identified through mental contrasting: "If distractions are getting on my way, then I will leave the building and find a place with no distractions"; "If I am falling behind schedule, then I will place other projects on hold and focus solely on writing until I get it done"; "If I lose motivation, then I will 'Think Values', reminding myself WHY this report is important." **Reappraisal:** Instead of perceiving the writing of this report as something burdensome, I will see it as "a great opportunity to make a difference in my organization" or "as an amazing learning opportunity."

E: Environment	A: Act	T:Think
Alone time: Foot traffic in my office can be quite high, diverting me from my goal. From 7–9 a.m. every morning will be fully devoted to this project; also train journeys; I may need to come on a Saturday or lock myself in my office for a full day to interpret data. **Set defaults**: On days that I dedicate to writing, I will set up an "out-of-the-office" reply informing colleagues that emails will be answered the day after. **Set tripwires**: If I am not on track, I will have to work at night until I catch up.	**Floss your teeth**: I need to prove to myself that when I put mind to something, I can get it done. During this time, I will go jogging at least four times a week. **Acting strategically**: All my time and energy must be focused, yet low-yield activities consume 80% of my day. I will determine what low-yield activities can be postponed, delegated, or solved in a simple and expedited way. **Archetype**: I will wear my report writing hat, and pretend I am a consultant for a major consulting company.	**Think values**: I will constantly force myself to ask WHY. The answer is simple—diversity is important to me and the findings could have a positive impact community-wide. **Hidden commitments**: A potential hidden commitment is my inherent need to protect myself from criticism. I will accept criticism as a natural part of the creative process and will embrace it willingly. **Mindset**: I will perceive writing the report as an exercise for my own personal growth and development. **Future self**: This project may be used as the foundation for future projects; by investing time and energy in it now, I am helping my future self.

E: Environment	A: Act	T:Think
	Delay action: I will take a break for a couple of days, to look at the report with a fresh eye.	**Pluralistic self**: When my self-critical self speaks loudly, I will need to bring my confident self to the forefront of the internal conversation. **Self-reflection**: My self-critical self engages in catastrophizing and other cognitive distortions that set me back ("this report will be horrible", "people will criticize me and question me"). But most of these distortions are never going to materialize, so I will let loose and go with the flow.

EXAMPLE 2.

Step 1. Goal: To get a competitive letter grade (B or A) on a difficult course.

Let's reframe the goal to make the goal exciting in itself:

Reframed Goal: To engage in deep learning on course X, leading to a good grade and opening a path to the graduate school of my dream.

Step 2. Pre-commit to commit: I will commit to the best of my ability all my faculties to achieving this important goal.

Step 3. Sub-Goals/Lead Measure **Step 4. Monitoring**

What actions are essential, under my control and will create the most impact toward my big goal?	How will I measure/monitor my progress?
Sub-Goal 1. Study every day after class for 45 mins	**One hour per day according to plan**
Sub-Goal 2. Answer all problems at the end of each chapter	**All questions answered**
Sub-Goal 3. Take advantage of faculty hours every time I encounter a concept I can't master, at least three times a semester	**Faculty consulted at least three times a semester and every time I feel stuck**
Sub-Goal 4. Study in groups before exams	**Attendance at study groups**

E: Environment	A: Act	T: Think
Shielding: My goal is being attacked by my need to constantly be on social media. I will turn my phone off while studying.	**Breaking bad habits:** I have the habit of going to the library to study but I just can't concentrate. I will now study in a different environment.	**Mental contrasting**: I know my smart phone is a distraction, my friends are always inviting to go out, I often don't feel motivated.

E: Environment	A: Act	T: Think
Structure: I will wake up at the same time every day and study for 45 mins. **Time leeches**: some of my friends are consuming too much of my time and I will need to have a conversation with them. **Manage FOMO:** Soccer practice, involvement on 4 on-campus clubs and organizations… something has got to go. **This 'r Nothing**: When I am studying, I will use the "This 'r Nothing" strategy. If I don't feel like studying, I will just stare at the book/screen. **Alone Time**: 7–8 a.m. is my quality time alone, just for me and this course.	**Eat a frog**: Studying every morning will be my daily frog. **No-thinking zone**: If I start doubting or questioning myself, I will stop thinking about the things that need to be done, and just do them. **Checklists & to-do lists**: Every morning I will write down what I want to accomplish that day as far as my studies are concerned. **Floss your teeth**: During this time I will go jogging at least four times a week. **Acting strategically**: I will determine what low-yield activities can be postponed or placed on hold. I will use campus resources when I get stuck.	**"If, Then" strategies:** "If my friends invite me to go out, then I will tell them that only Saturdays after I have caught up with all my work"; "If I am becoming demotivated, then I will remind myself that this course is very important for my future"; "If I can't control my urge to check my instant messages, then I will place my phone in a different room." **Think values**: Why do I need a good grade in the course? I want to become a doctor and this course is the key to my future. **Growth mindset**: If I apply myself, and spend enough hours and energy trying to master this subject, I do have a chance. **Labeling**: When having feelings that do not support my goal, I will relax, isolate the feeling, and ask why I was having them 5 times.

E: Environment	A: Act	T: Think
Set defaults: During final weeks I will have my social media sites and email set to "not available." **Set tripwires**: I will set my alarm 45 mins earlier than I am used to. I will set up an alarm to study for 45 mins.	**Archetype**: I will apply as much energy and focus to my studies as an athlete would apply to his or her sport. **Delay action**: I will take a break once in a while to gain new perspective.	**Future self**: This course is a foundation for my future self. I want my future self to be a successful, competent doctor. As such, I must align my present self with my future self. **Hidden commitments:** After doing this exercise, I learned that I may be committed to doing poorly. I am afraid that if I study and don't do well that I will feel embarrassed, so it is better not to put the effort in. I will revisit my big assumption and embrace the growth mindset—if I spend enough time and energy I can and will learn the material. **Pluralistic self**: Listening to my many selves, I realize that my self-critical, doubting self is dominating the conversation. I remind them that last semester I got some very good grades.

E: Environment	A: Act	T: Think
		Self-reflection: this course is hard and I find myself engaging in "all or nothing" and "catastrophizing" ("if I get a grade lower than a B, than all my chances are over"). After clarifying my thoughts with an advisor I learned that this is not necessarily true.

At this stage of the boot camp, in order to develop your self-control muscle, you are probably working on individual goals. But as you progress along in this journey it is important to shift the focus from merely achieving *goals* to creating *systems*, as previously discussed. The easiest way to accomplish this is by permanently incorporating some of the changes you have made through the exercise above into your daily routine.

If, when scanning the environment, you found that certain places, times and people were getting in your way, create a system for avoiding them. If there were certain actions you took that made you more likely to achieve your goals, such as eating frogs early or creating To Do lists before the end of the day, repeat those actions on a daily basis. If you identified a certain time of the day in which you were most productive, make that time of the day sacrosanct.

Above all, learn from the process. Have fun with it. Use it as a laboratory to learn more about your dark horse: what it wants and desires, when it bucks and why it bucks. Keep in mind that not all strategies will work for you. Find those strategies that best suit *your* personality and lifestyle. If a particular strategy does not work, move on to the next.

And above all, be accountable. Take responsibility for your achievements and failures. If you are not failing, you are not trying hard enough. If you are failing too often, you may have the wrong strategy.

And of course, when you do achieve a goal, even in small ways, celebrate that achievement.

CHAPTER 12

Seeking Balance

WHEN I DISCUSS SELF-CONTROL IN my seminars, people invariably ask me about the work–life (or study–life) balance.

It may be that I come across as too intensively focused on results, on doing, on action, or on achievement. Self-control can be misconstrued as a tool for endless engagement, when a fundamental part of self-control is knowing when to charge forward and when to retreat, when to engage and when to let go.

In fact, by deploying some of the strategies suggested here, such as the "This 'r Nothing" strategy, it's my experience that the focus they give you will allow you *more* time for a balanced life.

But we can't ignore the fact that seeking balance is a hot topic in an era of ultra-connectivity, endless distractions, and hyper pressure to perform and be competitive.

THE PURSUIT OF PERFECTION

One of the challenges with discussing "balance" is how it is construed by the experts and in our own minds. Most articles, books, and experts that discuss work–life balance portray it as a concrete, absolute concept, a target to be reached. In this view, work–life balance is represented by a scale in perfect harmony: on the one side is work or study, and on the other side is life (family, friends, sports, health, hobbies, and fun).

In my experience, work–life balance is far from being such a concrete, absolute concept. It is abstract, illusive, and very much like the weather. Although most of us desire beautiful blue skies, some days will be cloudy, others windy, and some wet and gloomy. In the long run, we want to have more sunny days than dreadful gloomy and windy ones.

When it comes to balance, the situation is no different. Balance may be achieved for some days, weeks, or even months, but for the most part you should brace yourself for interruptions, emergencies, urgencies, long periods of high demands on your time and energy, and many ups and downs.

Achieving a perfect balance is nearly impossible, particularly when we are on a mission to accomplish something relevant and significant.

There are several issues with the "perfect" work–life balance perspective. Firstly, it separates work or study from life, as if they were two completely separate entities. For most of us, work is a major, significant, important, and fulfilling part of our lives. Your studies are no different. In a society where lifelong learning is not only lauded but essential, study is, and will continue to be, a major part of all our lives.

Secondly, it implies that there is a perfect point on a scale that we should reach, creating major anxiety if we fall short of it.

Finally, it discounts the cyclical nature of life—the fact that at certain times in our lives, unexpected demands will pull us in different directions. These various demands will invariably throw us off balance.

A more realistic goal is to achieve some balance for some (or most) of the time. In the long-term, we want to have more balance than not. What follows are some simple measures to help with this.

Embrace a cyclical view of life

A linear view sees life as divided into separate, progressive time periods. The road leads ever forward. In this view, the struggles of tomorrow will be different from the struggles of today, and typically will not be as severe. In this view, you can achieve a truly balanced life because the steps you take today will pave the road for tomorrow and help you build your path towards true balance.

Although at first glance this view seems desirable, it can backfire as stressors keep coming back to haunt you. As a result, that rosy "the-grass-is-greener-in-the-future" picture never fully materializes, creating serious frustration.

A cyclical view, on the other hand, helps us realize that events will invariably repeat themselves—just as the four seasons keep on returning each year. Adopting a cyclical view when going through a period of imbalance helps us realize that we are stuck in a temporary cycle that will pass. It may take some time for the issue causing the imbalance to be resolved, and it may come back again in the future, just as the promise of a cold winter is always present. But so too is the promise of spring.

Expand your view of the present

By expanding our view of the present, we can build a bridge between the demands of our daily lives, including new projects and unexpected interruptions, and our goal of reaching balance.

We tend to think of the present as being today, right now. But this view is quite limiting and anxiety-producing: if you don't achieve balance today, then your goal to achieve life balance will have failed.

Daily balance is difficult to achieve, because 1) we can't afford to simply abandon a project or a task midway through to reach our daily dose of balance; 2) most projects and life issues that require our attention demand sustained effort over long periods of time; and 3) life's unexpected interruptions will distract us from our goals, requiring further effort to attend to both the distraction and to complete our original goal.

The solution is to redefine the present by expanding it to encompass a few days, weeks, or in some cases even months into both the past and the future. By doing so, yesterday, last week, or the week to come is still considered the "present." If you are involved in a project that requires complete focus (and will put you off balance for a couple of days), you are not frustrated that you are unable to find balance now, or this week (or this month), because if you don't reach it today, you can still reach it tomorrow or next week or next month.

It is important, however, to make sure that you do find a period of calm and quiet in the future, so that you can return to a sense of equilibrium.

Think values

Values give us a sense of purpose and direction. Whenever you feel overwhelmed by what life has put in front of you, focusing on your values helps to put things into perspective. It reminds you of the underlying reasons why you are facing these challenges in the first place.

For instance, if you are overwhelmed by a project at work, reminding yourself that you value customer satisfaction and teamwork will reinvigorate you and inject some new, refreshing energy into your approach.

Reframe

Try to reframe the situation in a way that is self-serving. Instead of thinking that a lack of balance will be detrimental to your mental and physical health, try to think about it in creative ways that give you the much-needed mental stamina to keep going through the tough times. Think about the project that is causing your unbalance as an exercise in endurance, as a great opportunity to learn, grow, and develop, and as something that will help to build your career.

Edit your Life

In times of extreme unbalance, certain things may have to go. Competing commitments drain energy, time, and resources that you can't afford to spare.

Letting go, as we established earlier, is not easy. The idea of extensively editing our lives might make us feel understandably anxious, but remember that we don't have to get rid of things forever. We can simply put less urgent and important projects, ideas, and activities on pause—at least temporarily, until our big goal is reached.

Take breaks

As much as possible, try and incorporate short breaks into your routine to give you a much-needed pause from your chores. This could be a quick run, a walk around the block, or a phone (or text) conversation with a loved one.

Remember, self-control is like a muscle. Over-extending yourself invariably diminishes your ability to push hard over more prolonged periods of time. We also become cranky when we're tired, and no one deserves to have to deal with our crankiness.

Celebrate small wins

A glass of wine, a night at the theater, lying down on your coach on a Friday night and binge-watching your favorite TV shows for hours on end—all these all examples of small rewards. You choose which suits you best. When you have worked really hard, reward yourself.

This is a great way to remind the dark horse that if it behaves, it will be rewarded. Most importantly, bear in mind that the reward does not need to be big, but you should make a big deal out of the celebration.

I recently had to write a long report. After a week of intense, unbalanced work, I bought a bottle of coconut water on my way home. I was exhausted, but I had accomplished a lot. To reward myself, I drank that bottle of coconut water with gusto! Yes, that was my reward. I think it's unacceptable to pay $5 for a bottle of coconut water, when in Brazil I could buy a whole coconut for 20¢. As a result, I had never bought coconut water in the US until that day.

And it made me feel good. That coconut water changed my internal state—I went from feeling depleted and exhausted, to triumphantly drinking from that bottle as if I had achieved a major win.

Why Now?

There is no time to be wasted. Life goes by in the blink of an eye.

After my seminars, scores of people often approach me to share how they too suffer from a lack of alignment between what they know they *want* and what they are actually *doing*. We fall into the knowing–doing trap because we too often equate thinking of, or desiring something with actually implementing it.

Thinking is easy. Implementing a thought, on the other hand, is energizing, draining, time-consuming, exciting, and ego-depleting.

There is also the "planning fallacy," in which we decide to do something assuming that it will be a breeze. But we soon learn that the real world works in mysterious ways, often going against our plans or just not responding to them in the way we anticipated.

It is in this cocktail of emotions—in this far-from-linear, messy reality, filled with highs and lows—that we become intoxicated and lost. But again, we don't have time for hangovers. The clock is ticking. The time is now.

We often subscribe to the notion that our future decisions will give us more control over our lives,[194] when in fact tomorrow we will be managing the decisions we made today. Our decisions today will keep coming back to either haunt or bless us. Our present selves cultivate and nurture the field in which our future selves will grow, flourish, and harvest the fruits of our labor. Cultivating and nurturing is hard, attentive work, the type of work the dark horse abhors and that it convinces you to delegate to your future self. Tame your dark horse and get it done

---

194 Jay, M. (2012). *The defining decade: Why your twenties matter—And how to make the most of them now* [Kindle 6.3 version]. Retrieved from http://www.amazon.com

today. Your future self will offer you their deepest gratitude in due time.

The accomplished novelist and human rights activist, and one of my favorite authors, Pearl Buck, summarized it perfectly: "if you want to understand today, you have to search yesterday." Following the same logic, if you want to predict tomorrow, examine today. She also said, "I don't wait for moods. You accomplish nothing if you do that. Your mind must know that it has got to get down to work." The dark horse speaks through moods and tries to convince you that tomorrow your mood will be better, you will feel more like getting things done. For the procrastinators reading this: don't wait for moods to drive your actions. The mood may never come. Action, on the other hand, often inspires more action. Once you start doing something you will find that it was not as bad as it seemed. Tame your dark horse, let the charioteer take control of the reigns of your life today, regardless of your mood, and get down to business!

I have adapted the following story from Benjamin Franklin's autobiography:[195] a man decided that he wanted his rusty chariot to be as bright and shiny as when he first got it, so he visited a blacksmith to get the job done. The blacksmith agreed to do the job, as long as the man turned the wheel for the polishing machine—which was very hard labor indeed.

After some time, the man asked the blacksmith how the work was progressing and the blacksmith reminded him: "You need

---

195 Franklin, B. (2012). *The autobiography of Benjamin Franklin* [Kindle 6.3 version]. Retrieved from https://www.amazon.com.

to keep on turning the wheel. Right now, it's still speckled with rust."

The man, fatigued, replied: "Yes, but I think I like a speckled chariot better."

A speckled chariot is what the dark horse tries to convince the charioteer to settle for. And sometimes the charioteer does succumb to the lures of the dark horse. I hope this book has offered you valuable resources for helping you to reach your final destination: your glory, and a beautifully polished chariot.

(PS: I pre-committed to commit to writing this book. I wrote it. I will now enjoy some coconut water.)

Made in United States
Orlando, FL
11 April 2023

32011360R00211